Yale French Studies

NUMBER FORTY-NINE

SCIENCE, LANGUAGE, AND THE PERSPECTIVE MIND:
STUDIES IN LITERATURE AND THOUGHT FROM CAMPANELLA TO BAYLE

Special Editor   Timothy J. Reiss

Managing Editor   Philip H. Solomon

Editorial Board   Victor Brombert (Chairman), Jean Boorsch,
Peter Brooks, Edwin Duval, Shoshanna Fel-
man, Joseph Halpern, Marie-Rose Logan,
Georges May, Maria Minich, Charles Porter,
Philip Solomon

Staff   Jed Rabinovitch, Mark Webber

Subscriptions (Beginning with Number 50):

$7.00 for two years (four issues), $4.00 for one year (two issues), $2.00 per
issue. 323 William L. Harkness Hall, Yale University, New Haven, Conn. 06520.

Cover: "Metaphor," pen and ink drawing by Timothy J. Reiss

Copyright © *Yale French Studies* 1973
Indexed in *Social Sciences and Humanities Index*
Forty-ninth in the series

PRINTED IN SPAIN
I. S. B. N. 84-399-1730-9
Depósito Legal: V. 4.475 - 1973

Timothy J. Reiss

Introduction: The Word/World Equation

> What a piece of work is man! how
> noble in reason! how infinite in faculty!
> in form, in moving, how express and
> admirable! in action how like an angel!
> in apprehension how like a god! the
> beauty of the world! the paragon of
> animals! And yet, to me, what is this
> quintessence of dust? man delights not
> me.
>
> SHAKESPEARE, *Hamlet*

> Mark all mathematical heads, which be
> only and wholly bent to those sciences,
> how solitary they be themselves, how
> unfit to live with others, and how unapt
> to serve in the world.
>
> ROGER ASCHAM, *The Scholemaster*

"For almost two centuries, the European scientific mind has put forward an unprecedented effort to explain the world, so as to conquer and transform it."[1] Only now is this mind—at least commonly—becoming aware that something is amiss in this desire for possession. If we have long since ceased to believe that the world was made for man by some divine intelligence, we have nonetheless continued to believe it was ours for the taking. Assuming the possibility of a total understanding of *nature, reality,* etc., we have supposed that possession only meant a harmless *using,* not a destruction. Still, Reimannian geometry has offered an alternative to the Euclidian, genetics has reduced organism to the inorganic, Marx, Freud, Einstein, have shown that the old adage remains truer than ever as the more we learn so the less certain becomes our knowledge. If we cannot be sure *whence*

[1] Mircea Eliade, *Forgerons et alchimistes* (Paris, 1956), p. 12.

3

came this original certainty (the precision of origins being a part of it), we can at least gain some idea of *when*.

Two events of immense symbolic significance lie at the doorway of what Whitehead has termed "the first century of modern science." The first, in 1600, is the burning of Bruno, the thinker who in so many ways suggests the effort to bind together two different modes of thought: "In his execution there was an unconscious symbolism: for the subsequent tone of scientific thought has contained distrust of his type of general speculativeness." [2]

The second event occurred a decade later, when in the latter half of 1609 the creation of modern technological thinking was given its most dramatic metaphor as Galileo interposed the distance of the telescope in the space between the human mind and the material world before it, the object of its gaze. The metaphor became distinctly literary and was to haunt, directly or indirectly, much of the imaginative writing of the following century from the moment the scientist chose to write it down and publish it as the *Sidereus Nuncius* in 1610.

Galileo's telescope, needless to say, is only a confirmation of a visual distancing whose entrance into consciousness this sign marks. For at least since the considerations of Cusanus upon perspective the abstractions of a continuous *interpretation* of the material signs were reduced by a certain visualization. And what Father Ong has been able to say of Ramus's "reduction" of the linguistic order to visual image (in *Ramus, Method, and the Decay of Dialogue*), Michel Beaujour and Jean Paris have been able to say already of Rabelais.

The telescope, though, may be taken as a fair representation of what happened to the linguistic sign. When it was felt to inhere in the thing, it was at once the subject and the object of an interpretative reading of the *signatura rerum*. Eventually the word, so to speak, passed down the telescope with the image until it was conceived of as a simple mental creation, having a quite arbitrary connection with the thing; but the very arbitrariness of the relationship between sign and object—or, more precisely, between signifier and referent—even-

[2] Alfred North Whitehead, *Science and the Modern World* (1925; rpt. New York, 1967), p. 1.

tually permitted a belief in the adequacy of word series in their association with things and their ordering.

The preoccupation with language throughout the century dates certainly from at least the beginning of the previous, the sixteenth, century. It is only to be expected that the multitude of *Arts poétiques,* from that of L'Infortuné (1500) to those of Laudun (1597) and Vauquelin (1605) should have made language one of their primary concerns. Less easy to account for is the similar preoccupation of nearly every published humanist, culminating towards the end of the century—after the briefer volumes of a Dolet or a Peletier—in the diatribes of Montaigne, of Charron, and in the longer and more formal works on the subject by Henri Estienne and Pasquier. At first they seek a language capable of expressing no more than the *interaction* of the human mind with the world of objects about it. More and more the *expression* of external "reality" is received as representing reality as it is. The difficulty many appear to have had in accepting the notion that the Copernican system was a merely useful mathematical model was compounded by the success of the empirical work of Gilbert, the discoveries of Galileo, and, a little later, those of Harvey. This development found an echo in writers and critics who aimed increasingly at an apparent clarity which would remove the awareness that language was capable of expressing only the human perception of things. There is a passage from a language conscious of itself as a human expression of the world of phenomena, and which does not try to take the place of that world, to a language which claims to represent "objectively" that world's phenomena.

The change, of course, is neither as simple nor as absolute as the above sketch seems to imply. Nonetheless, with Copernicus, Kepler and, most of all, Galileo—owing partly to his polemical turn of mind, notably absent in the other two—there was dealt a series of critical, if not mortal, blows not merely to an abstract system of ideas concerning the universe, but to the concrete, sensuous image of it. This was no doubt the result of those factors which we generally consider to have characterized the phenomenon known as the Renaissance—an

5

outburst of confidence in man's energies, in his capacity to know, in his ability to seize and conduct the world around him, *in his own name*.

The overthrow of the system under which this confidence grew had a not unpredictable effect. In so far as it had enabled the rejection of a system accepted until then as axiomatic, the confidence had shown itself a force to be reckoned with, if not well-placed. Its cost, however, was not merely the swaying of that confidence, but the revelation of the insufficiencies of our sense impressions and of the impossibility of our basing any intellectual system of the external world upon them. A contact between mind and matter was lost. Man placed himself to one side of matter.

The Copernican system, therefore, was presented by Andreas Osiander (anonymously) as a purely intellectual one. This preface would appear to be less cautious than it professes. It is certainly ambiguous. Implicit therein, as in the theory it preceded, is a rejection of the senses as a reliable source of knowledge and a new faith in what Descartes refers to as pure intellection. [3] As far as the ecclesiastical authority was concerned the axiomatic rejection in the Aristotelian (and Platonic) system of any ontological concordance between geometrical figures and physical bodies was thereby upheld.

Galileo himself seems, in fact, to maintain the separation to a considerable degree. This may be why the scientist cannot accept the Keplerian elliptical solar system but insists upon its circular form, continuing to assert the latter's perfection as a geometrical figure until his death. [4] The process that Galileo starts, as is made most clear, I think, in the *Letter to the Grand Duchess Christina*—because of its brevity and polemical purpose—but which is not much less apparent in the *Dialogue Concerning the Two Chief World Systems*, is the

[3] I say "implicit" deliberately—it is, of course, clear that its presentation as a mathematical model means it may be set *as such* against any other mathematical model, including the Ptolemaic. While this may ostensibly be intended to subordinate the new system to the authority of the older one, it is calculated to raise questions. It was not, in any case, until the observations of Galileo, the calculations of Kepler, and Newton's pattern, that *any* mathematical model was able satisfactorily to match observed phenomena.

[4] See Erwin Panofsky, *Galileo as a Critic of the Arts* (The Hague, 1954).

jumping of sense impressions and the making of direct contact between intellection and the physical world: hence, for example, the parable concerning the man on shipboard who thinks the shore is moving and its application to earthbound man who thinks the sun is moving (though this image is by no means original with Galileo, being used before him by, among many others no doubt, Virgil and, revealingly, Cusanus). As he remarks in the *Dialogue:* "... with regard to those few [geometrical and mathematical propositions concerning nature] which the human intellect does understand, I believe its knowledge equals the Divine in objective certainty ... " [5]

Still, the recognition that signs (whether mathematical or linguistic) fall in between the conceptualizing mind and the world of objects, in the space of the telescope itself, to keep our metaphor, having identity neither with the one nor with the other, is certainly made by Galileo himself—as Professor Drake makes clear in some detail in his essay. For him, discourse represents not the object itself but the *distance* between the object and the mind *per*ceiving and, then, *cc.n*ceiving it. The grave problem of representation that this poses (for we should not translate into discourse a conception that is an *individual* representation of the thing perceived as though it were the thing) is squarely faced by Galileo. In Bacon the solution is sought in what he terms "a gradual and unbroken ascent," in effect an endless chain of reasoning. Experimental language is not at first an attempt to describe the thing itself, so much as a description of the human *sighting* of that thing, of a *particular* relationship between an object clearly defined in space and time and the mind perceiving it under the same restrictions. Language stands for the distance. Not so for Descartes.

There is no question but that Descartes, from the *Regulae* on, is far more radical than this. He chooses to reject occular evidence altogether, or, more precisely perhaps, occular propositions (preferring to reconstruct them from "first principles," as he does in *Le Monde*

---

5 Galileo Galilei, *Dialogue Concerning the Two Chief World Systems— Ptolemaic and Copernican,* trans. Stillman Drake, 2nd ed. (Berkeley & Los Angeles, 1970), p. 103.

and the *Traité de l'homme*). The effect of this is ultimately to impose an intellectual structure upon the perceived world. And Descartes' aim is indeed possession. [6] The Galilean trinity of mind/language/ phenomena (curiously similar to the structural linguist's signified/ signifier/referent) is reduced by Cartesianism to a dichotomy: language reveals thought, and in so far as it refers to objects it can operate as a perfect stand-in for them. It is not, to be sure, the object itself; but it is conceived of as a sufficiently accurate representation for the purposes of discourse, into whose system it may be inserted. It is interesting to see how, at the beginning of *Le Monde,* Descartes plays on an ambiguity in the verb *concevoir:* meaning at once, "to understand," "to gain an idea of," and "to perceive." Thus his notion of conception comes to mean at once the thing itself as perceived *and* the idea one has of it. This ambiguity—it recurs constantly— permits the epistemological leap. Still, in Cartesianism, it is not the sign that has some kind of essential integrity in regard to its relationship with objects, such that the scholastic may hope always to find an identity. On the contrary, the division of the sign permits the assimilation of the "order" of things into the system of language. What is signified is the conception of the thing, but the conception is *also* its perception. While what is perceived is not to be confused with the reality of the thing (*viz.* the celebrated wax image of the second *Meditation*), the signifying of it within the sign is nonetheless *adequate* by virtue on the one hand of the signifier's very arbitrariness, but on the other, and more importantly, because perception and conception participate in the same moment in the ascription of meaning. This participation is already in Descartes, the adequation (explicitly rejected by him—e.g. in the third and sixth *Meditations*) will be the contribution of subsequent Cartesianism. When the Port-Royal theories of language and thought argue that the verb is an affirmation of things rather than a simple statement of perception, they are arguing that, grammatically speaking (and, hence, in their terms, epistemologically), the affirmation of things *contains* the statement of per-

[6] See, for example, the 6th part of the *Discours de la Méthode.*

ception and subsumes it. Again, I would suggest, this is because the signified is seen as congruent, if not identical in fact, with the referent. Port-Royal has already travelled some distance from Descartes to Cartesianism. By means of *conception* word and thing are brought to coincide. Possession is made possible.

This same desire is apparent in the Malherbian systematization of a literary code, seeking to give an adequate representation of a nature claimed as essentially objective. This is sometimes used, as in Racan, for example, to *prevent* the loosening of the structure "read" out of things. Instead of an ideal exchange between the scientist's encoding of nature and his perception of it, calling for a constant readapting of the code—such as Galileo seeks—Racan uses it to trap nature in a pre-Copernican form, just as Descartes, or at least the Cartesians, will assert the possession of it after Galileo. Both seem to be a function of a denial that the human view of the world is necessarily a perspectival one, and the second has come to it after a conscious search for some process to render this view a-perspectival. It is of considerable interest to know that it was just at this time in France that the need was felt for a word which would express the inexpressible as an "objective," describable *something.* The very fact of language, expressing the *exchange* between mind and matter, should make such a need unnecessary. Yet Professor Borgerhoff was able to note a first substantival use of the phrase *je-ne-sais-quoi* in 1628. [7]

From the notion that the word is in some way essential in the object that tends to prevail in popular writing even into the seventeenth century (in Claude Duret's anachronistic *Thrésor de l'histoire des langues* [1613], for example) to the idea that it is only a sign for the object it arbitrarily designates is, of course, an immense step; but both attitudes suppose that it is possible for the mind in some way to *know* nature. However, the first is open to constant interpretation: we can know details, we cannot know essential reality, for that belongs in a structure of which we ourselves are but a small

---

[7] E. B. O. Borgerhoff, *The Freedom of French Classicism* (Princeton, 1950), p. 190. The use occurs in Ogier's *Apologie pour Monsieur de Balzac.*

static part. The second rapidly comes to imply that naming an object or event is knowing it. The former can do with a relatively loose verbal structure, because things have a structure of their own; the latter requires a tight system because things otherwise become incoherent. For the mind that works in this way "every phenomenon is a moment in the theoretical mind, a stage of discursive thinking, a *prepared-for* result." [8] This mind Bachelard calls the "formal imagination." Its opposite he calls the "material imagination": a mode of thinking which uses the *images* of things, the immediately striking events, as its code. It is pre-conscious. It is what Lévi-Strauss refers to as mythical thought. [9]

In literature, as suggested, the manifestations of this change are quite rapid. The tension is visible between a "pre-Galilean" notion of language as a *means* of perception and a new distancing from language which permits the belief in an a-perspectival view of a nonhuman world: when the model becomes the reality of which it was previously but the expression. Thus the moving shore/stationary ship image is taken up in philosophy and literature by Cyrano, Bernier and Fontenelle, in morality and language by Pascal, with similar implications. But in Cyrano it is thrown into doubt by a critique of language itself, while in Pascal the ambiguities of its context serve to invalidate it. The invention of analytical geometry and calculus is obviously of great significance, but confusion as to the use of language subsists still in Newton, long after the strange mixture of the affective and the objective apparent, for example, in Mersenne's translation of Galileo's *Mechanics* (1634).

There is a contradiction between what language is and what it is being used for; between, on the one hand, language as the artist's best means of expressing and understanding *himself* in the world and, on the other, language as a descriptive instrument capable of

---

[8] Gaston Bachelard, *La Formation de l'esprit scientifique: Contribution à une psychanalyse de la connaissance objective*, 7ᵉ édition (Paris, 1970), p. 102.
[9] See, e.g., *The Savage Mind* (Chicago, 1966), pp. 19-21. It is from Bachelard that I take the titles of the first two parts of this collection: by the first, I mean the deliberate, logical thinking about the problems involved; by the second I mean their appearance (possibly unknown to their authors) in the very fabric of texts.

being regularized into geometrical, algebraïc, or even, perhaps, *précieux* forms. But the abuse of such regularization was leading to its takeover of the world of phenomena, and much of the agony of the critics of the period [10] is due perhaps to the realization that awareness of the truly perspectival nature of language is being replaced by the probably false premise that the expression of human perception is the exact reflexion of the external world. One result of this is the decidedly equivocal attraction of these critics to literary rules, whose possible analogy with an experimental language proves so attractive to the eighteenth century. This, too, may be the significance of the appearance of so-called *normative grammars* toward the second half of the seventeenth century: Bloomfield dismisses the grammarians responsible as contradicting linguistic principles, [11] but it is clear that any correspondence between the word and the world could have no meaning if the word side of the equation could not be fixed—a fact that would seem to be at the basis of Boileau's criticism of pastoral.

From the Cartesian attempt to substitute a logical human symbolic system for the natural signs within a mechanized universe, to the Pascalian critique of such a substitution and what would appear to be Bayle's optimistic effort to posit a kind of "passionate Cartesian reason," capable of organizing the world yet aware of its essential limitations, the whole dilemma of Western thought is fought out. That economic and spatial limitations oblige this collection to omit such important contributors to the process as Spinoza and Newton, Locke and Leibniz, is unfortunate but not, I think, a necessarily central loss. The process begun by Kepler and Galileo is only completed by Newton, and the views propounded by Bacon and Descartes can be traced through many successors; the objections of a Pascal or a Bayle resume those of others; Gassendi and Hobbes would seem to represent quite fairly the dynamics of change.

In concluding this introduction, lest it be felt that I am suggesting any precise origins, temporal or otherwise, for the processes here

---

[10] See Jules Brody, *Boileau and Longinus* (Geneva, 1958), and Borgerhoff, *op. cit.*
[11] Leonard Bloomfield, *Language* (1933, 1935; rpt. London, 1970), pp. 6-7, 496-97 & *passim.*

discussed, I would like to refer to a thinker who, almost exactly two centuries before the *Discourse on Method,* was considering just these problems. Writing that words and things are in no essential association, Nicolas Cusanus observes forcefully that all thought processes are but generalizations by slightly supported analogy, and that our arbitrary sign systems cannot be taken as representing any reality but an entirely subjective one. It is a lesson the post-Cartesian individual might well take to heart:

It so far surpasses human reason, however, to know the precision of the combinations in material things and how exactly the known has to be adapted to the unknown that Socrates thought he knew nothing save his own ignorance, whilst Solomon, the Wise, affirmed that in all things there are difficulties which beggar explanation in words... in presence of such difficulty we may be compared to owls trying to look at the sun.... [12]

---

[12] Nicolas Cusanus, *Of Learned Ignorance* [1440], trans. Germain Heron. Introduction by D. J. B. Hawkins (New Haven, 1954), p. 8.

Stillman Drake

Galileo's Language: Mathematics and Poetry in a New Science

> Names and attributes must be accommodated to the essences of things, and not essences to names; for things come first, and names afterward.
>
> GALILEO (1613)

> If the opinions of philosophers, and their words, have the power to call into existence the things they consider and name, why then I beg them the favor of their considering and naming "gold" a lot of old hardware I have about the house.
>
> GALILEO (1623)

In his famous *Dialogue,* written two decades after Galileo left his chair of mathematics at the University of Padua and took the post of chief mathematician and philosopher to the Grand Duke of Tuscany, he made his own spokesman declare that "Our discourses must relate to the sensible world, and not just to one on paper." [1] The demand would have been axiomatic to the practical Florentines at the Tuscan court. But to Galileo's former colleagues at the university it would have seemed in principle impossible of fulfillment, and in practice a revolutionary slogan threatening the very foundations of conventional philosophy.

Now, the latter is precisely what Galileo intended it to be, and that fact has much to do with his insistence on the title of "philosopher" to the Grand Duke. What he meant by that word is pretty much what we mean today by the word "physicist," a calling for

---

[1] Stillman Drake, *Discoveries and Opinions of Galileo,* Translated with an Introduction and Notes (New York, 1957), p. 113. Henceforth referred to in the text as *Discoveries.*

which there was as yet no place in the universities. Accordingly he set up shop outside them, and proceeded to inculcate a rival discipline to theirs, founded on a new physics that dealt directly with the world of sensible phenomena.

It is generally overlooked that the exposition of Galileo's new science was concerned in an essential way with language and its applications. He himself did not stress the point, but it is reflected in many passages such as the two that have been placed as mottoes at the head of this paper. The guiding idea is vividly illustrated in the *Dialogue,* where Galileo ridicules those who would deduce the nature of things from the writings of ancient philosophers and poets:

I have a little book, much briefer than Aristotle or Ovid, in which the whole of science is contained, and with some little study one may form from it the most perfect ideas. It is the alphabet; and no doubt anyone who can join and order this or that vowel with these or those consonants can dig out of it the truest answers to every question, and can draw from it instruction in all the arts and sciences. Just so does a painter, from various simple colors placed separately on his palette, by gathering a little of this one with a bit of that and a trifle of the other, depict men, plants, buildings, birds, fishes —and in short represent every visible object—without any eyes or feathers or scales or leaves or stones being present on his palette. It is indeed necessary that none of the things represented, or any parts thereof, should be actually included among the colors, if one wants them capable of representing everything; for if among these there were, say, feathers, then those would not serve for depicting anything but birds, or feather-dusters." 2

This started as an obvious sarcasm directed against men who thought that by consulting the indexes to Aristotle's works, they could answer every question. But Galileo's metaphor went far beyond that. Quite possibly it constitutes the first clear recognition of the powers and limitations of language as a means of discoursing about the nature of things. The elements of the language used cannot be found in the things themselves. We shall see presently how this bears on Galileo's novel (and much misunderstood) view of the role of mathematics, and on his neglected but important view of the role of poetic

2 Galileo Galilei, *Dialogue Concerning the Two Chief World Systems— Ptolemaic and Copernican,* trans. Stillman Drake (Berkeley & Los Angeles, 1967), p. 109. Henceforth referred to in the text as *Dialogue.*

metaphor, in science. For the present, let us note that he here asserted the possibility of discoursing in everyday language about problems that traditionally had always been dealt with by recourse to technical jargon. Galileo saw that what was really required in order to avoid turning the sensible world into a mere world on paper was not the artificial vocabulary of philosophers; rather, it was a certain kind of artistry in the use of the ordinary resources of language.

It may be that others before Galileo had used similar analogies, or had otherwise attempted to make clear the role of language itself in dealing with the world of sense. But if so, I think they can have been neither many, nor influential. Francis Bacon warned about the same time of certain pitfalls inherent in the structure of language that had escaped the attention of philosophers. But that is hardly the same thing. To make the actual world come alive on paper takes more than the avoidance of logical and semantic errors. A man does not become a painter merely by avoiding distortions of natural colors and forms; indeed, what often makes a painter great is his deliberate and skillful use of such devices.

"To depict burnished armor, for example, one must alternate pure black and white, one beside the other, in parts of the armor where [in fact] the light falls evently" (*Dialogue*, p. 79). Yet at the same time, craftsmanship is capable of abuse in philosophy as in painting:

> [Some philosophers] wish never to raise their eyes from those pages, as if this great book of the universe had been written to be read by nobody but Aristotle.... These fellows ... put me in mind of certain capricious painters who occasionally limit themselves, for sport, to represent a human face or some other thing by throwing together [on canvas] some agricultural implements, or different fruits, or perhaps the flowers of a given season. Such bizarre performances, so long as they are put forth in jest, are both pretty and pleasant, and they reveal more resourcefulness in some artists than in others. ... But if anyone ... should conclude in general that every other manner of representation was blameworthy ... he would be laughed to scorn by distinguished painters. (*Discoveries*, p. 127)

Galileo's avowed goal appeared unattainable in principle to many contemporaries because of the philosophical question, "How can words set down on paper deal with the sensible world that is quite independent of language?" Philosophers, lacking the artistry of poets (who manage that feat very well indeed), had long since abandoned the attempt to deal with the sensible world as such, leaving that part of physics to mere mechanics. In so doing, they had found a marvelous justification for their action. The sensible world is ephemeral, filled with illustion, and hardly worth the trouble of serious study. But behind it, they believed, there must lie permanent things, transcending the sensible world in interest and importance, and perhaps transcending it in reality. It was to such things that philosophers directed their attention, and that is why Galileo's demand threatened the very basis of real scholarship.

A typical dispute that occupied philosophers was waged between those who regarded mathematics alone as possessing eternal verities deserving of study for their own sake, and others who disparaged mathematics in favor of Aristotle's vocabulary and grammar as the key to lasting truth. These two persuasions are known as Platonism and Aristotelianism. If, with Josiah Willard Gibbs,[3] we consider mathematics itself a language, then the traditional dispute centers on which of two languages holds the key to our universe: geometry, or Greek? In place of this ancient dilemma, Galileo introduced a new conception, though its element of novelty has generally escaped notice. This has happened because historians of science, like philosophers, are usually more interested in the dispute (which is indeed eternal) than in Galileo (who was certainly ephemeral). His celebrated metaphor was this:

Philosophy is written in this grand book, the universe, which stands continually open to our gaze. But the book cannot be understood unless one first learns to comprehend the language and to read the letters in which it is composed. It is written in the language of mathematics, and its characters are triangles, circles, and other geometric figures, without which it is humanly impossible to understand a single word of it: without these, one goes wandering about in a dark labyrinth. (*Discoveries*, pp. 237-38).

[3] It is said that when Gibbs was professor of mathematics at Yale, shortage of funds made it necessary to consider the elimination of departments other than those of theology and languages. Gibbs rose to say, "Gentlemen, mathematics is a language."

Stillman Drake

In their understandable zeal to classify Galileo as one of the traditional disputants, most commentators regard this passage as putting him squarely in the camp of the Platonists. It seems to them that he here identified the universe we live in with that of mathematics, as so many other powerful thinkers have done. But in this they entirely ignore the linguistic consideration that was the source and whole point of Galileo's metaphor. This may be seen from the context in which it appeared, where poetry and fiction were being contrasted with science. There are in fact three elements in Galileo's metaphor, and not just the two which concerned all previous (and most subsequent) philosophers. The three elements are: a certain book, what is written in it, and the language in which that is written there.

Since the book is "the universe which stands continually open to our gaze," it can hardly be anything but the sensible world. Eternal mathematical truth does not stand open to our gaze, at least in the ordinary sense. We cannot gaze at partless points or breadthless lines. And Galileo was very keen on the ordinary senses of words, particularly such words as "gaze."

What is written in that book (the sensible world) is proper philosophy. To the extent that other books bear that title but fail to deal with the sensible world, they concern only worlds on paper. This notion is clear in many other places in Galileo's writings.

Finally, the language in which proper philosophy is written in the book (the sensible world) is the language of mathematics. This language is identified by Galileo neither with the sensible world nor with philosophy; still less is it treated as anything worthy of study for its own sake. Rather, Galileo speaks of the language of mathematics as the unique means to an understanding of something else; and that something else is precisely the sensible world which Platonists disparaged as ephemeral and illusory, and undeserving of special study.

Interest in the sensible world was anything but new, except perhaps to philosophers. But Galileo's linguistic metaphor was new, in that it presented mathematics as an instrument that would enable philosophy to discourse with accuracy about the sensible world. That was never Plato's conception. The desired end-product, however, need not be written in mathematical language at all, and certainly not exclusively. So far as Galileo was concerned, it was better written in Italian than in scholarly Latin. It was no accident that Galileo preferred a living language for the purposes of his new science; in the same way, his great Flemish contemporary, Simon Stevin, took Dutch to be the ideal language for science. The reason that Galileo once gave for his choice reflected a Renaissance penchant for popular education. (Another and more cogent reason will be given later.) When a German adversary could not read his book on sunspots, Galileo asked a friend who was a fine Latinist to translate it, writing to him:

I wrote it in the vernacular because I need to have anyone [here] able to read it; and for the same reason I also wrote my last little treatise [on hydrostatics] in Italian. The reason that moves me is my seeing how young men are sent indiscriminately to the university to be made into doctors, philosophers, and so on; and just as there are many who apply themselves to such professions but are most unsuited to them, so there are other men that would be apt, but who are taken up by family cares or other matters remote from letters. They have horse-sense, as Ruzzante would say, but because they cannot read things written in Latin, they persuade themselves that great new discoveries in logic and philosophy are published in awful books that remain way over their heads. Now, I want them to see that just as Nature gave to them, as well as to philosophers, eyes to see her works, so she has also given them brains capable of understanding those works. (*Discoveries*, p. 84)

Here, then, was a further linguistic characteristic (if not requirement) of Galileo's new science. The key was mathematics, but the goal was scientific discourse in easily intelligible terms. Popular education seems to have been only a part of the reason for this. It is at least debatable whether even today it would be possible to write physics without any intermediation whatever of ordinary language. Certainly that was not possible in Galileo's time. The answer to the question, "How is it possible to discourse of the sensible world when that is separate from and independent of language?" is, roughly speaking, "By constant allusions that redirect attention from words to the things of experience." That answer is not likely ever to satisfy philosophers, but it was adopted in practice by Galileo. And he realized that allusions to experience are far more effective, and much easier to manage, in the language of everyday life than in a specialized scholarly language.

Galileo's books are filled with such allusions, often quite colloquial in style. His readers are thus constantly reminded of familiar experiences and observations; of little puzzles that occur to everyone but are usually pushed aside; and of palpable absurdities that no one would ever expect to encounter. The backspin of a *bocce* ball delivered overhand, the curious rebound of a tennis ball struck with the racket slantwise, and the mingled kiss-and-bite on the ear of a slight dissonance are as much a part of Galileo's science as are the parabolic trajectory and the regular beat of the pendulum. The way to put the sensible world on paper without thereby reducing it to a paper world was to keep the reader's mind on things of experience rather than on verbal technicalities. The poets are great masters of this art. They bring experience to life by a single word or a brief phrase, when the same experience would remain lifeless through a paragraph of objective description. Galileo borrowed their technique, and he ascribed his own clarity of style to his intimate familiarity with the poetry of Ariosto. It was probably this poetic artistry that suggested to him the analogy, previously cited, between the alphabet and the simple colors on a painter's palette.

Poetry is acquired by continual reading of the poets; painting is acquired by continual painting and drawing; the art of proof, by reading books filled with demonstrations—and these are exclusively mathematical books, not books on logic. (*Dialogue*, p. 35)

Galileo's view of mathematics has already been touched on. His mistrust of logic will be mentioned again presently. In part, it mirrored his keen sensitivity for language and an attendant dislike for jargon. In this, he was indeed a follower of Plato, who "went to some pains to vary his terminology in what seems to be a deliberate attempt to resist the congealing of technical terms, and the implication of the Socratic-centered Platonic dialogue is still that two reasonably educated citizens can sit down and discuss these matters. ... With Aristotle, the professionalism implicit in the founding of the Academy comes of age in language." [4]

Aristotelian logic puts language in a straitjacket, expecting in this way to constrain it within any chosen universe of discourse—say that of the sensible world. But by its very insistence on precise definition, formal logic may sometimes remove words even further than necessary from the things of our experience. Freed from such restraint and used with artistry, ordinary words suffice to recall any common experience with remarkable efficiency and precision. Thus no logical description of the moon seen in daytime could be more effective in fixing its appearance than to say, with Galileo, that it resembles a little bleached cloud. Those words accurately present the moon of the sensible world under certain conditions. They fail utterly to present the mathematical moon of our astronomers, the physical moon of our scientists, or the Aristotelian moon that separates the elemental from the celestial regions. Galileo's phrase is one that poets might employ, though not for his purposes in invoking it. The phrase is poetic, but the purpose was scientific, as we shall see; and in his own words: "Nature does not delight in poetry. ... Fables and fictions are in a way essential to poetry, which could not exist without them; while any sort of falsehood is so abhorrent to nature that it is as absent there as darkness is in light." (*Discoveries,* p. 238) [5]

The use of a poetic device to portray anything in nature, when nature abhors fiction and poesy thrives on it, is logically unacceptable. On the other hand, the use of such a device not indeed to represent anything, but to call vividly to mind some actual experience, served a most useful purpose for Galileo. He saw in this the way to make sure that his discourse related to the sensible world, and not just to one on paper. How this was done will be seen below; since hardly

[4] F. E. Peters, *Greek Philosophical Terms* (New York, 1967), pp. xi-xii.
[5] This passage is an essential part of the context of Galileo's celebrated metaphor in which the language of mathematics mediates between philosophy and the sensible universe.

any physicist after Galileo employed such devices, I think it worth giving this one example in full. It is not as trivial as it may seem, and the technique is far from unique among Galileo's published writings.

Simplicio, who speaks for the philosophers, has just asserted that the gross and impure earth is unfitted to reflect sunlight as does the moon, a heavenly body and composed of the pure quintessential substance. The scientific question involved is Galileo's explanation of the moon's faint illumination near new moon, caused by reflection of sunlight from the earth. Ultimately coupled with this was the destruction of the Aristotelian dogma that the heavenly bodies are of a totally different substance from the elements surrounding us. This in turn relates to the principle of the uniformity of nature, on which all Galileo's new science (like the very existence of ordinary language itself) was made to depend. Thus the ensuing passage is an integral part of a vast program of reeducation intended to replace dogma with sensible evidence:

SALVIATI: Tell me; when the moon is nearly full, so that it can be seen by day and also in the middle of the night, does it appear more brilliant in the daytime, or at night?
SIMPLICIO: Incomparably more at night. It seems to me that the moon resembles those pillars of cloud and of fire which guided the children of Israel; for in the presence of the sun it shows itself like a little cloud, but then at night it is most splendid. Thus I have sometimes observed the moon by day among small clouds, and it looked like a little bleached one; but in the night that followed it shone very splendidly.
SALV.: So that if you had never happened to see the moon except by day, you would not have judged it brighter than one of those clouds?
SIMP.: I do believe you are right.
SALV.: Now tell me, do you believe that the moon is really brighter at night than by day, or just that by some accident it looks that way?
SIMP.: I believe that it shines intrinsically as much by day as by night, but that its light looks greater at night because we see it in the dark field of the sky. In daytime, because everything around it is very bright, by its small addition of light it appears much less bright.
SALV.: Now tell me: have you ever seen the terrestrial globe lit up by the sun in the middle of the night?
SIMP.: That seems to me to be a question that is not asked except in jest, or only of some person notorious for his lack of wit.

SALV.: No, no; I take you for a very sensible man, and ask the question in earnest. So answer just the same, and then if it shall seem to you that I am talking nonsense, I shall be taken for the brainless one; for he is a greater fool who asks a silly question than he to whom the question is put.

SIMP.: Then if you do not take me for a complete simpleton, pretend that I have answered you by saying that it is impossible for anyone who is on earth, as we are, to see by night that part of the earth where it is day; that is, the part struck by the sun.

SALV.: So you have never chanced to see the earth illuminated except by day, while you see the moon shining in the sky on the darkest night as well. Now that, Simplicio, is the reason for your believing that the earth does not shine like the moon; for if you could see the earth illuminated while you were in a place as dark as night, it would look to you more splendid than the moon. And if you want to proceed properly with the comparison, the analogy must be drawn between the earth's light and that of the moon as seen in daytime—not the nocturnal moon, because there is no chance of our seeing the earth illuminated except by day. Is that satisfactory?

SIMP.: So it must be.

SALV.: Now you yourself have already admitted having seen the moon by day among little whitish clouds, and similar in appearance to one of them. This amounts to your granting at the outset that those little clouds, though made of elemental matter, are just as fit to receive light as is the moon. More so, if you will recall in memory having seen at times some very large clouds, white as snow. It cannot be doubted that if such a cloud could remain equally luminous on the darkest night, it would light up the surrounding regions more than a hundred moons.

If we were sure, then, that the earth is as much lighted by the sun as is one of those clouds, no question would remain about its being no less brilliant than the moon. But all doubt on this point vanishes when we see the same clouds, in the absence of the sun, remaining as dark as the earth all night long; and what is more, there is not one of us who has not seen such a cloud, low and far off, and wondered whether it was a cloud or a mountain —a clear indication that mountains are no less luminous than those clouds. (*Dialogue,* pp. 87-89)

I think it hardly possible to read the foregoing dialogue without recalling to mind actual experiences of one's own; that is, I believe it would take superhuman effort to read Galileo's argument while keeping one's attention focused solely and strictly on its words, forgetting how the things named actually look, and how we might expect things to look if we could see them under conditions that never do exist for us. You would look in vain for any counterpart of this kind of persuasion in ancient and medieval commentaries on Aristotle's

Physica or *De caelo,* at least in those I have read. There you would indeed find compelling arguments, logically designed to convince you (with Simplicio) that gross earth is unfitted to shine like a heavenly body. In such arguments you are, it is true, invited to think of experiences, though not vivid ones: the experiences of grossness, of shining, and of the fitness of things. But it is not necessary that you do so, since the definitions suffice; and when we are reading dead languages, or technical terms in living ones, there is little stimulus to recall our own experiences.

Galileo would have been perfectly capable of writing the above argument in technical terms, and even with the objectivity that we associate with scientific writing of today. Whether that would have made it better science is an interesting question, that in turn would raise questions about the purpose or goal of scientific writing. On the whole, the goal of modern science seems to me to resemble that of the Platonists and Aristotelians of Galileo's time a good deal more than it resembles Galileo's goal. It is therefore fitting that modern science tends to be written in technical terms without the slightest tincture of poetic metaphor. It is of interest that Galileo rejected such a style, though it already prevailed around him. Had he adopted it, it is likely that he would have reached the top of the academic profession, would not have left the university to serve the Grand Duke, and would have died in universal esteem rather than as a condemned heretic.

The style used in writing a scientific work in any era requires respect for precision. Galileo's predecessors sought logical precision; his successors sought mathematical precision. Galileo did not turn his back on either of these; instead, he recognized and added other ways of making things precise. One, as we have seen, was that of invoking experience vividly. Another was the application of horse-sense, for which Galileo had a respect unusual in academics of his time.

Philosophers... attribute the rumbling of thunder to the tearing apart of clouds, or to their knocking together. Actually, during the brilliance of the brightest flashes of lightning, not the slightest movement or change of shape

23

is discerned in the clouds, and that is just when thunder is being created. I pass over in silence the fact that those same philosophers do not say that noise is produced by the striking of wool or hemp, but require the percussion of solid bodies to make sound. Yet at another time, when it suits their purpose, they assert that mists and clouds on striking together will render the loudest of all sounds. Tractable and benign indeed is such philosophy, so pleasantly and readily adapting itself to men's needs and wishes! (*Discoveries*, p. 269)

Galileo's mistrust of logic may originally have grown out of its frequent abuse in such cases as the above; for only by misapplied logic could such a theory of thunder have originated. His preference for mathematics over logic may be attributable in part to the relative difficulty of similarly misapplying mathematics. Geometric shapes, or numbers obtained from measurement, are not the least bit tractable. Where mathematical expressions happen to apply to the sensible world, they do not readily adapt themselves to men's wishes. Often they do not apply at all, "But in this," Galileo wrote to a friend late in life, "I have been lucky; for the events of falling bodies do correspond punctually with the properties I had found" in the hypothetical treatment of accelerated motion. [6]

It is evident from that remark that Galileo did not believe that everything mathematical has a counterpart in nature. No more did he believe that everything in nature must have some mathematical counterpart. That astounding revelation was reserved for his younger contemporary, René Descartes. In the Cartesian scheme of things, which quickly supplanted Galileo's, every phenomenon in the universe was in principle capable of explanation in terms of matter and motion, and hence mathematically—at the expense, of course, of reverting to the earlier custom of discoursing about worlds on paper. Galileo had said:

There is not a single effect in nature, not even the least that exists, such that the most ingenious theorists can ever arrive at a complete understanding of it. The vain presumption of understanding everything can have no other basis than [that of] never having understood anything. For anyone who had experienced just once the perfect understanding of one single thing would

[6] Letter to G. B. Baliani, 7 January 1639.

recognize that of the infinity of other truths he understands nothing. (*Dialogue,* p. 101)

Galileo was, however, by no means pessimistic about the progress of science, so long as its objectives were kept with the bounds of men's powers:

All things among which men wander remain equally unknown, and we pass by things both near and remote with very little or no real acquisition of knowledge. When I ask what the substance of clouds may be, and am told it is a moist vapor, I shall wish to know in turn what vapor is. Peradventure I shall be told that it is water, which when attenuated by heat is resolved into vapor. Equally curious about what water is, I shall then seek to find this out, ultimately learning that it is this fluid body which runs in our rivers and which we constantly handle. But this final information about water is no more intimate than what I knew about clouds in the first place; it is merely closer at hand and dependent on more of my senses. Similarly, I know no more about the true essences of earth and fire than I do about those of the moon or the sun....

But if what we wish to fix in our minds is the apprehending of some properties of things, then it seems to me that we need not despair of our ability to acquire this with respect to distant bodies as well as those close at hand—and perhaps in some cases even more precisely in the former than in the latter. Who does not understand the periods and movements of the planets better than those of the waters in our various oceans? Was not the spherical shape of the moon discovered long before that of the earth, and much more easily? Is it not still argued whether the earth rest motionless or goes wandering, whereas we definitely know the movements of many stars? (*Discoveries,* pp. 123-24)

Galileo's new discoveries in the heavens had widely expanded the sensible world of which he wished to discourse, but he was in no great hurry to set forth any general theory about it. The first step was to take care that the words applied should obey the analogies of the sensible phenomena to which they were applied. In answer to a rival who argued that spots on the sun were impossible because all men agreed the sun to be lucid and pure, and who suggested instead that the appearances were stars, Galileo wrote:

Men were in fact obliged to call the sun 'most lucid and pure' as long as no shadows or impurities had been perceived in it. But now that it shows itself partly impure and spotty, why should we not called it spotted, and not pure? (*Discoveries*, p. 92)

Nor are the sunspots stars. It is indeed true that I am quibbling over names, when I know that anyone may impose those to suit himself. So long as a man does not think that by names he can confer inherent and essential properties on things, it would make little difference whether he calls these "stars." Thus the novae of 1572 and 1604 were called "stars," and meteorologists call comets and meteors "stars," and for that matter, lovers and poets so refer to the eyes of their lady-loves:

> "When Astolfo's successor is seen
> By the glance of those two smiling stars." [7]

For like reasons, the sunspots may also be called stars; but... stars are always of one shape and quite regular, while the spots are of various shapes and most irregular; the former are consistent in size and shape, while the latter are always changing.... Now, I fail to see any reason for putting the spots with things that differ from them in a hundred ways. (*Discoveries*, pp. 139-40)

But most men did think, and had always thought, that by bestowing names they could confer essential properties on things, and little attention was paid to Galileo's cautious program and limited objectives for science. His considerable discoveries, both in the heavens and with regard to terrestrial physics, passed into the common stock of science, while his view that the search for the essences of things and the causes of events was a waste of time gave way quickly to the mechanical philosophy of Descartes, in which a new world on paper was established from a few principles of breathtaking generality. Galileo, who had not managed to overthrow the physics of Aristotle, would not have been in the least surprised at the speedy success of Cartesian physics if he had lived to see it. For he had written, long before:

Dealing with science as a method of demonstration and reasoning capable of human pursuit, I hold that the more this partakes of perfection, the smaller the number of propositions it will promise to teach, and fewer yet will [be those] it conclusively proves.... Grandiose promises attract the natural curiosity of men and hold them forever involved in fantasies and chimeras, without ever offering them one single sample of that sharpness of true proof

[7] Ariosto, *Orlando Furioso*, VII, 27, 1-2.

by which the taste may be awakened to know how insipid is the ordinary fare of philosophy. (*Discoveries*, pp. 239-40)

Galileo's science offered a brief interlude between the all-inclusive system of the Aristotelians and the all-inclusive system of the Cartesians. It was an interlude marked by the invasion of horse-sense and poetic metaphor into the alien territory of sober philosophy and science, bulwarked by eternal verity. Galileo knew well enough the chances of a successful or lasting invasion when he wrote:

There is no danger that a multitude of great, subtle, and wise philosophers will allow themselves to be overcome by one or two of us who bluster a bit. Rather, without even directing their pens against us, they place us under universal scorn and derision. It is vanity to imagine that one can introduce a new philosophy by refuting this author or that one. It is necessary first to teach the reform of the human mind, and render it capable of distinguishing truth from falsehood, which only God can do. (*Dialogue*, p. 57)[8]

[8] The text reads "them" rather than "us," because Galileo's view is put in the mouth of an interlocutor.

Karsten Harries

Descartes, Perspective, and the Angelic Eye

Few philosophers are initially as accessible and, in the end, as elusive
as Descartes. Consider the *Meditations*: with his methodological doubt
Descartes makes an effort to take nothing for granted; the thought
of his predecessors is bracketed; the reader is asked to participate
in an effort to philosophize *de novo*. As commentators have shown,
this attempt fails; Descartes' arguments are more dependent on the
tradition than his principle of doubt would allow them to be. Yet
even if we keep in mind the many ways in which Descartes follows
his predecessors, his work does represent a new beginning which
helped to shape our understanding of man's place in the world. Just
this poses a difficulty. We find ourselves already caught up in ways
of speaking and thinking which rest, at least in part, on Cartesian
foundations. Not only the course of modern philosophy was set by
his conception of proper method; our science and technology, even
our common sense with its faith in reason and reason's power to
grasp and manipulate reality owe much to Descartes. And yet, while
this faith still tends to be taken for granted—in spite of the fact that
ever since Kant it has come under increasing attack—Descartes himself was unwilling to do so. For him it was the result of reflections
which had their origin in a doubt which puts even the reality of the
world into question. To a baroque audience which would tend to
view life as a dream this doubt may have seemed familiar enough;
from our post-Cartesian point of view its meaning is more difficult
to understand: how can Descartes doubt the reality of a world which
is just being torn apart by a very real war? Granted that he does
so only as a philosopher, can philosophy afford to fly in the face of
what is generally accepted and taken for granted? But if we cannot
make sense of Descartes' doubt, we cannot even begin to participate

in his *Meditations*. The basis of his and to some extent still our trust in reason remains obscure.

Descartes introduces his doubt as a device guarding against error. If what claims to be knowledge is to deserve that name, it must be placed on a secure foundation. In order to establish such a foundation Descartes demands that we take as false all that is not so patently true as to resist all our attempts to doubt it. Too often we accept what is questionable and are content with appearance and conjecture. Not that we can dispense with this altogether; we simply don't have time to examine carefully all we see and hear. But until such an examination has taken place our thought cannot really be secure, it will be belief, not knowledge.

The demand for knowledge and a need for security are closely linked. Security again demands stability and order. Descartes thus refuses to accept things as they offer themselves in all their fleeting and confusing variety; they are to be transformed in such a way that they can be grasped and mastered. This is the goal of his method.

Be it with our hands, be it with our mind, we can grasp only what endures. All that is evanescent—melting snow, fog rising from a meadow, fireworks, a smile—eludes us. How can we hold on to time? The baroque's fascination with time keeping devices comes to mind. Góngora tells of our futile attempts to build for time prisons of glass which would let us hold it in our hands. Descartes' *mathesis universalis* is a related effort.

To wish for mastery of the world is not only to wish for a conquest of time, for a view of the world *sub specie aeternitatis*. It is also to wish for an Archimedean point, a place which will permit us to seize reality as it is, not only its representations, perspectival appearances which present themselves to us only because our point of view happens to be what it is. Along with the dread of time, this dread of the distorting power of perspective is at the center of Cartesian doubt as it is at the center of much baroque thought.

In the second of his *Rules,* where the principle of doubt is first announced, Descartes asks us to reject all merely possible knowledge. Doubt is tied to possibility. In order to doubt we must be able to conceive of the possibility that something may be different from the way it presents itself to us. Essential to doubt is the contrast between what is and what appears to be. It is thus quite possible to doubt whether the world which I naively take to be more or less as I see it really is that way. In this connection philosophers have always appealed to the fact that our senses can trick us; we do not even have to appeal to optical illusions and the like; something like the distinction between appearance and reality is inseparable from sense experience. For example, as I look at the table before me, I am also aware that that same table will look different to those whose point of view is not my own. The table looks to me the way it does because I happen to be at this moment in this particular place. But in thinking the limits imposed by my point of view, I am already beyond these limits: thus I can imagine myself occupying different points of view. Were someone to ask me to draw the table as it would look from a point of view at the center of the ceiling, I could attempt to do so. That this is possible shows that my location here and now does not imprison my thoughts. As soon as I recognize that a perspective is just a perspective and that there are others, I am already in some sense beyond all these perspectives. This transcendence of the self over the here and now makes it possible to demand an a-perspectival description of the thing in question.

Historically the rising awareness of and interest in the phenomenon of perspective, as it expresses itself for instance in the development of renaissance and baroque art, goes thus hand in hand with the emergence of the objective conception of space which is presupposed by the new science. Already in the fifteenth century Cardinal Nicolaus Cusanus raises the question whether the earth is not taken by us to be the center of the cosmos simply because this is where we happen to find ourselves. Could not a man drifting on a boat in the middle of the ocean take his boat to be the unmoving center of the earth with equal right? And would not a lunarian tend to take the moon, a Martian Mars to be the center of the cosmos? When we maintain the central position of the earth, are we not ascribing to reality itself what only appears to us because of our point of view? This reflection on the phenomenon of perspective has explosive consequences. Not only does it lead Cusanus to question the geocentric world view. The very idea of a natural center of the cosmos is put into question. And if this idea has to be given up, it also makes no longer any sense to speak of the limits of the cosmos. Instead we arrive at the conception of an objective, homogeneous, infinite space. The overthrow of the limited and hierarchical medieval cosmos has its origin not in the new science of Copernicus, Kepler, and Galileo, but in rather simple speculations on the nature of perspective. [1] That such speculations gained wide currency is shown by a woodcut from Nuremberg, dating from about 1530, which shows a man breaking out of the shell of the medieval cosmos. [2] The sixteenth century was ready for the discoveries of Tycho Brahe and Galileo.

But while such reflections on the phenomenon of perspective lead to doubt in that picture of the world presented to us by the senses, they hardly lead to the radical doubt with which Descartes would have us begin. Just the opposite would seem to be the case. Doubt provides its own cure in that it leads to a more adequate grasp of what is—where one should perhaps question the identification of the more adequate with the more objective which is being taken for granted here.

We can generalize from this example. To the extent that I can think the perspectival nature of my world—and the point of view in question need not be the here and now, but could be my history or

---

[1] "Origin" is used here to suggest a historical and a logical priority. In another paper I hope to show that Cusanus' speculations about the infinity of the cosmos have their roots in Rhenish mysticism and in the hermetic tradition. Thus when Cusanus describes the cosmos as an infinite sphere, which has its center everywhere and its circumference nowhere, he uses a phrase which first appears in the pseudo-hermetic *Liber XXIV philosophorum* as a metaphor for the being of God, whose creative vision is without limit and beyond all perspective. Meister Eckhart used the same metaphor to describe man's soul, whose reach surpasses the perspectival limitations of all sense-bound knowledge. With this reflection we are on the threshold of a new objectivity.

[2] Reproduced in Nikolaus von Cues, *Die Kunst der Vermutung*, Hans Blumenberg, ed. (Bremen, 1957), facing p. 186.

my language—I must already be in some sense beyond it, capable of conceiving other points of view. Consider the following case: someone asks us to think of the Eskimos and of their way of life which forces them to be attentive to aspects of their environment which we would not even notice. We should expect this to be reflected in their language. They are caught in a linguistic framework different from ours—we live in different worlds. But to make sense of this thesis we have to have some understanding of both perspectives. To understand how or even that their world differs from ours we must possess the resources to do justice to this difference. If our perspectives are indeed different, we have to add that these perspectives are not prisons, but can be transcended in thought.

This transcendence of thought makes it possible to oppose to the embodied, concrete "I" and its vision of the world an angelically pure or transcendental "I" whose "vision" of the world would be objective and a-perspectival. The idea of such an angelic "I," and perhaps it is no more than that, is implicit in our experience. It can be uncovered and made the measure of what presents itself to us. Using this measure we can try to redescribe reality in such a way that all those aspects which presuppose a particular point of view, including all secondary qualities, drop out. The move to objectivity appears to defeat doubt. The ascent to the pure ego promises something like the sought Archimedean point, a transcendental absolute, a place where it is possible to stand without fear that this place, too, will be recognized as relative.

To think an a-perspectival vision of reality is not yet to possess it. We have to keep in mind that the objective world pictures provided by science are not based on some a-perspectival mode of vision, but are conjectures which, if they are to be more than idle invention, must retain their foundation in the data provided by the senses and, in spite of all the striking successes of the new science, it is by no means obvious that the silent and colourless world now revealed to us does greater justice to reality than the richer world of our senses of which it is only a redescription. Given his insistence that we take as false all that is not so patently true as to resist all our attempts to doubt it, Descartes would have us dismiss such conjectural knowledge. If we are to escape from doubt there must be in us a faculty which lets us grasp what is as it is, free of the limits of perspective. Only if we can learn to see like the angels can Cartesian doubt be defeated, can there be science in the Cartesian sense of clear and evident cognition. [3]

In the *Rules* Descartes makes a first attempt to show that we do indeed possess an intuition which unlike ocular vision is not marred by perspective. Mankind is said to have "no roads towards certain knowledge open to it, save those of self-evident intuition and necessary deduction." [4] The former, more fundamental in that it is presupposed by deduction, is tied to an apprehension of simple natures. By their very essence such simple natures do not permit doubt as to what they are. We either grasp them or we fail to grasp them. We cannot grasp them partially, for they have no parts. They could thus not possibly be other than they present themselves to us. Simple natures are necessarily clear and distinct, while all clear and distinct ideas are or can be analyzed into simple natures.

Descartes leaves the status of these simples somewhat uncertain. He certainly suggests that they are recognized, not invented—they are more than figments of the mind; they are the building blocks, not only of science, but of reality. Among his examples of simple natures Descartes includes existence, unity, duration, extension, things that are the same as a third thing are the same as one another, the triangle is bounded by three lines only, $2 + 2 = 4$, I exist, and I think—a rather mixed group which blurs the distinction between notions and propositions and thus between intuition and judgment. But whatever his simples may be, we know that if there are such

---

[3] Alexandre Koyré thus thinks it very likely that Aquinas' discussion of angelic knowledge served as the source of Descartes' account of human knowledge. See *Essai sur l'idée de Dieu et les preuves de Son existence chez Descartes* (Paris, 1922), p. 93. Also, Etienne Gilson, *Etudes sur le rôle de la pensée médiévale dans la formation du système cartésien*, 3ᵉ édition (Paris, 1967), p. 12.

[4] *Rule XII;* vol. I, p. 45. Page references are to *The Philosophical Works of Descartes*, Elizabeth S. Haldane and G. R. T. Ross, trans., 2 vols. (New York, 1955).

simples they cannot be sensed, for all objects of sense are given perspectively; they will present themselves differently to different points of view and consequently must have more than one side; but this is incompatible with the demanded simplicity. If there is indeed an intuition of simples, there would also appear to be an escape from perspective.

Unfortunately Descartes himself raises some doubts. There are passages in the *Rules* where Descartes separates the orders of being and knowing and does not insist that they run exactly parallel. What seems simple to us may not be simple in reality. "Here we shall treat of things only in relation to our understanding's awareness of them and call those only simple, the cognition of which is so clear and distinct that they cannot be analyzed by the mind into others more distinctly known." [5] Are Descartes' simple natures simple only relative to our understanding? In the *Rules* Descartes appears willing to admit this. But with this admission we find ourselves back in the theatre of perspectives. The foundation of Cartesian science in intuition is rendered questionable.

If Descartes is to show that the move to the clear and distinct does indeed offer an escape from perspective, he has to establish clarity and distinctness as an adequate criterion for the truth of our representations. Only if this is possible can the gap between knowledge and being which opened up in the *Rules* be closed. In the *Meditations* an attempt is made to provide the necessary bridge by an analysis of the *cogito*: I cannot doubt that I, a thinking thing, exist, and, if Descartes is right, what makes it impossible for me to do so is nothing other than the clarity and distinctness of the idea involved. But is Descartes not presupposing here what is still to be established, the trustworthiness of the clear and distinct? If the clarity and distinctness of our ideas is sufficient to free us from doubt, what reason is there to begin with the *cogito* rather than with any other clear and distinct idea. Any of the simples mentioned in the *Rules*

[5] *Rule XII;* vol. I, p. 41.

should do equally well. An explanation of why at least some of these simples won't do is given in the *Principles*: "And when I stated that this proposition *I think, therefore I am* is the first and most certain which puts itself to those who philosophize in an orderly fashion, I did not for all that deny that we must first of all know what is knowledge, what is existence, and what is certainty, and that *in order to think we must be,* and the like; but because these are notions of the simplest kind, which of themselves give us no knowledge of anything that exists, I did not think them worthy of being put on record." [6] Descartes now draws a distinction between "notions of the simplest kind," which do not claim to give us a knowledge of existence and are therefore of comparatively little interest, and "propositions" which do make that claim and just because of this are subject to doubt.

The doubt of the *Meditations* presupposes that our thoughts represent or at least claim to represent reality. Following medieval tradition Descartes distinguishes between *realitas objectiva* and *realitas formalis.* The representation (idea) intends another reality which it claims to represent. By its claim to representation the idea has a meaning, i.e. is *realitas objectiva.* This suggests that the objective reality of our ideas cannot be grasped as a simple nature, for what is grasped here is not simply an idea, but this idea taken as a representation. Our understanding of objective reality involves not only intuition, but judgment as well and just this makes it dubitable. Even if our representations claim to represent reality, how can this claim be justified? Is not all our knowledge of reality mediated by ideas? And if this is so, is not the attempt to reach beyond representations to reality itself futile?

Cartesian doubt recalls the baroque view of this life as a theatrical performance, the world as a stage, and of God as the author of a play in which we are given parts we do not fully understand. Only death puts an end to our performance; only then does real life begin, only then will we see reality as it is. With his hypothesis of an evil deceitful demon Descartes transforms the already distant divine

[6] *Principles I, no. X;* vol. I, p. 222.

author of the baroque into a being quite indifferent to man's desire to grasp what is as it is. Descartes' demon has his origin in the Occamite conception of an omnipotent God in whose will all truths have their foundation. Our truths, and this includes even the truths of mathematics, must correspond to the creative thoughts of God if they are to be true in an absolute sense. To this view Descartes adds the suspicion that we may not be attuned to God's will. A transcendent ground of what we take to be true is posited only to be declared inaccessible. But this thought experiment, which threatens to transform the baroque theatre into a labyrinth, is introduced only to show us that despite the demon's schemes we can escape from conjecture and doubt. The truth of what we comprehend clearly and distinctly cannot be doubted while we so comprehend it. Here there is no need to appeal to God. To the traditional view which would seek truth in the correspondence of human and divine knowledge Descartes opposes another which would found truth in the way in which things appear to the perceiving subject. "What is it to us, though perchance someone feign that that of the truth of which we are so firmly persuaded, appears false to God or to an Angel, and hence is absolutely speaking false? We have assumed a conviction so strong that nothing can remove it, and this persuasion is the same as perfect certitude." [7] With Descartes the subject begins to replace God as the foundation of truth and thus of reality. That other Copernican revolution which Kant claims for his *Critique of Pure Reason* announces itself. The baroque view of the world as a theatre, resting as it does on the subordination of the human to the divine point of view, is replaced by another which understands reality in terms of man's ability to grasp and manipulate what is.

But Descartes provides us with no more than a beginning. The very fact that he thinks it necessary to secure our trust in the clear and distinct, first by an analysis of the *cogito,* later by proofs of the existence of God, shows that the traditional view which seeks truth in the adequacy of our ideas to things which in turn have their foundation in the creative will of God continues to be operative. Descartes

[7] *Reply to Objections II;* vol. II, p. 41.

turns to the *cogito* rather than to any other clear and distinct proposition because in this one case I am the reality being represented. No longer imprisoned in my ideas, but outside, I can hope to show that the clear and distinct is indeed like transparent glass which lets me see what is without distortion.

But do I have a clear and distinct idea of myself? We have to grant Descartes that the existence of the self cannot be doubted as it is presupposed by all doubt, but how much content can I give to this knowledge of my own existence? Certainly, and this would be granted by Descartes, all that is connected with my having a body is as dubitable as any other matter of fact. But what remains? More than the mute certainty that I am? Descartes would point to the idea I have of myself as thinking substance. But this idea is hardly gained by simple intuition. It depends on a particular and questionable interpretation of being, according to which "to be" means "first of all to be as substance." [8] Descartes' description of the self as thinking substance rests thus on theory and is in that sense hypothetical and dubitable.

Is there any description of reality which is not inadequate in comparable ways. Descartes' own interpretation of being as substance can be turned to suggest that there is not. Substance, Descartes tells us, is known only as that in which attributes reside. Man has no unmediated cognition of substance. This recognizes that our knowledge of reality is marked by a kind of double awareness: our knowledge of what something is mediates, but does not exhaust our knowledge of it. But does not our knowledge of what something is depend on antecedently given, usually linguistic frameworks which determine how that reality can present itself to us? How definitive are these frameworks? Do they offer us more than possible points of view? Once again a labyrinth of perspectives threatens. To answer this threat Descartes could point out that in the case of language, too, we can move from our language and its perspective to a more perfect

---

[8] *Meditation V;* vol. I, p. 182. *Principles I, nos. LI, LII,* and *LIII;* vol. I, pp. 239-40.

a-perspectival language. To be sure, there is no logical reason why there are just these languages and no others. The multiplicity of languages is part of facticity and like all facticity groundless. But given the already mentioned possibility of an ascent from the concrete "I" and its vision to the pure "I," can we not similarly arrive at a conception of language which is equally pure, an *a priori* form which all languages must share in order to be languages at all? Such an *a priori* form could not be imagined to be other than it is. Its mode of construction would guarantee that it would present itself to us *sub specie aeternitatis,* i.e. as ground. The idea of this form can be used to judge one supposed *a priori* more certain than another. The greater the degree to which particular perspectives have been transcended, the more ideal, the more certain the *a priori.* In this sense the rules governing our use of the word "good" transcend my particular perspective; they provide us with a common measure and in this sense they furnish something like an *a priori,* but this *a priori* lacks the certainty of, let us say, the rules governing counting or of such logical principles as the law of noncontradiction. Does this movement to the progressively more certain come to an end, e.g. when we arrive at the conditions of all possible experience? If so, it should be possible to establish solid ground.

With his "notions of the simplest kind" Descartes took a first step in this direction. Unfortunately his discussion is too sketchy to provide more than suggestions. Perhaps even the principles of logic can be considered perspectival phenomena, as e. g. Nicolaus Cusanus tried to show with his discussion of a *coincidentia oppositorum.* If so, man can transcend them. With Cusanus the step beyond all perspectives becomes a step beyond the finite to which we can give no content. But this must remain no more than a suggestion on which little depends. What I would like to emphasize here is that this move to a purer language which offers an escape from possibility and perspective is also a move to the increasingly formal and therefore empty. Again the search for security leads away from concrete reality.

A more serious threat to the Cartesian program is posed by a second consideration. To know what something is is to have assigned it a place in a logical or linguistic space which has room not only for this, but for countless other possible worlds. This place is never so fully determined that is could not also be occupied by some other, very similar thing. To give just one example: outside my window I see a linden tree, light green now and wet with rain, almost ready to bloom. But when I try to describe this tree I also know that no matter how rich my descriptions might become, they would still fail to do justice to this particular tree. The measures which we bring to reality, for instance when we call something a linden tree, cannot capture the individual in its individuality, but only in certain respects which make it comparable to other objects. We should not be too quick to see in our inevitable failure to close the gap between language and reality a defect. Were it not possible to subject the infinite richness of reality to our measures, all attempts to secure our place in the world would be in vain. Reality would drown us. But if, as Gryphius writes, "through language we rule," that rule is very incomplete. [9] The Cartesian demand for fully adequate representations of reality cannot be fulfilled. Reality reveals itself to us as such precisely where it reveals itself to us as surpassing all our forms of representation.

Just as I cannot provide a definitive description of the things which surround me, I cannot provide a definitive description of my own self. Least of all does Descartes' thinking substance provide such a description. In it I grasp myself not concretely, but at best as the abstract form of my and any other possible consciousness, an abstraction which can appear so hard and simple only because it is so formal and empty. As soon as I grasp myself as this individual,

[9] Andreas Gryphius, *Grösse und Elend der Sprache* [*The Grandeur and Misery of Speech*]. The poem is in two parts. The first praises the gift of speech: "Das Wunder der Natur, das überweise Tier, / Hat nichts, das seiner Zungen sei zu gleichen. / Ein wildes Vieh entdeckt mit stummen Zeichen / Des innern Herzens Sinn; durch Reden herrschen wir!" [The wonder of nature, the more-than-wise animal, / Has nothing to compare with its tongue. / A wild beast discovers with mute signs / The meaning of the inner heart; we rule through speech!"]. It concludes with the line: "Des Menschen Leben selbst beruht auf seiner Zungen" [Man's life itself rests on his tongue]. The second part offers the antithesis. It concludes with the line: "Der Menschen Tod beruht auf jedes Menschen Zungen!" [Men's death rests on every man's tongue!].

existing here and now, the illusion of transparency disappears. Again the search for a secure foundation leads to an attempt to lift the self out of this world, to leave behind the prison of the body and to become the pure "I." But far from leading to reality this ascent to angelic heights leaves only the emptiness of abstraction. The attempt to make this form of self-knowledge the paradigm of our knowledge of reality has to lead to a similarly abstract picture of the world.

For very different reasons Descartes felt that his analysis of the cogito failed to provide an adequate foundation for our faith in the clear and distinct. After that analysis has been completed, doubts return: How do I know whether what presents itself to me clearly and distinctly is really true? Have I not been deceived in the past and may I not be deceived again? Doubt reappears as a doubt in the destructive power of time.

This fear of time makes a first appearance in the *Rules*. In his discussion of deduction, on which we have to rely if we are to move from the simples provided by intuition to more complicated structures, he suggests that while intuition takes place "at the same time and not successively," deduction takes time; its certitude is "conferred upon it in some way by memory." [10] But is memory reliable? In the *Rules* Descartes tries to minimize this danger by suggesting that we can learn to perform our deductions so quickly as to all but cut out this dependence on memory. The measure of knowledge is thus provided by instantaneous intuition. Deduction is suspect because of its tie to time.

These suspicions were to increase. In his *Replies* to Mersenne Descartes even goes so far as to maintain that God's guarantee is necessary only to guarantee the reliability of memory. This doubt concerning memory is no more to be reduced to the empirical problem of how reliable an individual's memory is than Descartes' doubt concerning the reality of the world is to be reduced to the problem of the reliability of our senses. In both cases the question is whether

[10] *Rule III;* vol. I, p. 8. *Rule XI;* vol. I, p. 33.

my reach extends beyond the theatre of representations which here and now presents itself to me. This moment may be mine, but is the past mine? The future? Doubt appears here as a function of the attempt to give truth a foundation in the intuition of the moment. That attempt threatens to imprison the knower in the instant, making him like an infant "whose power of thinking is asleep." [11] According to Descartes the infant does think, he is even conscious of his thoughts, but he cannot grasp himself in his successive thoughts. The infant has neither past nor future. Similarly our attempt to make the momentary grasp of the clear and distinct the foundation of truth cuts us off from our own past and future. And yet, just as reflection shows my point of view in space to be just one of infinitely many possible points of view, it also shows this moment to be just one of infinitely many possible moments. But can we call truth what has its foundation only in what I now happen to grasp clearly and distinctly? Is the very essence of truth not destroyed when it is thus subordinated to time? With his proof of the existence of God who guarantees the reproduction of the past in the present, both as continued existence and as memory, Descartes retreats from his attempt to found truth in the subject.

But is this retreat not premature? Can we not replace God with the subject, not with the concrete subject, bound to the here and now, but with the transcendental or pure subject. It is indeed in such a replacement that our own objective view of reality has its foundation. Our truths have their measure in what such an ideal observer would find true, where it is important to note that the ideal observer need not exist to provide this measure. It has been suggested, by Heidegger for example, that all this talk of a pure "I" rests on a confusion of theology and philosophy and it is indeed easy to show that there are historical and systematic connections between the Christian God and the transcendental subject which comes to replace God as the foundation of truth and reality. [12] But to point this out is not to discredit the latter conception. As I have tried to show, the

[11] *Reply to Objections IV;* vol. II, p. 103.
[12] *Sein und Zeit,* 7th edition (Tübingen, 1953), p. 229.

pure "I" has its foundation in the self-understanding of concretely existing man who, as he becomes aware of himself as occupying a particular point of view here and now, also learns to transcend it.

There is, however, a crucial difference between the ways in which God and the transcendental subject can function as foundation of reality. While God functions as the ground of all that is, providing both form and matter, the transcendental subject provides only its empty form, a form which has room not only for this, but for endless other possible worlds. Part of the ascent to the transcendental subject is an ontology which reduces reality to groundless facticity.

Here we come to what is perhaps the fundamental reason for Descartes' retreat from his own attempt to make the subject the foundation of truth and to a final formulation of Cartesian doubt. Again doubt presupposes that we measure what presents itself to us as reality by our idea of reality. Following the tradition Descartes ties being to perfection and perfection to self-sufficiency. What supports itself in its being is thus more perfect than what depends for its being on another. Substances are more perfect than attributes; God, in whose will all things have their foundation, is the most perfect being. Measured by this idea of reality, the objective world of science has to appear unreal. The world of Descartes' dream is one which is neither maintained by God in its being, nor, like the Cartesian God, the foundation of its own being; it is a world without a foundation, a bubble floating on the nothingness of time which has replaced God. Given a very different understanding of reality which stresses objectivity and makes man's power to grasp and manipulate the measure of what is, this doubt ceases to be intelligible. But that understanding of being, which owes much to Descartes and his method, is more an expression of our will to rule than a conclusion drawn from being itself. Perhaps we find it so difficult to understand Descartes' dream because this dream has become our reality.

Olivier René Bloch

Gassendi and the Transition from the Middle Ages to the Classical Era

"In the *English* materialists, nominalism is an all-important element and broadly speaking it constitutes the *first expression* of materialism." The philosopher Pierre Gassendi (1592-1655) was the compatriot and contemporary of Descartes. Yet this remark of Marx in the *Holy Family* concerning the birth of modern materialism from the womb of medieval theology may equally well be applied to him. [1] The very real role played by him in the history of ideas is due no doubt less to his work's immediate public than to the loud echo it provoked in the English scholars and philosophers of the second half of the seventeenth century. In a way they acted as the intermediaries who transmitted his message to the thought of the eighteenth century; such that I feel we may speak of a veritable fusion, beginning in the years 1660-70, of Gassendism with the British philosophical tradition. [2] His role and message, in any case, move towards materialism, a materialism of which his attempted restoration of Epicurean atomism certainly served as a basis, though perhaps more in the sense of a point of reference than in that of foundation. And it is certain that in his case the "first expression" of this materialism was the acceptance in his early *Exercitationes Paradoxicae* of the essential theses of medieval nominalism. [3]

We may thus see in Gassendi the last link binding the materialism, or rather the prematerialism, of the Middle Ages with the thought of the classical era, in so far as its materialist aspects are concerned,

---

[1] *Marx-Engels Gesamtausgabe* (Frankfurt, 1927-35), Part. I, vol. III, p. 304.

[2] We may note that in the above-quoted text, Marx, for his part, linked Gassendi with Hobbes in materialism's opposition to Cartesian metaphysics (*op. cit.,* p. 302).

[3] *Exercitationes Paradoxicae adversus Aristoteleos*, in Pierre Gassendi, *Opera Omnia* (Lyon 1658), III, pp. 95-210. Saving indication to the contrary, all future references here will be by volume and page to this posthumous edition.

whatever may be the diversity, contradictions and ambiguities of that thought in other ways, like that of Gassendi himself. Taking up once again some of the conclusions to which I have previously come,[4] I would like to demonstrate here this transitional function of Gassendist thought as it applies to certain aspects of his conception of nature, his theory of knowledge, and his views on society.

If we are going to talk about Gassendi's world view, it is *view* that must first of all be emphasized. The importance of the theme of visuality in the seventeenth century is well known: if we want to use a term made fashionable by one of those who have recently brought out its importance,[5] it is an integral part of the substitution of a classical *episteme* for the medieval and Renaissance *episteme* of word and sign. In the seventeenth century this theme of visuality is vastly over-determined. It institutes, in a way, a structure in which come together significations of a technical, methodological and scientific, epistemological, and ideological kind. For the first, we need but think of the perfecting and use of optical instruments; for the second, those concerning for instance the role and import of celestial observations; for the third, the notion of vision as the model of knowledge; and, finally, the substitution of a universe which reveals itself to man through the transparency of his gaze for a world which was the mediator of the divine word. It is a structure elaborated via a return to the thought of antiquity—Platonism and the view of essences, Epicureanism and the primacy of sensuous vision.

There is no doubt that Gassendi is at once a privileged witness to and a founder of the polysemous structure thus elaborated. The theme of visuality runs through his work and thought in all its dimensions and its ambiguities: from the astronomical observations that he was making and recording without interruption from 1618 to his last days,[6] and the anatomical ones undertaken with his friend Peiresc in 1634-35 in a study of the eye, together with the psycho-

---

[4] O. R. Bloch, *La Philosophie de Gassendi: Nominalisme, matérialisme et métaphysique* (The Hague, 1971).
[5] Michel Foucault, *Les Mots et les choses* (Paris, 1966).
[6] *Commentarii de Rebus Caelestibus*, IV, pp. 75-498.

physiological, methodological and epistemological reflections that both inspired in him, [7] to the theological position he takes, particularly during the polemic with Descartes of 1641-42, [8] and in the posthumous *Syntagma Philosophicum*, [9] of assigning to metaphysics the mission of contemplating divine finality at work in the universe. Between these two poles, the same theme is revealed in the epistemological critique, stemming from his initial nominalism and reinforced by the contribution of the Epicurean theory of knowledge, that he never ceased making of the idea of intellectual intuition which constitutes one of the axes of the *Disquisitio Metaphysica:* if it is true that knowledge has no other function but that of representing reality, then man has no other material for such a representation than the visual sense, and intellectual processes, presupposed by the latter in any case if it is to have any objective value, can only serve to extend this sight by applying discursive operations to its decipherment. [10]

In Gassendi, as his contemporaries, this visualization of object, situation, and processes of knowledge is one with a mechanistic representation of the universe, in the sense according to which it is considered as a complex of displacements of matter in space; which first of all supposes a new conception of the latter and, correlatively, of time. It is indeed such a conception that Gassendi strove to evolve, or rather, it was he who was the first to express, in formulae of a striking clarity, the characteristics which constitute the classical

[7] See for example the *De Apparente Magnitudine Solis Humilis et Sublimis*, III, pp. 420-77.

[8] *Disquisitio Metaphysica seu Dubitationes et Instantiae adversus Renati Cartesii Metaphysicam, et Responsa*, III, pp. 269-410.

[9] This essential work occupies in their entirety the first and second volumes of the Lyon edition cited in note 3. The text of volume I goes back to 1649-55, that of volume II to 1644-45 (or perhaps 1646). It was preceded by a work of quite different appearance but whose content is essentially identical, the *Animadversiones in Decimum Librum Diogenis Laertii,* which was published at Lyon in 1649. Manuscripts of almost the whole of a previous version, entitled *De Vita et Doctrina Epicuri*, exist in the libraries of Tours, Carpentras and Florence. It is the end of this version which, for lack of anything more recent, was reproduced as the second volume of the printed *Syntagma*, while the beginning, which dates from 1633-34, had already been published as early as 1647, also at Lyon, with the title *De Vita et Moribus Epicuri* (the manuscript of which has not survived). The remainder, written between 1636 and 1643 (with a long interruption between 1637 and 1641), remains unpublished.

[10] On this point, see my article, "Gassendi critique de Descartes," *Revue Philosophique* (1966), pp. 217-36.

notions of space and time. [11] Space, an entity at once immobile, homogeneous, infinite and infinitely divisible, indifferent of all content, freed of the traditional ontological categories of substance and accident, is conceived as a kind of object/medium of an ideal visualization of the sensible, which is achieved only by its negating itself in its abstraction as a limit case: it is a seeing which is view of nothing, of a nothing which is object, and site of all viewing of objects. At the same time it serves as the model for the new representation of time, which is conceived and defined from now on—by virtue of its "parallelism" with space—as an infinite, continuous, invariable flow, indifferent of events, the frame of succession in the same way as space is the condition of localization.

Linked with the "geometrization of space" which is responsible for the transition from the "closed world" to the "infinite universe," [12] these notions, which are none other than the presuppositions of classical mechanics, were in fact constructed by Gassendi from his contact with the work of Galileo, of whom, like his friend Mersenne, he made himself the vulgarizer and propagandist in several minor writings of the 1640s. [13] Indeed, the comparison of published and unpublished texts reveals that it is in these very years that he perfected the central element—and the one most difficult to establish— of this conceptual edifice: the strict parallelism of time and space for which he was obliged, whether he would or no, to break with the Epicurean thesis which held time to be the "accident of accidents." And, together with the representation of matter provided by the atomism of antiquity and with that dynamism, drawn from, though doubtless surpassing, Epicurus—Democritus, rather— which he posited in the thesis regarding the "active matter" and the "innate mobility" of the atom, [14] it is these notions which for him condition

---

[11] See, in the *Syntagma Philosophicum*, the Book *De Loco et Tempore* (I, pp. 179-228), and earlier the substantially identical development in the *Animadversiones* (pp. 605-30).

[12] See Alexandre Koyré, *From the Closed World to the Infinite Universe* (Baltimore, 1957).

[13] See the *De Motu impresso a Motore translato* (III, p. 478-563) and the *De Proportione qua Gravia decidentia accelerantur* (III, pp. 564-650).

[14] See, particularly, I, pp. 335b-336a.

the principles of mechanics: the principle of inertia of which he was the first, as we know, to publish a correct statement, [15] principles of conservation which he tried, in a very concise if not quite precise formulation, to deduce from the "mobility" of the atom. [16]

It may be that this visualization of science and the world helped him to extend this mechanism to chemistry for which, taking seriously methodological and experimental elements which were as much hidden as revealed in the researches of the "chymistes" of his age, he proposed an atomistic and "molecular" interpretation. [17] Even more likely is it at work in the cosmological descriptions in which, despite the restrictions he imposed—partly out of prudence, but just as certainly from a real concern for orthodoxy—upon his scientific and philosophical tendencies in this area, he maintained as far as possible the Copernico-Galilean heliocentric theory, and in which, despite his theological creationism and finitism, he revealed his partiality for Bruno's thesis of the infinity of worlds, and narrowly managed to repress the temptation of proposing a materialist cosmogonic model. [18]

In brief, if we but take the trouble of freeing them from the mass of erudition in which they are enveloped, Gassendi's work in the realm of physical thought provides quite an imposing array of astonishingly modern ideas which lead essentially in the direction of scientific materialism, such as it was in his time, and many of which form an integral part of the seventeenth- and eighteenth-century world view. This is particularly striking in the case of his ideas on space and time, where it is clear that the Gassendist formulae, prior even to his publication of them, were a direct inspiration to Pascal in his writings on the vacuum, [19] and will be taken up again in very similar terms by Newton in the celebrated opening pages of the *Principia Mathematica*. And yet to a very great extent

[15] In Letter I (dated November 20, 1640) of the *De Motu impresso*, published in 1642 (see III, pp. 489a-b and 495b-496b).

[16] I, p. 343b.

[17] Particularly, I, pp. 243b-245b and 472a.

[18] For the first, see especially, I, pp. 667b-669a; for the second, see I, pp. 480b-486b—particularly if this passage is read in the light of the earlier unpublished version.

[19] See the letter to Le Pailleur of February or March 1648, in the Brunschvicg and Boutroux edition (Paris, 1908), II, p. 188.

Gassendi worked out these novel expositions *on the basis of the past:* the distant past represented by the atomism of antiquity and the past of the Renaissance, whose "humanistic" concerns permitted the reintroduction of this atomism in the presence of the new science; the past of the Middle Ages, whose theological notions of "imaginary" spaces and times and, more precisely perhaps, the nominalist theologians' arguments,[20] provided a primary support for the new concepts he was proposing; and the more recent past of the Italian naturalism of *novatores* like Patrizzi and Telesio, of whose speculations he certainly made use, correcting and surpassing them, fertilizing them through contact with scientific development.[21]

This process of transmutation by means of which old-style thinking and data come to furnish the bases of the philosophy of modern times is no doubt even more apparent, or at least, other things equal, better known, in the Gassendist concept of knowledge. Because it is better known, but also because there is less originality evident in it, we need not discuss this point at any great length. I will limit myself to a few reminders and comments.

There is no doubt that nominalism is a feature common to all the important philosophies of the seventeenth century: with greater or less explicitness, with more or less divergence of meaning and intention, Descartes is as much of a nominalist as Hobbes, Spinoza as Locke. But their common refusal to attribute the value of real essence to general concepts formed by the understanding through the abstraction of individual characteristics, appears within their systems without direct reference to medieval nominalism. Gassendi, on the other hand, as I indicated at the beginning, refers explicitly to it in 1624 in Book II of his *Exercitationes Paradoxicae* in order to maintain that universals exist only in the understanding, that only individual cases

---

[20] Alexandre Koyré, "Vide et espace infinis au 14e siècle," in *Etudes d'histoire de la pensée philosophique* (Paris, 1961), pp. 33-84. The matter was also treated in Paul Vignaux's lecture given at the XXVIIIe Semaine de Synthèse in Paris in 1967, though to my knowledge this remains unpublished as yet.

[21] I, pp. 245b-246b.

Olivier René Bloch

are real, that concept and essence have no common measure. [22] But for the name alone, it is this same nominalism that he will oppose to Cartesian metaphysics: if, as far as the reality of all things is concerned, existence and essence are one, then we must beware of confusing this undivided and individual reality with existence as an idea or with essence as an idea. For this last is nothing but the universal concept which, for lack of intellectual intuition, is forged out of experience by the human mind and which, as such, is no more than a relative instrument inadequate to the profound nature of things. It is from this confusion that is born the illusion of "eternal essences" to which existence is supposed to be added as a real "property" and as a "predicate" of judgement, an illusion on which rests the ontological proof of God's existence in Descartes' Fifth Meditation. [23] While Gassendi, then, links himself from the outset with medieval nominalism, and while, in a more general sense, he draws on the scholastic sensualist tradition according to which the understanding cannot think without an image, both this nominalism and sensualism eventually meet in him with the more distant past represented in the Epicurean doctrine which he first sought to restore then to defend, but only from 1626 on. The unpublished version of the *Logique* of what was to become the *Syntagma Philosophicum* reveals furthermore that it is his initial nominalism which forms the link between the "skeptic" critique developed in the *Exercitationes Paradoxicae* and the Epicurean gnoseology which serves henceforth as Gassendi's inspiration, though he never adopted it unequivocally. [24] It is this encounter and inspiration indeed that led him to the constitution of a relatively original empiricism, which gains in coherence at the time of the polemic with Descartes, and whose structure seems quite close to that of Locke's. The latter certainly draws on Gassendi, and not only through such intermediaries as Boyle, Charleton or Bernier, but also

[22] III, pp. 159a ff.
[23] See, particularly, III, pp. 374b-383a.
[24] See above, note 9: the *"Logique"* of the *De Vita et Doctrina Epicuri* was written in 1636; a manuscript of it (not an autograph one) is to be found in the Bibliothèque de Carpentras.

doubtless as a result of a direct acquaintance with his writings: [25] the critique of the notions of essence, substance, or infinity, the rejection of intellectual intuition and Cartesian innateness, the construction of a system of knowledge on the basis of sensation and reflection, all these major themes of the *Essay Concerning Human Understanding* are often more than merely prefigured during the polemics of the *Disquisitio Metaphysica,* then later in the *"Logique"* of the *Syntagma Philosophicum* and the Books on *"Imagination"* and *"Entendement"*, [26] and even before in many a passage of the *Exercitationes Paradoxicae.* By means of this intermediary, Gassendi's empiricism, itself due to the inspiration of the Middle Ages and antiquity, acts to a considerable degree as the remote source of the dominating stream of thought throughout the eighteenth century which took Locke's *Essay* as its breviary, up to and including the issue it finds in Kantian philosophy.

While these facts are relatively well known, Gassendi's ideas concerning the social world and political order are much less so. We may almost say that they are not known at all. However apparently minor may be their place in his work, and however doubtful their coherence, certain of their aspects seem to me of great interest, taking into consideration their historical significance and the very real role they may perhaps have played in the history of juridico-political ideas. There may therefore be some point in emphasizing them here somewhat.

As often in the *Syntagma Philosophicum,* Gassendi presents these ideas in a traditional framework: the treatment of questions of political Prudence and Justice, of Right and Laws, [27] the classic theme of the theological treatise, to which indeed, if we are to believe his secretary and biographer La Poterie, he had intended to devote his

[25] Valuable indications on this point are to be found in Locke's manuscript notebooks, especially those of the Lovelace Collection owned by the Bodleian Library, and in the *Medical Commonplace Book* preserved in the British Museum.

[26] I, pp. 31-124; II, pp. 398-468.

[27] II, pp. 754b-765a; II, pp. 783a-808a.

Olivier René Bloch

first theological teaching as early as 1616. In the case of the chapter of the *Syntagma* entitled *De Justitia, Jure ac Legibus,* it is furthermore at the moment of a commentary on Epicurean doctrine and texts (the *Principal Doctrines* of Epicurus, the fifth canto of Lucretius' poem, and a long fragment of Hermarchus cited in Porphyry's *De Abstinentia*) that the most striking concepts appear. But it is quite clearly Hobbes' doctrine of the *De Cive,* whose name is never mentioned, that forms the center of Gassendi's reflections in these pages. It is this that is paraphrased and indeed criticized there on the basis of positions inherited from the sixteenth century, not to mention the medieval traditions. At the same time this reflection and criticism take their place, *de facto,* in the history of theories concerning the social contract and natural right.

Like Hobbes and Lucretius, but also such theologians as Mariana for example, [28] Gassendi in fact connects the problem of Right with that of society's origin, as though to its source. He thus refers it back to the state of nature taken as preceding it and to the process by which men are supposed to have passed from one to the other for reasons of utility. [29] But when he comes to give his own opinion, he in fact opposes to the Hobbesian theory a kind of dualistic one resting on a distinction between the point of view of man considered in himself, singly and "absolutely," and that of man considered in his relationship with others. [30] The first corresponds to a state of pure nature, basis of a "primary" natural Right, a state and a Right of which Gassendi draws a picture no different from Hobbes': a state of struggle and warfare in which there is a confrontation resulting from everyone's equal claim over all things, and where each man's right is none other than his strength. But according to Gassendi, this state is joined from the start with a state of nature which, though no less natural, is "as though modified," and predisposes man naturally to the social condition as it establishes a "secondary" natural Right of a contractual kind. It is nature itself that, having already and always placed in man

[28] Juan Mariana, *De Rege et Regis Institutione Libri III* (Toledo, 1599).
[29] II, pp. 787b ff.
[30] II, pp. 794a ff.

the desire to escape from the state of "pure" nature, grants him the capacity to conclude agreements with others for that end. Man is possessed, in short, of a social predisposition no less fundamental than the individual's tendency towards the satisfaction of his egoistic needs by any means whatever. On the other hand, in so far as the first agreements themselves are concerned, Gassendi substitutes for the single pact by which, for Hobbes, all by common accord place the totality of their rights and powers in the hands of a third party and thus by a single act constitute at once society and absolute power, a series of three basic contracts: the first, veritable birth certificate of the social condition, by which each individual renounces his right over all things so as to retain it only over a few, institutes property therefore; the second, according to which each gives over to the collectivity his power of "vengeance" *(vindicandi facultatem),* constitutes sovereignty, laws and penal justice; the third, finally, which for reasons of convenience confers on one or more leaders the exercise of the sovereign power thus constituted, is properly speaking the foundation of the State. [31] The separation of these contracts, particularly that of the last two, has the explicit effect of rendering conditional in theory the transfer of collective sovereignty to the chosen leaders whose power is supposed to respect previously established laws or modify them only with the at least tacit consent of the collectivity. [32]

By conferring on "nature" itself the principle of sociability which for Hobbes was only the calculation of a reason which, in order to survive, is obliged to denature nature, by splitting into successive contracts the single pact which in Hobbes is the result of this calculation, there is no doubt that Gassendi is interpreting and correcting the Hobbesian doctrine in the light of a return to the traditions of antiquity and the Scholastics, and to the contractualist theories that had been born or reborn as a result of the politico-religious struggles

[31] II, pp. 795b-796a.

[32] II, p. 796a. This explicitness is true at least of the development I am resuming here, but the parallel development of the *Prudentia* (II, pp. 755a-b) seems to lean in the opposite direction, though it is true that it is less explicit. It must needs be said that the *De Prudentia* is strongly marked by the influence of Jean Bodin, which helps to explain the contradiction.

of the sixteenth century. In doing so he reveals, it seems to me, the "feudal" orientation of his political leanings. In the context of the first half of the seventeenth century, and particularly of the 1640s in France, the presentation of the act which constitutes the State's power as a *last* act, incapable of annulling those which precede it, as an act of delegation of power rather than of transfer, presupposing laws antedating it and of which it is not the basis, such a presentation is very likely to be used to justify the feudal claim to oppose the progress of absolute monarchy with the "fundamental laws of the kingdom," in other words with the prerogatives of constituted bodies and the privileges of the feudal orders. At the same time, the placing of this claim within a contractualist theory inspired by Hobbes, the correction thus imposed of the views of the author of the *De Cive* by the appeal to "nature," in short the critical conceptualization of a political concern, result in the production of a schema which at the very least prefigures the classical theory of contract of the school of Natural Right and the liberal doctrine of the State as they will appear in the second half of the century.

Indeed, despite the antecedents which have been claimed for it, to my knowledge it is only in Pufendorff that the first explicit formulation of the double contract is to be found, generally held to be typical of the traditional conception of the State and society held by the school of Natural Right. [33] While the "contract of submission" by which the subjects promise obedience to the monarch in exchange for protection is clearly expressed during the sixteenth century in the libels of the protestant monarchomachs, followed by those of the Ligue, while the "contract of association" by which individuals decide to become a society can be connected with such traditional—and vague—formulations as those found in Cicero, and while it is also true that the Hobbesian concept aims at placing in a single contract the origins of society and State, I do not think that the explicit statement of two successive contracts instituting first the one then the other can be found before the end of the seventeenth century.

[33] Samuel Pufendorff, *De Jure Naturae et Gentium Libri octo* (Lund, 1672), Book VII, Ch. II.

On the other hand, nothing seems nearer to it than the Gassendist distinction between the three contracts which establish in succession the right of property simultaneously with the social condition, then sovereignty and laws, and only afterwards the State. And it may be asked, though I do not for the moment see a way to answer the question, whether the indications contained in the *Syntagma* could have been used by the theorists of Natural Right, and if so how. [34] Furthermore, the liberal theory of the State in the form whose foundations are laid by Locke rests precisely for him upon the preexistence to the State of rights which already have a value in the state of nature, and in particular of the right of property, such that, far from being endowed with an absolute power, the State has as its first function that of making sure these rights are respected. Now, whatever may have been Gassendi's no doubt very different intentions, and however much his affirmation of the monarch's or the "magistrates' " obligation to respect preexisting laws may have remained a matter of theory, the schema he proposes arrives expressly at the same conclusion. In this case the certainty we have otherwise of Locke's knowledge in other areas of Gassendist ideas and texts may lead us to suppose that here, too, the views of the *Syntagma*'s author may not have left him indifferent.

We can discover here again then, in so far at least as the question of the foundations of political right is concerned, a process analogous to that which I have tried to describe in the area of the theory of knowledge and the conception of the world. Using old theoretical bases, retrograde political concerns even, to approach the problem of the politics and political doctrine of his age, Gassendi manages in a sense to open the way to the theses which will he fundamental to the thinking of the following century.

The ambiguity which characterizes the content of Gassendist thought is thus joined by that of his historical situation. While Gas-

---

[34] Despite the personal relations between him and Gassendi, I think we must set aside any mediation on the part of Grotius here, for his ideas, on this subject, are not relevant.

Olivier René Bloch

sendi seems at once a materialist thinker and one eager to remain within the bounds of orthodoxy, he also stands out as one of the last—the last?—thinkers of the Middle Ages and Renaissance, as well as one of the first classical thinkers. As I have tried to show, this pivotal position, this privileged transitional moment reveals itself characteristically in the application of the same thought process to the most varied objects. It is a process which, starting with old schemas and concepts drawn at one from Greco-Latin antiquity, from scholastic traditions, and from the humanism of the Renaissance, ends with the formulation of theses and themes which inaugurate the science, gnoseology, and even political thought, of modern times.

Translated by T. J. Reiss

T. A. Heinrichs

Language and Mind in Hobbes

It has often been noted that Hobbes combines a materialist account of the workings of mind with a rationalist preoccupation with the workings of words. One commentator has argued that this particular combination makes Hobbes' thought "everywhere a masterpiece of exquisite paradox." The two, he claims, send Hobbes' philosophy wandering in different directions along irreconcilable paths which lead in the end to destinations far removed from what Hobbes himself had envisaged. His materialism supposedly transports him to the borders of impossibility, while his rationalism "comes near to carrying him over into an abyss of subjectivism." [1] This essay will examine this contention by focusing on Hobbes' analysis of experience and thought on the one hand and language on the other. I shall argue that Hobbes' attempt to combine materialism with rationalism does indeed result in paradox, but that this paradox does not stem from the attempt itself but from the particular manner in which Hobbes attempts to combine them. Materialism and rationalism are of one piece for Hobbes because neither could stand alone: his materialist account of the workings of mind is ultimately dependant for its comprehensibility on his rationalist preoccupation with language, while his rationalism, in turn, would be pointless without this materialist account. Furthermore, it is not his rationalism that is in danger of dropping him into a subjectivist abyss, but his materialism. If anything, Hobbes' rationalism saves him from this fate; for it is language and not mind that guarantees for us the reality and objectivity of the world outside. In Hobbes' philosophy language puts mind into perspective because it is only from the standpoint of language that experience and thought are at all visible.

[1] D. G. James, *The Life of Reason: Hobbes, Locke, Bolingbroke* (London, 1949), pp. 39, 20.

T. A. Heinrichs

In what appears to be the earliest statement of his mature philosophy Hobbes declared "Every thing is eyther Substance or Accident." [2] From this fundamental principle he never wavered, though as he sharpened his attack on the "incorporeal substances" and "sensible species" of the "dogmatici," body replaced substance as his central material category, and his theory of accidents underwent drastic surgery to accomodate this corporeal emphasis. Body, for Hobbes, signifies anything subsisting of and by itself, independent of thought or imagination, and "coincident or coextended with some part of space" (*E.W.* I, p. 102; *L.* p. 428). Bodies are *real* things, and Hobbes is insistent on this point. They are "there" whether or not we perceive or think they are. Moreover, all that has real being in the world is body:

> and hath the dimensions of Magnitude, namely, Length, Bredth, and Depth: also every part of Body, is likewise Body, and hath the like dimensions; and consequently every part of the Universe, is Body, and that which is not Body, is no part of the Universe: And because the Universe is All, that which is no part of it, is *Nothing;* and consequently *no where.* (*L.* p. 689)

Accidents, on the other hand, are not bodies, consequently they are not real things. They are instead the properties or qualities on the basis of which we distinguish one body from another. According to Hobbes, a body is "subject" to accidents, and these accidents account for its particular appearance to us. Accidents are the causes of all variations in our reception of bodies: "they answer best that define an accident to be the manner by which any body is conceived," or "that faculty of any body, by which it works in us a conception of itself" (*E.W.* I, p. 103. Emphasis omitted). Accidents *are not.*

---

[2] "A Short Tract on First Principles" in *The Elements of Law: Natural and Politic,* Tönnies, ed., 2nd ed. (London, 1969), p. 194. Hereafter, all references to Hobbes will be included in the text and abbreviated as follows: *English Works* (*E. W.* followed by volume and page numbers of the Molesworth edition). Exceptions to the use of the Molesworth texts are Tönnies' *Elements* (*E*), and C. B. Macpherson's edition of *Leviathan* (*L*) (Penguin, 1968).

They are epistemological rather than ontological entities, mere functionaries in the manufacture of conceptions. And because they are epistemological entities, when they are said to be "in" a body it is not to be conceived that some "thing" is "contained" within that body "as blood is in a bloody cloth." For if this were the case, it would then be possible to move an accident from place to place and physically add it to or subtract it from a body which would, in turn, make the accident just another body (*E.W.* I, p. 104).

Accidents are faculties of bodies that cause us to perceive them. Without accidents our minds could not make contact with matter. Now Hobbes never drew a major theoretical distinction between what other theorists termed primary and secondary qualities, but in practice he assigned what amounted to primary status to magnitude and motion and secondary status to all others. He claimed that magnitude and motion were "the most common accidents of all bodies" (*E. W.* I, p. 203). Magnitude is the one quality necessary for a body's existence—without it a body would perish (*E. W.* I, p. 104). Yet if a body were possessed only of magnitude, it would be unobservable. This is because it is only by means of motion which is the cause of our phantasms that we are able to perceive at all. Though not necessary to the existence of a body, motion is nonetheless critical for our perception of it. Hence, without magnitude nothing would exist, and there would be nothing for us to notice: without motion nothing would happen, and we would be unable to notice a body even if it did exist.

Phantasms are generated by the motions of bodies of determinate magnitude pressing against our sense organs. This motion, according to Hobbes, is not terminated on contact but is transmitted by means of nerve impulses to the brain and to the heart. Here it causes a "resistance, or counter-pressure, or endeavor of the heart, to deliver itself: which endeavor because *Outward,* seemeth to be some matter without. And this *seeming* or *fancy,* is that which men call *Sense*" (*L.* p. 85). Motion coming into the heart colliding with and resisting motion coming out produces—if the reaction is strong enough—a phantasm. This is the whole act of sense experience, an act which, Hobbes says, is begun and completed in an instant.

For our purposes, there are three features of Hobbes' account of the act of sense experience that are particularly important. First, by "generate" Hobbes means "cause," and his analysis of the generation of phantasms is therefore a causal analysis. Second, in the act of sense motion is both cause and effect. This is consistent with one of Hobbes' fundamental metaphysical postulates, namely, motion can only cause motion. Phantasms are internal accidental motions of the mind caused by the external accidental motions of bodies, and it is only on the basis of this internal generated motion that we can perceive anything of the world outside us. At bottom, variations in the motions of external bodies account for the variety of all things received in sense experience. It may seem like reductionism in the extreme, but Hobbes claimed different phantasms, that is, different colors, tastes, sounds, shapes, and the like were nothing but variations in the motions of bodies (*E. W.* I, pp. 69-70; *E. W.* VII, p. 83). Hobbes, however, had good reason to make this claim. Without it, he could not hold to his causal theory of sense perception. Since motion can only cause motion, it would be impossible to explain how phantasms could be caused unless they were held to be but various motions. Hence, depending on the level of consideration, secondary qualities are both subjective and objective: subjective in that they inhere in the sentient, but objective in that they are nothing more than motion. Finally, as it is itself simply a species of motion, a phantasm is an inner picture only of some particular variety of motion outside the sentient. Phantasms reproduce not the body outside us, but only its accidents. Considered "*Singly,*" our phantasms "are every one a *Representation* or *Appearance*" not of some body, but "of some quality, or other accident of a body without us (*L.* p. 85; *E.* pp. 2-3; *E. W.* I, p. 411). In sense experience mind and matter are connected only through the mediation of accidents, yet at the same time it is not to be conceived that accidents interpose themselves between the two in such a way as to draw attention to themselves. Accidents are not for Hobbes, as they were to be for later empiricists, objects of perception but merely the vehicles of this perception: "The *subject* of sense is the *sentient* itself. . . . The object is the thing received; and it is more accurately said, that we see the sun, than that we see the light" (*E. W.* I, pp. 391, 116, 404-05, 411). Accidents are vehicles and not objects of perception because of the speed by which individual phantasms are formed and compounded by the mind into whole ideas of bodies: "For a phantasm is the act of sense, and differs no otherwise from sense than *fieri,* that is, being a doing, differs from *factum esse,* that is, being done; which difference, in things that are done in an instant is none at all; and a phantasm is made in an instant" (*E. W.* p. 392). [3] In sense experience discrete and individual phantasms are formed so rapidly that we derive a complete and compounded picture of the object even though these phantasms singularly reproduce only individual accidents.

In the act of experience body and accident appear as one indistinguishable unit. We cannot perceive bodies apart from accidents or accidents apart from bodies. Of "pure" body we can have no experiential awareness, and of accidents severed from bodies we are likewise in the dark. This is an important point for Hobbes; indeed it is the basis of his argument against the theory of sensible species. By suggesting that in experience "species" are sent out from an object and received into the organs of a sentient, the theory, according to Hobbes, converted the appearances of a body into a species of body itself. In Hobbes' own view accidents mediate between mind and matter in such a way that though we may perceive or experience bodies, we do so on the basis of their accidents. We perceive the body, but the body we perceive is the body as it appears. At the frontier of awareness in experience we encounter the inseparability of body and accident. As we shall see, however, this situation obtains only in

---

[3] Hobbes is not always consistent in his use of the word "Phantasm". Sometimes he uses it as a synonym for "image," "idea," or "conception," and at other times to denote simple sense date such as color, figure, hardness, and the like—i. e., as "representations" of accidents. However, that he did distinguish between imagery and sense data is obvious from the quote given above (p. 58), and from the opening pages of his discussion of method (*E. W.* I, pp. 65-68).

the sublinguistic world, for when we reason in words the nominal separation of bodies and accidents is not only possible, it is necessary.

Hobbes' account of thought closely parallels his account of experience. This is because unlike most rationalists, he did not distinguish between the acts of perception and conception except to say the latter can transpire in the absence of any sense object. Hence, the experiential act could just as legitimately be characterized as either conceptual or perceptual. And indeed Hobbes himself often used "conceive" where more appropriately he should have said "preceive." It makes no difference which word is used, however, because the processes involved are the same in both cases: thinking as well as experiencing involves nothing more than the compounding of phantasms. The process of thinking might be considered in its "purest" form when no experience is involved, and the idea produced does not refer to anything existing in nature. Yet even in this case, the process is identical to the act of experience. For the mind "composeth an imagination of diverse conceptions that appeared singly to the sense." A "golden mountain," for example, is compounded out of "the figure of a mountain" and "the colour of gold" (*E.* p. 10).

But if, for Hobbes, the processes involved in experiencing or thinking are identical, so as well are the ideas these processes produce. Whether the outcome of experience or thought, all ideas are images compounded out of phantasms. There is no such thing as a pure imageless concept in Hobbes' vocabulary. The importance of this is that our mental awareness extends always and only to images of particular bodies appearing in diverse ways. In thought just as in experience, no separation of body and accident is possible. Hobbes' treatment of experience and thought shows his materialism, therefore, to be thoroughgoing and complete. All knowledge, he says, is evidence, all evidence conception, all conception imagination, all imagination "decaying sense," all sense the outcome of experience, and the experience itself of bodies as they appear (*E.* pp. 25, 55; *L.* p. 88).

61

In the world we inhabit by nature, the world of sense and thought, everything is individual and determinate: "a man can have no thought representing any thing, not subject to sense. No man therefore can conceive any thing, but he must conceive it in some place; and indued with some determinate magnitude" (*L.* p. 99). All existents are determinate individuals which in experience are broken up into accidental representations, and which, in turn, are pieced together instantly by the mind to produce an image which is itself of determinate dimension. Individuality is the key to Hobbes' account of the sensible world. It is also, as a result, the key to our experience and thought of this world. Universals exist neither in nature nor in the mind, and, for that matter, even if they did exist in nature, the composition of mind is such that they would escape our notice. Since all imagery is singular, we could have no conception, no evidence, and consequently no knowledge of them.

According to Hobbes, what our minds know of the world is known on the basis of ideas derived in whole or in part from sense experience. And because these ideas are always images, they reproduce in mind the singularity of the world outside. There is more than just a touch of irony in all this. For if it is granted that all ideas are images of determinate bodies, then mind alone is powerless to explain both the individual things experienced or thought and the processes by which these things are experienced or thought. A thing or an event can be explained only if it is fitted into some more general category of things or events, only, that is, if it can be placed within some universal context. This context mind cannot possibly provide because ideas or images simply multiply the singularity of the sensible world. Moreover, since in imagery body and accident compose one undifferentiated unit, and since imagery is the extent of our awareness, it is impossible to know by means of mind alone what the causes of sense or thought could possibly be. No idea or set of ideas could give us grounds for supposing that the way we perceive or conceive any particular body is determined by the variety of that body's motion. This knowledge is not given us by means of experience or thought but only, as we shall see, by means of language. Now, in the space that remains I wish to explore some of the implications of this materialist interpretation of mind for Hobbes' treatment of language. I shall begin with a discussion of the resemblance between the thinking and reasoning processes, for it is here that we get a clue as to the unique position language occupies in relation to Hobbes' materialism.

If one examines Hobbes' remarks on the process of reasoning in words and compares them to what he says about the processes of thought and experience, one is struck by the similarity between the two. In experience and thought, he says, our minds compound individual phantasms into whole determinate images, while when we reason we compute the names of individual accidents (abstract names) to arrive at the particular names of bodies (concrete names). Moreover, just as any particular body appears as it does in sense or thought because of the peculiar composition of its accidents, so as well the determination of any particular name of a body is a result of the names of the accidents it comprehends. To be sure, this is the process of reasoning at its most elemental definitional level, but the process is the same as we move up the scale of generality to propositions, syllogisms, and demonstrations. Reason, therefore, as well as experience and thought is calculative. The only difference is in the nature of the materials calculated: reason computes names, the mind phantasms.

There are good reasons to suspect this similarity between the processes of mind and of reason is more than simple coincidence. For the fact, according to Hobbes, that names were invented as instruments of mind to mark and signify thoughts seems, if anything, to suggest reason was created after mind's own image and patterned after the processes of thought. If this is granted, the similarity would appear to be the result of the modelling of reason on the operations of mind.

Indeed Hobbes' very treatment of experience and thought tends to reinforce this interpretation. He often writes as if he were considering these matters from the inside—as it were, looking at them from the point of view of one who had not the use of language or reason. This, of course, is common procedure for Hobbes. It is only one instance of many where he employs the resolutive-compositive method he recommends so often as the method of all philosophy. The trick is to "feign away" speech and reason in order to inspect the pure and natural residue that remains. In this case the residual faculties remaining after the feigning operation has been performed are experience and thought. The point here is that if it is possible to observe the workings of mind without the aid of language, then it is also possible to construct a language which is based on these workings. There are a number of reasons, however, for thinking that while Hobbes' method might suggest the feasibility of such a project, his own understanding of experience and thought, in fact, rules it out. For there are a number of assertions Hobbes makes in his account of experience and thought that, given the nature of this account, could not conceivably be made from the standpoint of someone unacquainted with language. First of all is Hobbes' insistence on the reality of bodies. His analysis of experience and thought supplies no ground whatsoever for this insistence, since the only messages received from the world outside—our phantasms—picture only its accidents. Second, to our mind's eye, body and accident always appear as one inseparable unit. If this is granted, then the mind in experience and thought cannot be said to be capable of distinguishing between them. Since we can have no awareness of one apart from the other, we can have no awareness even of the distinction. Third, Hobbes' contention that phantasms are the materials of mental computation conflicts with his view that they are unobservable: observability extends only to images. Last, Hobbes' observation that phantasms are formed and compounded by the mind so rapidly into determinate images as to make the process itself unobservable contradicts, if strictly adhered to, the very observation. Each of these difficulties turns around the central paradox that Hobbes at one and the same time suggests that experience and thought can give us information that his analysis of these faculties shows to be impossible.

T. A. Heinrichs

Because this information cannot be furnished by the faculties in question, it seems reasonable to conclude we must look elsewhere. My suggestion is that we reverse direction and look in the region of language, for how else could we explain Hobbes' search for the equivalent of a syllogism in the mind? (*E.W.* I, pp. 49-50).

What I shall suggest here with regard to Hobbes' account of thought and experience is what has elsewhere been argued with respect to his reading of the "estate of man by mere nature." [4] The experiencing and thinking being that remains after the feigning operation has been performed looks suspiciously like the linguistic creature with which Hobbes began. In fact, if not in intention, Hobbes reads back the logic of language into his analyses of both the process and substance of experience and thought. This reading is possible because though neither materials nor processes of thought or experience are observable, both the process of reason and what is processed by reason are. And it is plausible because without it Hobbes' materialism would take him straight over the precipice into the subjectivist abyss. In order for Hobbes to avoid this fate, he has to do more than explain experience and thought in words: he has to explain them on the basis of words.

Experience and thought on the one hand and reason on the other differ as to the nature of the respective materials compounded by each as well as to the speed of the compounding process. When we reason we add and subtract names while when we experience or think we add and subtract phantasms, and while phantasms are immaterial and unobservable, names are both material and observable. Names, for Hobbes, are "sensible marks," and this sensibility lends characteristics to the reasoning process that thought and experience by their very natures cannot possess. Names allow us to slow down the reasoning process, stop it altogether at will, inspect each element separately, reverse it at any point, and begin it again at our leisure.

---

[4] C. B. Macpherson, *The Political Theory of Possessive Individualism: Hobbes to Locke* (Oxford, 1962), pp. 19-29.

Like a film with all the possibilities of what in the jargon of the day are termed "stop-action" and "instant-replay," words can be calculated in slow-motion. We can observe the reasoning process because we manipulate observable entities. We can construct, dissect, analyze, and piece together again a linguistic proposition, syllogism, or demonstration which, because the mind traffics in insensible phantasms moving at unobservable speeds, cannot be done in sense or thought. In the mind there is an unobservable flux of phantasms, while from the mouth there flows a discrete ordering of words. This is the great advantage reason enjoys over thought—an advantage which is strictly a result of the nature of its medium.

Two features of this medium are particularly important for us. First, in words we are able to construct the abstract universal entities that are without equivalents in nature or in mind. And second, we can separate in words the names of accidents from the names of bodies, whereas in mind bodies and accidents always appear as a single unit. Language gives us the power to speak the inconceivable. We can say "man" though our minds can only produce images of particular men because language is the region of the unthinkable universal: "there being nothing in the world Universall but Names; for the things named, are every one of them Individual and Singular" (*L.*, p. 102). To take the argument a step further, there are no universal thoughts precisely because imagery always portrays bodies as they appear. To the mind bodies and accidents always compose a single sketch. Language, on the other hand, gives us the power to split this picture in two and consider each element as if it were a separately existing thing. Names of accidents (abstract names) can be separated from names of bodies (concrete names) and either added to or subtracted from the latter. In discourse, though not in mind, we can empty a body of all its accidents to arrive at an unimaginable universal entity, and then, in turn, we can add them back one at a time to produce an entity that is imaginable.

The existence of linguistic universality along with the separation of the names of bodies and accidents are the two indispensible prerequisites for the description of experience and thought that Hobbes provides. Reason has to be the model for Hobbes' understanding of mind because neither experience nor thought could produce this understanding. Putting together a proposition involves, for Hobbes, nothing more than the "copulation" of abstract and concrete names by means of the verb "is." In propositions concrete names function as subjects of assertions while abstract names denote their causes, or why it is the name of any one body differs from the names of all other bodies. Abstract names, therefore, define concrete names by separating out and designating the various accidents or qualities according to which any particular body named is to be distinguished. In language just as in perception or conception we find an interplay of "figure" and "ground." Abstract and concrete names cooperate to produce an object visible to the mind's eye. On this score, however, the difference between language and mind is that by its very nature mind must be unaware of the distinction between figure and ground and, therefore, unaware of the interplay itself.

The importance of language for Hobbes' account of experience and thought extends further than to its use as the model on which his description of the processes of mind is based. Because of his radically materialist account of mind, language becomes the very source of our information about the real character of bodies external to mind, and of the preconditions for their receptivity in sense experience. To see how this is possible we must lift the discussion to its most abstract level, for it is here that we encounter the universals "body" and "accident".

At this point it should be clear that nothing derived from experience could lead us to think what Hobbes said when he wrote "Every thing is eyther Substance or Accident." This knowledge could only come from a familiarity with the use of words because "substance," or "body," and "accident" exist only in language and refer to no entities existing in nature or mind. But though these words do not refer to any experiential or conceptual entities, they do refer to the conditions under which experiencing and thinking occur. Consider Hobbes' definition of "body": "The Word *Body,* in the most general acceptation, signifieth that which filleth, or occupyeth some certain room, or imagined place; and dependeth not on the imagination, but is a reall part of that we call the *Universe*" (*L.,* p. 428). By the word, Hobbes simply *asserts* the necessity of some "thing" apart from mind that does not depend for its existence on our mental recognition of it. This "something real" is all that the word "body" denotes. This makes it, indeed, a "word-body," since no image could ever furnish us with grounds for such an assertion. "Body," for Hobbes, states one precondition of perception and thought, namely, that there be some thing to perceive and to think about, without which we would unable to experience or think at all. In the universal language of names, "body" signifies the "objectivity" of objects, and the real character of all the particular things that appear to us in sense and in thought. Just as when we reason concrete names function as the ground and referent for abstract names, so in pointing to the real and objective character of bodies, "body" points to the ground and referent, the locus of all experience. Bodies are "there." Without them we could not perceive. This "thereness" of bodies denoted by the word "body" is underscored by Hobbes' claim that the one accident without which any particular existing body would perish is magnitude, or as he otherwise terms it, "real space."

If the word "body" denotes the reality and "thereness" of all particular bodies, the word "accident" denotes universally the appearances all bodies must possess if they are to be perceived. Thus, while "body" designates the object, "accident" indicates the agency whereby the object is transformed and received by the mind as an image. Together, "body" and "accident" tell us what we experience as well as how and why we experience what we experience in the manner that we do. By defining the necessary conditions of experience, they explain how both experience and thought are possible, though they themselves refer to nothing in particular that exists. This understanding is impossible outside of language because only in words can we reach the universality necessary to account for experience and thought *per se*. For that matter, however, since all ideas are images of bodies as they appear, and since, therefore, mind is incapable of distinguishing between bodies and accidents, not only can we not reach the universality necessary to understand thought and experience *per se*, but we cannot understand what is happening to us in any particular instance. Outside of language any individual image is just as mysterious to us as imagery itself.

Only if it is assumed that Hobbes' account of experience and thought is modelled on the workings of words can we explain how, in the instances noted above, Hobbes could "observe" what his account of these processes states cannot be observed. It is only with an eye fixed on language that we can know bodies are real, distinguish a body from an accident, be aware of phantasms, and of the process by which they are compounded into determinate images. Reasoned discourse describes this sublinguistic universe for Hobbes by stipulating its preconditions and by designating its processes. Mind needs language to understand the preconditions and processes of its own operation because awareness is limited to ideas, ideas are but images, and images simply reproduce the singularity of the sensible world. Because we cannot think a universal thought it falls, for Hobbes, on language to supply the universality necessary to measure and explain the singular content of experience and thought. And because it is only in words that we can distinguish bodies from accidents, it is only on the basis of language that we are able to know how the outer, real, and objective world of nature is connected to the inner, apparent, and subjective universe of mind. Science, or knowledge proper, for Hobbes, is concerned only with connections or causes. This is why it is entirely an affair of language, and why, as well, it often seems as if Hobbes carries rationalism to an extreme. Mind can produce an awareness only of particular experiences, not, however, of the connections among them. It is language alone that can fill this need, but it fills it at the price of a magnificent irony: for the connections observed are simply connections among words.

Language and experience or thought constitute separate but parallel worlds that intersect in Hobbes' philosophy only analogically. This combination, I have suggested, is a consequence of a materialism that portrays mind in such a way that it needs language to enable it to understand both the world it observes and the conditions and processes of its own operation. Hence the interdependence of Hobbes' materialism and his rationalism. Without his materialist interpretation of mind, his rationalist preoccupation with words would not be necessary. On the other hand, without an eye to the workings of words, his materialist reading of mind would not be possible. In Hobbes' philosophy the Idea is not the measure of all things, language is. The name rather than the idea is the measure because thought is collapsed into experience, the idea into the image. At the same time, of course, the Name is not the Idea since it is a sensible and invented commodity. The invention of the mark is the invention of an intermediary screen between mind and its objects. It is as true for Hobbes as it is for Wittgenstein that though we think we are "tracing the outline of a thing's nature over and over again," we are "merely tracing around the frame through which we look at it." [5] When we search after the Idea or the "nature" of anything, we always encounter language, for language is the mould into which the contents of mind are cast. Thus, the attempt to remove language in order to gaze upon thought and experience in their natural simplicity must inevitably fail: mind cannot be seen as it is given to us by nature, but only as it has been shaped and hardened by the mould that covered it. Wherever we look we always see language. To see the world as Hobbes saw it, we must inevitably look at the workings of words.

[5] *Philosophical Investigations*, I, p. 114.

D. E. Curtis

Pierre Bayle and the Range of Cartesian Reason

At first sight, Bayle appears a most unlikely object of Cartesian influence. His preoccupations are less philosophical than moral, religious
and historical, less theoretical than practical. For when in his erudition
he painstakingly establishes the truth of a historical fact and when
in his philosophical criticism he delimitates the range of reason, his
purpose transcends these disciplines. His constant aim, proclaimed
as clearly in the *Nouvelles de la République des Lettres* as in the
Dictionnaire, is to lead his reader to accept the necessity of tolerance.
His rationalism is critical rather than architectonic: he practises the
analysis of ideas and facts rather than their synthesis and, as Professor I. O. Wade points out in his *Intellectual Origins of the French
Enlightenment,* appreciates the "interesting points" of philosophical
systems rather than the unitary vision which inspired them. [1] And
underpinning his criticism is a religious world-view which colours
his conception of the whole nature of knowledge. Nevertheless, the
very preoccupations which led Bayle to circumscribe the range of
Cartesian reason in the fields of physics and metaphysics led him to
extend Cartesian pretensions to areas ruled out of bounds by the
distinction of metaphysical and moral certainty and to envisage
Cartesian method as applicable in principle to all aspects of knowledge.

One finds in the first place that, for all his enthusiasm for the
achievements of the new corpuscular physics, Bayle is excluded by
his lack of mathematical knowledge from understanding both Descartes' idea of a *mathesis universalis* and the mathematical origins
of self-evidence. Ironically, it is partly in the name of Cartesian self-
evidence as he understands it that he rejects the mathematicisation

[1] (Princeton, New Jersey, 1971), p. 605.

71

of physics in favour of the most outdated part of Descartes' work, the tying of a physics to a metaphysic of clear and distinct ideas. Bayle is even prepared to justify his ignorance of mathematics by claiming that the mind may be formed equally well and more easily by the study of other disciplines, notably Aristotelian logic. And his practice shows that he finds physics the most interesting when its inquiries have metaphysical and religious implications: thus the Cartesian attempt to extend mechanical principles to biology and the effects this had upon the vexed question of animal souls, never ceased to stimulate Bayle's critical mind. When however it is a question of the application of mathematical concepts to physics, Bayle declares on many occasions that this enterprise can never succeed.

His argument is firstly that the self-evident truths of mathematics contradict certain self-evident common notions which no one can doubt because, apart from their intrinsic self-evidence, they are also corroborated by the senses: mathematics claim to prove for example that a finite quantity and an infinite quantity are equal. Secondly, taking up the sceptical arguments of Gassendi and Huet and reviving those of Sextus Empiricus himself, Bayle concludes that mathematical quantity cannot exist outside the mind: a similar misunderstanding of Descartes' distinction of imagination and understanding vitiates Bayle's interpretation of Malebranche and, more spectacularly, of Spinoza. Bayle is led therefore to condemn the pioneering work of Kepler and the new mathematics of Leibnitz and Newton and to judge the new mathematically based concepts of relative time, space and motion, developed by Bruno, Kepler and others just as incomprehensible as the old absolute concepts of the Scholastics and the new absolute theory of Newton. Thus Descartes' kinematic idea of motion as relative geometrical change, which had to concede that the forces causing motion could not be conceived clearly and distinctly because they formed part of neither thinking substance nor extended substance, Bayle declares roundly to be unworthy of a schoolboy. Characteristically, the criterion of his judgment is of Cartesian inspiration: Descartes' idea of motion, itself obscure, merely refers us to the equally obscure idea of rest. And when Bayle discovers that mathematicians claim to be able to demonstrate the existence of the vacuum in the face of the clear and distinct idea of spacial extension, which he regards as "l'Orthodoxie Philosophique" [philosophical orthodoxy] and the most important contribution of the century to the understanding of the physical world, he can feel that his opposition has been well justified.

However, Bayle's invocation of the empiricist criterion of truth against mathematical self-evidence appears to be due to more than the misunderstanding of a non-specialist. Bayle is concerned to find a place for alternative passages to knowledge, to rehabilitate experience and even prejudice against the defenders of ahistorical reason. This he does, not by claiming that each branch of this threefold path is of equal worth, still less that experience must be the final judge: nor does he argue, as Montaigne did in his essay *De l'Experience,* that experience serves where reason fails—a conception of truth which retained the supremacy of reason but denied that it had only one form. Bayle's argument is that factual knowledge can be made to approximate to the ideal of metaphysical self-evidence and that irrational knowledge will one day be, as it were, absorbed into the latter—a process which can be brought about only by re-defining the boundary between the Cartesian categories of moral and metaphysical certainty. Thus Bayle defends historical knowledge as capable of attaining self-evidence by the use of a method inspired by that of Naudé and other *libertins érudits* of the first half of the Seventeenth Century, a method which, as Mme. Labrousse showed in her important work on Bayle, is in essence that of the Cartesians. No doubt, the self-evidence of a historical fact is on a lower level to that for example of the common notions of arithmetic. Nevertheless, it cannot be reduced to the status of a moral certainty as the Cartesians understood this term. Again, human instincts and passions may be not only a means to knowledge—impartiality leading only too often to indecision—but also a means of knowledge. That this defense of prejudice is no idle paradox, or, as some critics have maintained, a ruse to confuse the orthodox, is suggested by the fact that Bayle justifies it in terms of a doctrine of natural providence which appears in his work as early as the *Pensées diverses sur la Comète* of 1682-83 and as late as the *Dictionnaire.*

Bayle first distinguishes practical reason, which is preceded by the passions, from speculative reason, the realm of self-evidence. Of the former he says that were it not the slave of passion it would counsel self-regarding action and destroy monagamous marriage and society itself. Of the latter he says that it is so vacillating and self-destructive that "si la Philosophie venoit à bout de faire agir tous les hommes, selon les idées claires et distinctes de la Raison, on peut être très-assûré que le genre humain périroit bien-tôt" [were philosophy to succeed in persuading men to act according to the clear and distinct ideas of reason, the human race, one can be quite sure, would soon perish]. Once again, by this supposition, meaningless to a Cartesian, he is declaring the notion of moral certainty redundant. For the time being, he goes on to argue, the dominion of passion and prejudice is a necessary evil, a dispensation of Providence, a plank after the shipwreck of the Fall. However, Bayle prophesies, "son Empire (i.e., of instinct) cessera un jour, et alors la Religion et la Raison seront la regle des actions de l'homme" [one day the reign of instinct will come to an end and religion and reason will be the rule of men's actions]. Until then, reason will find in the supremacy of the irrational a solid demonstration of the existence of God and unreason will perform the functions of reason. [2] Bayle appears to be suggesting then that unreason may be more than false knowledge, but may be seen as prereason which it is the philosopher's task not simply to reject, but to make explicit. In practice, however, does the weakness of speculative reason permit him to accomplish this?

In Bayle's hands metaphysical self-evidence, divorced from its mathematical base and contaminated by its incursions into the domain of moral certitude appears to survive as an intellectual and moral ideal realisable in only a fragmentary way, an ideal of a moderate and critical rationalism. It seems that Bayle's historical studies did nothing to shake his youthful belief in the absoluteness

[2] *Nouvelles Lettres sur l'histoire du Calvinisme* in *Œuvres Diverses,* II (Amsterdam, 1727), 274.

of reason, for him, that faculty which, on the foundations of the self-evident common notions of arithmetic, metaphysics and ethics, attempts to build an edifice of deductive truths. On the contrary, his tendency to see philosophy as a mixture whose elements could be broken down and recomposed in different ways or, to change the image, as a play in which the same characters—Immanentism and Atomism for example—reappear in different situations, confirmed his conception of the Cartesian criterion of clear and distinct ideas as reason becoming conscious of itself. Understood in this way, Cartesianism absorbs and perfects aspects of Pyrrhonism and even of Acatalepticism, in as far as the former can be equated with impartiality and the latter aimed to stop men from passing judgment until they had found self-evident truths. Again, the Scholastics cannot doubt the truth of the Cartesian criterion of truth without doubting their own principles, because it has shown them why the common notions they use are true.

However, if reason has a certain number of clear and distinct ideas at its disposal, it is incapable of synthesising them, of combining them to realise the Cartesian ideal of an irrefutable deductive system. In practice, the obscurity of our knowledge is such that principle opposes principle and doctrine opposes doctrine. Thus Gassendi could choose from the number of self-evident ideas furnished by reason those which opposed divisibility to infinity and reject those which supported it. Is this weakness of reason due to the ambiguity of the Cartesian criterion itself? Certainly, Bayle talks of Gassendi and others seeing more self-evidence in one doctrine than in another. Has Bayle therefore made self-evidence an ideal to which individual *évidences* may correspond to a greater or lesser extent? Or does the resort to the Cartesian criterion mask a doctrine of probability? The ambiguity of the texts does not permit more than a hesitant answer to these questions. Bayle's rejection of mathematical self-evidence illustrates his tendency to grasp the significance of an individual doctrine such as that of spacial extension rather than the relationship of this doctrine to the philosophy as a whole. The same defect appears to be present in his treatment of metaphysical truth as the example of divisibility to infinity shows. For the Cartesian, divisibility is an inseparable property of spacial extension and clearly conceived as such: furthermore it is of the very definition of divisibility that it is infinite—a point made clear, admittedly, only in the *Méteores* and in the *Principia*. Bayle appears to believe that the world is transparent in the clear and distinct ideas of an attentive mind and that Cartesianism has succeeded in discovering part at least of the world's mechanism. His aim appears to be to show not that such knowledge is impossible, but that it is, because of reason's tendency to destroy rather than to construct, very limited in scope. His argument is not that Cartesianism can escape insoluble objections but that other philosophies are subject to even stronger objections. Bayle never ceased to maintain that metaphysical doctrines may be open to insoluble objections and lead to incomprehensible consequences and yet still be true. To illustrate this point he takes in the *Dictionnaire* what he sees as a certain Cartesian doctrine, that of spacial extension, and shows that Malebranche's objections against it are feeble in comparison with those that Zeno could put forward were he to return to earth. Metaphysical reason's inability to see things whole must not lead it to abandon those insights it does possess.

Bayle's insistence that the incomprehensibility of a doctrine is no proof of its falsity allows him to make a bridge between the natural world and the world of faith and to sketch a semi-fideism based upon Cartesian self-evidence as he understands it. He does not tire in the *Dictionnaire* of reminding his reader that since reason has to accept the existence of spacial extension and other incomprehensibilities in the natural realm, there is no justification in reason for rejecting the mysteries of faith. In his later works he develops this idea further. He argues that in the religious domain as in the natural, reason is incapable of erecting a coherent and indubitable system. However, if a rational theology of the Socinian type is impossible, reason may still prefer one self-evident truth—above all, the veracity of God—to another self-evident truth—for example the self-evident maxims which contradict the mysteries. Unfortunately, Bayle does not make it any clearer here than he did in his discussion of natural truths why one self-evident truth is to be reckoned more certain than another, why, for example, the maxim "l'incompréhensibilité d'une chose n'est pas une raison sufisante *(sic)* de la révoquer en doute" [the incomprehensibility of a thing is not a sufficient reason to doubt it] is more certain than the rules of Aristotelian logic. [3] It may be that once again Bayle has retained the core of a Cartesian doctrine: Descartes did talk after all of the existence of God as more certain than any geometrical demonstration. But Bayle's attempt to use the speculative truths of natural reason to justify the body of revealed truths necessary for salvation, two realms carefully distinguished by Descartes in the *Discours de la Méthode* and in the 4ème *Méditation* would have appeared meaningless to the philosopher, whose fideism was content with the belief, shared wholeheartedly by Bayle, that Christian dogmas are more certain than clear and distinct ideas. Bayle, it appears, also wished to prove that they are.

This conception of the nature and range of metaphysical self-evidence Bayle puts forward both against dogmatists, who believed that reason could render itself quite invulnerable to objections, and against sceptics, who believed that reason could establish no truths at all. With obvious pleasure Bayle showed the blinkered abbé of the article *Pyrrhon,* who had reached the age of forty-five fondly believing that no Pyrrhonist objections could shake him, that even his continuing personal identity as a dogmatist was doubtful—an argument that Hume was to take up to good effect. Against the sceptics Bayle argued first that even the most determined Pyrrhonist must accept the validity of the Cogito. Indeed, Bayle refuses to believe, whatever Seneca and Cicero may say to the contrary, that any sceptic ever has doubted it—an example of Bayle's a priorism overcoming his historical method which is as rare and as instructive as his belief, held independently of the evidence provided by European travellers, in the universal predominance of evil. Second, sceptics must accept that, as something exists today, there is a being which is eternal: Yet the objections to this belief are insurmountable, and so

[3] *Réponse aux Questions d'un Provincial* in *Œuvres Diverses,* III (Amsterdam, 1727), 770.

the Pyrrhonist, like Bayle, must accept a self-evident truth subject to insurmountable and self-evident objections.

It is clear that in Bayle's mind this conception of metaphysical self-evidence is inseparable from the idea of tolerance. His argument is first that moral and intellectual qualities are interdependent. For just as the intellectual vice of dogmatism leads to the moral vice of intolerance, the intellectual vice of complete scepticism represents bad faith and, in its acataleptic form, leads to inactivity or "quié-tisme" [quietism], a doctrine denounced in the *Dictionnaire* almost as much as Spinozism, to which it is linked in Bayle's mind. However, in the last decades of the Seventeenth Century as, Bayle suggests wryly, in any other epoch, men had little to fear from the sceptics and in some spheres, that of witchcraft for example, much to gain. But they had much to fear from intolerant dogmatists in both the Protestant and Catholic camps. Here religious faith was accompanied by a naïve faith in reason and, what was worse, the rational demand for self-evidence was being applied to religious controversy, the realm of probability, to justify forced conversions. Thus the article *Pyrrhon* condemns explicitly the dogmatism of Jurieu and implicitly, by its portrait of the purblind abbé, the dogmatism of Catholics who, like Nicole at the time of the Revocation of the Edict of Nantes, claim self-evidence for their cause. Against these zealots, Bayle defends a more modest conception of the range of metaphysical reason, but one sufficient he believes to establish the moral rationalism of the *Commentaire philosophique*. What is more, Bayle tends to see self-evidence itself as a moral ideal of impartiality which it is the philosopher's duty to attain by a process which resembles an examination of conscience more than Cartesian methodical doubt.

The only public check that the method has been properly applied becomes that of the discussion of the reasons for and against the metaphysical doctrine in question, a discussion which, given Bayle's religious and moral preoccupations, tends to take the form of controversies against real or imaginary opponents. Thus in the *Réponse aux Questions d'un Provincial* Bayle introduces Descartes' four rules into a discussion of the difficulty of knowing God and asserts that, as Cartesian doubt requires the knowledge of all one's prejudices, it is finally impossible. That for Bayle the essential part of Cartesian method is the removal of prejudice is shown in another way by the fact that he gives a quite different account of philosophical doubt in the *Dictionnaire,* arguing not only that when one is trying to prove the existence of God to an atheist there is no need to reject ones's belief, only to put it, as it were in brackets, so that it does not distort one's reasoning, but also that this attenuated and vulgarised form of Cartesian doubt is in fact what Descartes understood by radical philosophical doubt. Finally, Bayle concludes from the ultimate impossibility of knowing whether the method has been used the necessity of tolerance. Too often men impute to malice or *amour-propre* the results of a man's sincere attempts to reach impartial judgment. This is most common in debates which concern religion directly or indirectly, and Bayle gives as an example of this behaviour the attribution of evil motives by Protestants to one of their number who becomes a Catholic. The use of this example reveals not only Bayle's personal stake in his championing of the ideal of impartiality but also that Cartesian method understood as a means to this ideal is now being applied to what Bayle recognises to be part of the realm of moral certainty, religious controversy. Here there is no attempt to annex an aspect of moral certainty to the realm of self-evidence. It is rather that Cartesian method has lost all necessary connection with its object and is therefore applicable in principle to any field of knowledge.

In the *Discours de la Méthode* Descartes had bemoaned the fact that men he considered intelligent and who seemed to have understood his views, changed them beyond recognition. The Seventeenth Century, which saw his principles reconciled with those of Gassendi and even with those of Aristotle, was to corroborate his worst fears in this respect. And yet, what Paul Mouy wrote of the development of Cartesian physics in the seventeenth century appears true of that of Cartesianism as a whole. Noting "la médiocrité des résultats obtenus par les *professeurs cartésiens*" [the mediocre results obtained by Cartesian teachers], too often servile compilers, he stresses the fruitfulness of the work of "soit des demi-cartésiens soit des cartésiens d'inspiration" [half-Cartesians and those inspired by Cartesianism]. [4] Of this latter category is Pierre Bayle. No doubt, Bayle's evaluation of his work expresses his intentions rather than his achievement. It appears that in his own mind he is erecting a cautious rationalism which, equally removed from the extremes of dogmatism and scepticism, will teach men, in the words of his first biographer, to "douter des choses douteuses" [doubt doubtful things]. In his own lifetime, Bayle's readiness to concede that his options were subject to insuperable objections was inevitably interpreted as the most dangerous skepticism: that those who knew him better were able to interpret his aims more equitably is shown by the case of Shaftesbury. A modern critic, without in any way minimising the incoherence of Bayle's treatment of the nature and range of Cartesian reason—his own considerable contribution to the "downfall of Cartesianism"— [5] may feel that if Bayle destroyed the epistemological foundations of this philosophy he did so largely in the name of a conception of self-evidence made possible by the subjectivism inherent in the Cartesian criterion of truth itself. [6] For if Bayle's preoccupations make him one of those who in reading Descartes "veulent y trouver la solution de plusieurs difficultés dont il ne dit rien, et auxquelles il n'a peut-être jamais pensé" [seek the solution of several difficulties he does not mention and of which he has perhaps never thought] [7] he is also of those who follow Descartes' exhortation in the *Principia* to yield only to what they find self-evident. That Bayle sought the self-evident in the temporal realm and found a place within a philosophical framework of Cartesian inspiration for alternative passages to knowledge was his most fruitful infidelity to the Master. Thus the Eighteenth Century could see in Bayle more than the "skeptic,"

[4] *Le développement de la physique cartésienne (1646-1712)* (Paris, 1934), p. 321.
[5] Cf. Richard A. Watson, *The Downfall of Cartesianism 1673-1712: A Study of the Epistemological Issues in Late 17th Century Cartesianism* (The Hague, 1966).
[6] See the forthcoming article in *French Studies* by E. D. James entitled, "Pierre Bayle on belief and 'évidence'."
[7] *Discours de la Méthode*, part 6.

that is to say a thinker whose incoherent defence of Cartesianism unwittingly hastened its demise. For the new age Bayle was also the wielder of a formidable historical method and a moralist whose doctrine of natural providence could be put to good if very limited use to rehabilitate *amour-propre,* soon to become the keystone of eighteenth-century ethical thought.

Timothy J. Reiss

Structure and Mind in Two Seventeenth-Century Utopias: Campanella and Bacon

The Utopian thinker, according to Marx, writes as a bourgeois who, in the silence of his study, gives free play at once to his reason and his imagination, [1] and it may be supposed that this acknowledged duality of cause has its reflexion in the result. For the utopian ideal is at once a meditation upon history or an historical situation and a proposing of an "ideal" solution to that history. Indeed, to the extent that the utopia represents at once myth *and* the reasoned attempt to permit the insertion of that myth into the stream of History, it clearly partakes—as a literary text—of that epistemological division of thought which appears to characterize the sixteenth and seventeenth centuries in Europe. Insofar as the utopia is dynamic, it may offer an idealized *continuation* of that history, and it may thus be said to be adapted rather to the serial process of rational (logico-mathematical) thinking. Insofar as the utopia is static, it suggests a halt to History; and this halt can be found only in the creation of a myth, a retreat from social praxis into a mental figure of social stasis, the freezing of that praxis. In a way one may doubtless argue that an utopia is always static—as has recently Alexandre Cioranescu [2]—since it always suggests to some degree the sublimation of a pre-existing social order, or of a model abstracted from that order. Nonetheless, that a profitable distinction can be made between the

---

[1] Paraphrased by Georges Duveau, *Sociologie de l'utopie et autres "essais,"* ouvrage posthume (Paris, 1961), p. 7. The "utopiste" is here opposed to the "scientifique."

[2] Alexandre Cioranescu, *L'Avenir du passé: Utopie et littérature* (Paris, 1972): "The very structure of the genre forces it to remain within horizontal structures, in which epic details provide only an artificial relief: the great enterprise of vertical or diachronic cross-sectioning is not open to it" (p. 23). "One may say," he adds later, "that Bacon's utopia is not utopian" (p. 149).

Timothy J. Reiss

dynamic and the static utopia is what I hope to demonstrate in this essay.[3]

The two best-known utopias of the early seventeenth century represent an almost exemplary demonstration of the two seemingly opposing thought systems which collide at this time. Campanella's *Civitas Solis*[4] stands virtually as a paradigm of the process that seeks knowledge by analogies, Bacon's *New Atlantis* is as much a paradigmatic suggestion of the new experimentalism, of the reach for knowledge by the inductive process.

Certainly, Campanella was anything but ignorant of the expansion of knowledge and technical "know-how" occurring in his lifetime: he is aware (obviously) of the voyages—the form of his dialogue between the steersman and a "Grandmaster of the Knights Hospitallers" is reminiscent of Pigafetta's relation of Magellan's voyage to the Grandmaster of the Knights of Rhodes,[5] his seaman served with Columbus—his Solarians have discovered flight,[6] various forms of sea and land travel, and other mechanical devices; he hesitates between the systems of Ptolemy and Copernicus (p. 177), recognizes Gilbert's work with magnets (p. 179), avoids pronouncing on the question of the infinity of worlds (p. 179), and refuses authority in learning, claiming preference for a direct experience of things (pp. 151-

[3] This "introduction" is necessarily elliptic, and for further remarks on the dualism here suggested in this context I must refer the reader to my introduction to this collection (and to the entire volume).

[4] Started in 1602, published "a Thobia Adami" in 1623. All quotations for *The City of the Sun* are taken from the translation by T. W. Halliday, which can be found in at least three collections: Charles M. Andrews, *Ideal Empires and Republics* (1901, 1937); Frederic R. White, *Famous Utopias of the Renaissance* (1946, 1955); and Henry Morley, *Ideal Commonwealths* (London & New York, 1901) the last is the edition to which my page numbers refer. The translation is abbreviated and somewhat rearranged in places thanks to Halliday's or Morley's censorship of "indecent," theological, and astronomical and astrological discussions (where these last became, apparently, too abstruse). Thus I have checked all references with the first Latin edition, which appears as an *Appendix Politicae Civitas Solis Idea Reipublicae Philosophiae* on pp. 417-64 of F. Thomae Campanellae... *Realis Philosophiae Epilogisticae Partes Quatuor*... (Frankfurt, 1623), and with the modern Italian edition in *La Città del Sole e Scelta d'alcune poesie filosofiche* a cura di Adriano Seroni (Milan, 1962), pp. 1-49, whose text is based on the mss., and to which I refer when Halliday omits or alters.

[5] See, Charles E. Nowell, ed., *Magellan's Voyage Around the World: Three Contemporary Accounts* (Evanston, Ill., 1962), pp. 85-260.

[6] These last two details are omitted by Halliday.

52).[7] All this one may gather from the most superficial reading of no more than *The City of the Sun* itself. Campanella was also, of course, so ardent a supporter of Galileo as to offer himself in 1632 as the scientist's defender before the papal commission, and he had previously risked his life and successfully put a stop to the process leading to his own freedom by his *Apologia pro Galileo* (1622, commenced 1616), in which, as Santillana puts it, he "had called Aristotle and the Scholastics all sorts of names, had come out boldly for the Copernican system, and had propounded new and arbitrary interpretations of scripture."[8]

However, as Santillana elsewhere observes,[9] these particular "perilous fantasies" serve rather to affirm than deny that science is, if anything, the handmaiden of an humanism based in theological speculation and that its discoveries are more or less satisfactory explications, in the form of geometrical structures, of the miriad workings of divine providence. The Copernican system struck Campanella as a particularly happy model; but in this he varies scarcely at all from Osiander's position in his preface to the *De Revolutionibus*. He accepts the new cosmology as a suitable mathematical model for purposes of human knowledge, but denies that it is reality.[10] This position, rather Renaissance humanist than medieval, is the very echo of the mode of thinking of the pre-Galilean philosopher. Speaking of Urban VIII, Santillana again makes the following remark:

[7] This obviously does gross injustice to Campanella's thought, but I am concerned here in the main with what can be gleaned from the *Civitas Solis*. For a thorough discussion, see particularly, León Blanchet, *Campanella* (Paris, 1920).

[8] Giorgio de Santillana, *The Crime of Galileo* (Chicago, 1959), p. 199, n. 7. See Thomas Campanella, *The Defense of Galileo*, trans. and ed. with Introduction and Notes by Grant McColley, Smith College Studies in History, XXII, 3-4 (Northampton, Mass., 1937): "Before presenting in Chapters IV and V the arguments from ancient and modern theologians which support and oppose Galileo, I shall construct from Holy Doctrine, the laws of nature, and the agreement of mankind, *the most probable and substantial hypotheses or foundations* essential to their foundation" (p. 14—my italics).

[9] Santillana, *op. cit.*, pp. 19, 168.

[10] See Blanchet, *op. cit.*, pp. 244 ff.

Timothy J. Reiss

This is where his thinking was backed by the great schemes of the Renaissance and its hope in unknown harmonies. "There is nothing that is incredible," Marcilio Ficino had said. "For to God all things are possible, and nothing is impossible. There are numberless possibilities that we deny because we do not happen to know them." This was also what Pico della Mirandola had maintained, hinting at reaches of "natural magic" beyond our dreams; and Campanella, too, was supporting Galileo in the hope of results such as no scientist could ever produce. It was "Platonic theology" itself, urging man to extend his imagination beyond what he could see and test; it was Leonardo's belief in the creative power of artistic "fantasy." [11]

Campanella's criticism of scholastic learning, when the Solarians argue that the bookman "has contemplated nothing but the world of books and has given his mind with useless result to the consideration of the dead signs of things" (p. 151), is in essence no different from his acquiescence in the Copernican system:

They praise Ptolemy and admire Copernicus, but put Aristarchus and Philolaus ahead of him; but they say that the one counts with stones, the other with beans, while neither with the things themselves that are counted [*le stesse cose contate*], and they pay for the world with money of account, not with gold. But they research this transaction [*questo negozio*] with extreme subtlety, because it is important to know the workings [*le fabbrica*] of the world... [12]

The signs of things serve only, he argues here, to conceal them. Between the bookmen's world of playing with the signs for themselves, and that of the future technocrat, who will take the signs for their referent, the choice is that of two sides of the same coin. The phrase, "*stesse cose contate*," is a revealing one, and it is to this goal that the Solarian will bend his energies: to the knowledge of things in themselves without the mediation of signs, whether monetary or linguistic. This, of course, brings us almost to Descartes' "idées claires et distinctes," the static knowledge at the center of all human knowing. Impossible goal, no doubt, but this is the reason for Campanella's dual rejection of signs.

This is why the form looks back to the concept of the great chain of being, and also why Campanella refers back to the *Critias*, and to

11 Santillana, *op. cit.*, pp. 167-68.
12 My translation from Seroni, p. 40. Halliday (p. 177) omits all the central portion.

the Renaissance utopias of Doni and Stiblin for the outward shape
of his circular city. The structure of *Civitas Solis* is entirely directed
inwards, and ultimately through the microcosm of the individual mind
to God. [13] In the light of the above brief commentary, there is little
remarkable in that its theme is *ostensibly* directed more to the future
and a knowledge of the natural sciences: "It represents an unlimited
will to know [*Wissen-Wollen*], which is directed at all natural objects." [14] For, in fact, the knowledge of nature is not simply a "will
to know," but a will to know God, and it is to this end that the
Solarians direct all their science.

The city "is divided into seven rings or huge circles named from
the seven planets, and the way from one to the other of these is by
four streets and through four gates, that look toward the four
points of the compass" (p. 141). After the visitor has entered through
the outer walls, of which, the traveller remarks: "so thick are the
earthworks and so well fortified is it with breastworks, towers, guns,
and ditches" (p. 142), that they would be impossible to storm, one
arrives, by passing through the subsequent rings, at the foot of an
ascent: "On the top of the hill is a rather spacious plain, and in the
midst of this there rises a temple built with wondrous art" (p. 143).
This temple is not divided from the city, but, like the intellect—or
perhaps soul—that it appears to represent, it is opened to it, so that
a constant intercommunication can, and does, take place: "... it is
not girt with walls, but stands upon thick columns, beautifully
wrought," and in its center is to be found the dome with, beneath it,
the altar (p. 143). The occupants of the temple are the 49 "priests
and religious officers" (p. 144) of whom the principal is Sol: [15] this

---

[13] See, e. g. Charles Rihs, *Les Philosophes utopistes: le mythe de la cité
communautaire en France au xviie siècle* (Paris, 1970): "*The City of the Sun,*
a political work, is a description of the ideal State, an image of the divine
order" (p. 293). "The Solarian approaches knowledge more as a Platonic
philosopher than as an expert technician" (p. 299, n. 8).

[14] Martin Schwonke, *Vom Staatsroman zur Science Fiction: Eine Un-
tersuchung über Geschichte und Funktion der naturwissenschaftlich-technischen
Utopie* (Stuttgart, 1957), p. 10.

[15] Seroni (p. 5, n. 9) notes that all the mss. have the astrological sign for
Sol, rather than a word: the first Latin edition "translates" this as "Sol,"
the second as "Hoh."

is a godlike figure of all-knowing, not unlike the Cartesian image of human possibilities:

The principal of the sciences, except Metaphysic, who is Hoh himself, and is, as it were, *the architect of all science, having rule over all,* are attached to Wisdom. Hoh is *ashamed to be ignorant of any possible thing* (p. 171—my italics).

Indeed, the manner in which the priests, *who are named after various human virtues,* moral, intellectual, and physical are described, is not unrevealing: for they are essentially the mediators between the ordinary citizens and the government of Sol or Hoh:

The priests, moreover, determine the hours for breeding and the days for sowing, reaping, and gathering the vintage, and are, as it were, the ambassadors and intercessors and connection between God and man (p. 175). [16]

The situation of the city is such that we pass through the material walls to the pure intellect at the center, and this system informs life within the city in all its forms. The learning process, which we would expect to follow this pattern, is indeed impressed upon the citizens by it. The rejection, but the necessity for purposes of communication, of mere signs is also indicated in this process. The relegation of the purely human symbolic languages of alphabet and mathematics to the outer wall (though the latter are given pride of place on the inner surface) of the city would seem to suggest that though the way to knowledge must initially lie through them, we must, and can, so to speak, come out on the other side. Things are learned less by talking about them, than by direct observation; that is to say, "by walking around them" and through them (p. 149). These symbols are replaced, as the visitor approaches the inner temple, by the depiction (perforce) of natural objects: successively, minerals, rivers and streams, vegetables, fish, birds and animals, until he comes to "the mechanical arts" and "the inventors in science, in warfare, in law" (p. 146), the prophets of natural religion, before arriving at the

[16] The Italian has "... e serveno come mezzani tra Dio e gli uomini" (p. 37).

final resolution of the microcosm/macrocosm tension with the world on the altar where is also to be found the central intellect, the ruler of the *City of the Sun.*

This plan is quite clearly the old one of the scholastics. And it is by a logic which accords with this that the city is communistic. Here the dynamism of the individual, the impulse behind possession, has no role. The static grandeur of nature which, properly, neither is controlled by man nor does it control him, informs the city. Within each step of the hierarchy there is equality of possession (save of honors), if not of talent: but each talent has its place in the *organized* hierarchy of the city. Given the static form of things, all works in harmony, and it is to be expected that things are done by the inhabitants only "when it is a pleasure to them" (p. 167), and because it is natural to do so (p. 158): "each one [works] according to his natural propensity doing his duty well and pleasantly, because naturally" (p. 146).

Campanella's depiction of his city as a world in harmony (the outer surface of the first wall contains, not only alphabets, but also "an immense drawing of the whole earth" [p. 145]), which is at the same time the individual mind and its way to knowledge, is summed up by one of the Solarian's pieces of wisdom: "The world is a great animal, and we live within it as worms live within us" (p. 178).

Campanella's city is indeed a static refuge (not, I would remark, a *retreat*) from the problems posed by a century about to confirm the adaptability of directed thought, with the concomitant problems of a metaphysical, ethical and social nature suddenly bursting in from a now strange outside. It is "an enchanted island, miraculously preserved at the Ocean's end, a perfect ark rediscovered at the end of a dream." [17] Well aware of the new developments, the Solarians are bent on seeking knowledge:

And when I asked with astonishment whence they had obtained our history, they told me that among them there was a knowledge of all languages, and that by perseverance they continually sent explorers and ambassadors over the

[17] Jean Servier, *Histoire de l'utopie* (Paris, 1967), p. 26.

whole earth, who learn thoroughly the customs, forces, rule and histories of the nations, bad and good alike (p. 147).

This dynamism is absorbed into the monolithic structure of the city. Absorbed as a force of change into a form that can accept no change. Where the harmony is perfect, the only hope for survival is, very precisely, no change. The circles that are the image at once of the mind and of the world cannot but predicate their essential identity and continuity. This is why the movement to knowledge, the visitor's advancement, is inwards, toward the divine intellect, towards the spirit of the world, into the static knowledge at the center of being.

Speaking of the necessary structure of Utopian fiction, Cioranescu has noted that its articulation is most similar to that of a lawyer's brief: "The hypothesis is its basic fact: the deduction is its logical scaffolding." [18] This, of course, forms the whole fiction—a static mass presented as a finished city. This may not be a wholly inapt characterization of the *Civitas Solis,* nor, come to that, of *Utopia* itself. But what if the fiction makes of deduction (or induction) not merely the means of its scaffolding, but also the subject of it? A most recent utopia, Skinner's *Walden Two* (1948), for instance, sets the idea of logical (experimental) progress at the very basis of its functioning; and what is most frightening *for us* about *Brave New World* or *1984* is just exactly their static nature and the quashing of the hope of experimentalism by extending it to one of its logical ends. Sir Francis Bacon lies at the other end of Huxley's and Orwell's dreary ladder, and in the *New Atlantis* it is to be expected that a serial progress should become its own subject. The essential structure controlling this utopia is based on a movement towards the outside, whether it be as voyage (and, in this connection, those of Columbus or Magellan are as symbolic as they were real), or as gaze. If the *Civitas Solis* can be compared to a contracted prey trapped in a corner—situated, may it be said, near the Taprobana of an already-outdated cosmogony—then the *New Atlantis* is the octopus, situated in a New World, sending out its tentacles to the Old.

[18] *Op. cit.,* p. 25. This position is common to most commentators of utopian fiction.

Where Campanella dismisses the voyage itself in a word (as he does those of the Solarians), Bacon, on the contrary, insists upon it. In his fiction, this movement and its accompanying troubles take on what would at first appear to be an inordinate emphasis:

We sailed from Peru (where we had continued by the space of one whole year) for China and Japan by the South Sea, taking with us victuals for twelve months, and had good winds from the east, though soft and weak, for five months' space and more. But then the wind came about and settled in the west for many days, so as we could make little or no way, and were sometimes in purpose to turn back. But then again there arose strong and great winds from the south with a point east, which carried us up (for all that we could do) towards the north, by which time our victuals failed us, though we had made good spare of them. So that finding ourselves in the midst of the greatest wilderness of waters in the world without victuals, we gave ourselves for lost men, and prepared for death (pp. 449-50). [19]

In passing we may compare the tone of this passage to Pascal's anguished cry before the fearful silence of immense space which will come shortly after. It is an awe which fails to daunt Campanella, but certainly affects Bacon's travellers. For them, however, as initially for Pascal, the voyage comes to a halt at a land in an utterly unknown area of an unexplored sea (p. 450). There they enter a welcome harbor before a beautiful city.

It is now, just when one would expect the journey to be at an end, that in fact there begins a whole series of journeys. The main voyage from the shelter of the old, safe world to this unknown region is to be repeated in several forms; and it is this dynamism of the voyage that becomes the central figure of *New Atlantis*. Anchored in port, they are not yet allowed to disembark, nor even approach the town, and it is only after several trips to-and-fro, after much discussion and ceremony, that the islanders permit them to land, and then only after a night's wait. From the prison their boat has become, they then make the short trip (in distance, but immense spiritually) which brings them to the "Strangers' House" (p. 453-54), where they

---

[19] I have used the edition found in Francis Bacon, *Essays, Advancement of Learning, New Atlantis, and Other Pieces,* ed. Richard Foster Jones (New York, 1937). All subsequent references are to this edition.

will once again find themselves sequestered; this time for five days (p. 455).

After these five days, they do not yet leave. Instead there recommences the islanders' trips to-and-fro that characterized their wait in port: the governor of the House of Strangers comes for discussions. However, these are no less centered on sea-travel than the account itself to date: on the first day, he relates how a mysterious "ark or chest of cedar" (p. 460) brought them by sea the word of an apostle of Christ, to which they owe their faith. The following day, he describes to them the state of navigation in the past, the Flood, and how his country was alone in maintaining a knowledge of foreign lands and the means to go there (p. 466). He goes on to tell how one of the principal activities of New Atlantis is the dispatching every twelve years of two ships to go out into the world:

appointed to several voyages; that in either of these ships there should be a mission of three of the Fellows or Brethren of Salomon's House, whose errand was only to give us knowledge of the affairs and state of those countries to which they were designed, and especially of the sciences, arts, manufactures, and inventions of all the world, and withal to bring unto us books, instruments, and patterns in every kind... (p. 468-69).

It is only after the revelation of this archetypal voyage of research, that the visitors, strangers, begin to go out of their "refuge" to see the country. Ultimately, one of the voyagers from the House of Salomon comes back and they watch the ceremonial passage that he makes from the harbor, through the town, to some solitary retreat. There, after three days, the narrator is given permission to join him in discussions. This is followed by a kind of meditation upon the reason and justification for the House of Salomon, its activities, its journeys:

The End of our Foundation is the knowledge of Causes and sacred motions of things, and the enlarging of the bounds of *Human Empire,* to the effecting of all things possible (p. 480—my italics).

What follows is a description of a veritable experimental institution with its means and its experiments (pp. 480-91). "It is," as Cioranescu remarks, "a veritable programme, to the extent that all programmes remain open and leave the door open behind them. It was thus that it was understood immediately: and as early as 1645 a philosophical College was founded at London, in the imitation of Salomon's House, and which was the ancestor of the illustrious Royal Society." [20]

After this description, and after the traveller has left the narrator, the story comes to a close, or rather does not, with these words, "The Rest was not Perfected" (p. 491). But this end serves as an explication of the series of voyages within voyages, and suggests the goal obtained by the inductive movement. It is a journey which takes the traveller out towards the exterior to bring him back, ultimately, upon himself (here in the form of a second traveller) with the new knowledge he has acquired, and which will serve for the meditation I mentioned. The story, in a way, could not end otherwise. The experimental system must be an open-ended, repetitive one. The continual voyages, their halts for consideration, the arrival at empirical knowledge which leads the narrator back into another journey, and so on, are quite precisely the image of the experimental sequence. This dynamism is reinforced by the use throughout the fiction of the first person, both singular and plural; a use which may be contrasted with the almost exclusive use in the *Civitas Solis* of the third person, and that despite its superficial use of the dialogue.

Bacon's seeker is an individual "I" in search of knowledge which will allow him to enlarge "the bounds of Human Empire." It is a way to personal possession, with all the difficulties, hesitations, and fears that this may involve. The fellows of the House of Salomon are as much seekers of *personal* honor and riches as they are enrichers of the general store of knowledge: "For upon every invention of value we erect a statua to the inventor, nad give him a liberal and honourable reward" (p. 490). It is not without significance that the narrator's own temerity is rewarded by a sum of money (p. 491). To be sure, so were Campanella's Solarians rewarded: but these *all* could gain honors, and such as were no more than symbolic. Here

[20] *Op. cit.,* p. 149.

they are represented by material possession, the image of that permitted by the invention itself. Here, moreover, the wise men do not consider the State an harmonious organism: it is an almost foreign body of which they are scarcely a part: "[they] take all an oath of secrecy for the concealing of those [inventions] which [they] think fit to keep secret, though some of those [they] do reveal sometimes to the state, and some not" (p. 489).

There is little doubt that Uscatescu is right when he comments: "... Machiavelli's conception of politics was in agreement with the fundamentals of the Baconian experimental philosophy. In addition, the idea Bacon has of politics is essentially utilitarian and activist." [21] There is nothing new in a statement of identity between the politics of possessive individualism and the scientific stance of experimentalism: that the structure of Bacon's sea voyage should illustrate this is scarcely a cause for surprise. What is less generally remarked upon is that it is not only at the level of content that this attitude is revealed. The very form is built up from the impulse to control the other, to impose the self.

There is a fundamental difference of impulse between these two fictions. The access to both is by a long sea voyage, to be sure; but how speedily does Campanella jump the southern ocean to go to earth in his island, bound tight by its circular foundations, closed off as far as possible from the outside expansion of the sea. The City of the Sun is an attempt to create an unchanging world where all necessary knowledge has been not only acquired, but fixed for all time on its walls.

There is a more essential way, then, in which Campanella's structure recalls the Platonic, and that is not merely in its outward shape but in the very impulse of its functioning. In the *Republic* knowledge is equated with being itself: "And knowledge is relative to being and knows being" (477, Jowett translation). And absolute knowledge, knowledge of Unity, of Idea, is by definition accession to total being. Translated into Campanella's terms, the perfect

---

[21] George Uscatescu, *Utopía y plenitud histórica* (Madrid, 1963), p. 89.

knowledge aimed at by the City will be quite precisely coincident with that identity of the self with God found at the altar of Hoh. Just as Plato's State is ideal *because* it is at once the homologue *and* analogue of the ultimate guardian, the perfect philosopher, *because* its perfect harmony is that of the just soul (in the absolute sense given to *Justice* by Plato), so also with Campanella's City. Moreover, though it aims at this unity with the Divine, it can only do so in response to the aura of the Divine. Its light does not proceed from within. Although it must, of course, be completely receptive, it receives its light from without and beyond: "Then the sun is not sight, but the author of sight who is recognized by sight" (*Republic,* 508b).

Bacon has taken each of these terms and inverted them. For him, as he remarks in *The Advancement of Learning,* "the truth of being and the truth of knowing are one, differing no more than the direct beam and the beam reflected." This may well be, but however close he keeps them still, they are nonetheless divided: knowledge and being are split into two separate fields, and, for Bacon, their generalization into concepts is the responsibility of, and will result in, at least two different systems. His island has its base in two different motives. Furthermore, the sun of the New Atlantis is an entirely human one, and the mind, no longer recipient of light, is rather imposer of it. The twelve seekers who go out from Salomon's House are known as "Merchants of Light," while the three members of the House who are responsible for the formulation of "new experiments of a higher light" are known as "Lamps" (pp. 488-89). If Salomon's House "is the very eye of the kingdom" (p. 459), it is a very self-contained eye, and quite unlike the reactive soul of Plato's State or Campanella's City.

Bacon's Atlantis is a city trying to have the best of both worlds: it, too, has its well-placed and long-lasting foundations. But its impulse is to the water. It is the travelling sages who are most honored and for whom there is most rejoicing. It is a city whose spirit is towards flux, danger, the transitory—in a word, progression: "The being destined to water is an ever-changing being [*un être en vertige*]. At each moment he is dying, some part of his substance is endlessly crumbling away." [22] What is represented by these islands, lying in the midst of uncharted seas, is perhaps the attempt to seize the processes of intellection, a certain form of the unconscious. Each narrator sails through "an oneiric experience" towards "the revelation of his reality and of his ideality." [23]

The utopian structure would appear to be understood best as the objectivization of a mode of thought, perhaps common to an era but certainly characterizing an individual view, and not as its opposite, a thinking about an object. Whatever may have been Campanella's attempts to externalize his ideal had the Calabrian revolt of 1599 been successful, [24] alters this not in the least: our text would then have been in the field instead of in the library, but its form and meaning would have been the same. It would simply dramatize Cioranescu's point that "man's future remains still and always a mere literary image." [25] That *New Atlantis* is without a conclusion emphasizes the apparent conflict between a static literary (and philosophical) mode, and the desire for the dynamism of possession; which perhaps suggests why Campanella's revolt had no conceivable hope of success. In that, it was the image of the mental structure which fostered it.

---

[22] Gaston Bachelard, *L'Eau et les rêves: essai sur l'imagination de la matière* (Paris, 1942), p. 9.

[23] *Ibid.*, p. 34.

[24] In an essay, "The Communism of Tommaso Campanella," Benedetto Croce remarked that "it is now firmly established that the aim of the Calabrian plot, for which so many men were executed and for which the monk suffered 29 years of prison, was precisely to put into practice the ideas laid forth [later] in *The City of the Sun*," quoted by Blanchet, *op. cit.*, p. 66.

[25] Cioranescu, *op. cit.*, p. 15.

Sylvie Romanowski

Descartes: From Science to Discourse

Although many labels have been attached to Descartes,[1] that of philosopher of language is not one of them, nor is he regarded as an exceptional practitioner of language, save for some quick comments praising him for his style and for using the French vernacular. While the purpose of this article is not to transform Descartes the mathematician, philosopher and moralist into something else, it can nevertheless be shown that language played an important role in Descartes' thought on at least two levels: on the level of conscious thought, as an object of theorizing, and on the level of practical use, where the linguistic medium eventually becomes an integral part of philosophizing, and of philosophy itself. The interplay between his reflections on language and his early works cannot be ignored if both his early writings as well as the later, well-known works (*Discourse on Method, Meditations*) are to be properly understood. Specifically, I will examine first the theories of Descartes on language, their relation to the scientific thought of the time, for the purpose of understanding his first major work, all too neglected though of great, even crucial importance, *Le Monde ou Traité de la Lumière* [*The World, or Treatise on Light*].

The very first writings of Descartes that are extant are the *Cogitationes Privatae* [*Private Reflections*], which consist of short fragments dealing principally with science—which kind we shall see presently; a few statements are concerned with the relation of science to language, more exactly, with the problem of finding an adequate language for discovering and expressing scientific truths. In these

---

[1] For the works of Descartes, references are given to the edition by Adam and Tannery (abr. AT); for the correspondence, to the edition by Adam and Milhaud (Paris, 1936-63) (abr. Corr.). Descartes's spelling, save for capitalization, has been modernized. The translations are all my own.

96

early notebooks, the ambitious young scientist does not consider language as a given, but already examines it critically in the light of a certain vision of the physical world.

The early view of the universe that Descartes expounds in the *Cogitationes* consists of a mixture of religious, animistic, stoic and platonic notions: belief in the unity of nature, the correspondence between the spiritual and the sensory worlds, the harmony of sympathies and antipathies, of attractions and repulsions that maintain the universe in a dynamic equilibrium. Descartes asks the question, what kind of signs will man use to convey this knowledge? The signs will consist of language, but what kind of language and what kind of sign? Given the postulate of universal harmony, language will have to correspond to the knowledge that it is to express. Since Nature is essentially a harmonious system of attractions and repulsions, it can itself be viewed as already a language—a complex system of signs referring to each other—and the language of man will be one more system of signs having as its referent the sign-system of Nature. This rather complex language-sign can be called a symbol (i.e. a sign referring to another sign), to distinguish it from the signs of Nature. In Nature, all is harmony and correspondence, and nothing is haphazard: the signs of Nature are anything but arbitrary, and it is man's main task to discover the motivated signs of the universe through his symbols, which in turn will be motivated and resemble the natural signs:

Cognitio hominis de rebus naturalibus, tantùm per similitudinem eorum quae sub sensem cadunt: & quidem eum verius philosophatum arbitramur qui res quaesitas feliciùs assimilare poterit sensù cognitis.[2]

If the symbols are motivated, and therefore uncreated by man, the searcher of knowledge can only uncover them as they pre-exist in the world; on the other hand, is it not possible for the poets to give

---

[2] "The knowledge that man can have of natural things can come only through similarity with those things that our senses perceive; and we will judge him to be truly a philosopher who can make the things he seeks more similar to the things known to the senses" (AT, X, 218-219).

us new insights into Nature: "Mirum videri possit, quare graves sententiae in scriptis poetarum magis quam philosophorum. Ratio est quod poetae per enthusiasmum & vim imaginationis scripsêre." [3] The two functions of language are not distinguished from each other, no more than human language is separated from the language of Nature. [4]

From this integrated synthetic view of man and Nature, of human symbols and natural signs, to the analytical and mathematical operations of the *Regulae ad directionem Ingenii* [*Rules for the Direction of the Mind*]: such is the extraordinary leap that not only Descartes took, but other scientists and thinkers in going from a geocentric, Aristotelian or animistic view of the world to a heliocentric, Copernican, mechanistic one. The scientific revolution of Galileo and others, which has been amply analysed, will not be examined here in detail, save for a few remarks in order to understand the numerous repercussions on the role of language in this new science.

In brief, both the Aristotelian, geocentric view of the universe and the animistic view as well had the characteristic of corresponding to a common-sensical, intuitive view that any man has of his physical environment: for example, the sun does in fact seem to rise in the East and set in the West, revolving around a perceptibly immobile Earth, and scholastic physics incorporated this into its cosmogony. If a stone falls, it is because it wants to, because some spirit, akin to man's mind or soul, guides it towards a more preferred position. Neither Ptolemaic nor animistic views did anything to disturb man's common-sensical perspective of the universe, whereas the Galilean and Copernican views go counter to every perception we have of our world. The scholastic and animistic sciences allowed a continuous contact between perception and conception of the cosmos; the Copernican-Galilean view instituted a radical break between perception and conception of the world, not only by putting the sun at the center rather than the earth, but, more fundamentally, by positing

---

[3] "It may seem remarkable that deeper pronouncements are in the writings of poets than those of philosophers. The reason is that poets write with enthusiasm and with strong imagination" (AT, X, 217).

[4] For a more complete discussion of Descartes' early excursions into symbolism, see H. Gouhier, "Le refus du symbolisme dans l'humanisme cartésien," in *Umanesimo e Simbolismo* (Padova, 1958), pp. 65-74.

that the essential nature of the cosmos is mathematical and mechanical, i.e. quantitative rather than qualitative.[5] If the previous scholastic or animistic views corresponded to (and merely amplified) man's common-sensical perceptions, man's natural language was basically adequate, whereas, for the mathematical and mechanical nature of the world to be known, a new language had to be elaborated, and a break had to be made with natural language as a tool for knowledge.

The new scientists faced not only the problem, internal to science, of elaborating the needed mathematical tools to measure the cosmos, but faced also a more external problem, though not less urgent: that of convincing the public-at-large of the validity of the new quantitative, heliocentric science. Galileo and Descartes both expended much effort in this direction. In order to understand why this problem of persuading the public arose, one must remember that the shift in the seventeenth century from the qualitative to the quantitative physics was a more radical and disturbing one than a change from one quantitative physics to another, such as we have witnessed in our time (e.g. with the introduction of the physics of relativity, which still involves measurement as much as the classical physics).

For the purpose of persuasion, natural language could not be discarded, as it could within the domain of science itself. However, Descartes, now converted to the new mathematical science, does not concern himself yet with this problem, and, as the *Regulae*'s main aim is to explain his method for obtaining scientific truth, the statements about language concern only the language of science.

The new science being totally divorced from man's usual, common-sensical perception, it is not surprising that natural language should be regarded with great distrust by Descartes. Even if one uses ordinary words, one must take great care not to be misled by them, and to define them carefully. When Descartes wishes to define the mathematical nature of the universe, he spends a whole paragraph

---

[5] See Michel Foucault's description of the evolution of Western science from a basis of resemblance to one of difference, in *Les Mots et les Choses* (Paris, 1966), tr. *The Order of Things* (London, 1970).

discussing the word "mathematics," its etymology and its use (Rule IV). Similarly, in the thirteenth Rule, he stresses the necessity of knowing the exact meaning of the words "nature" and "magnet" when enunciating a problem such as, what is the "nature of a magnet," and he shows that the riddle of the Sphinx turns on the definition of the one word "foot." In the fourteenth Rule, he discusses at length the meaning of such critical words as "étendue," "lieu," "corps" [extension, place, body] before setting forth his view of the physical world.

And even if preliminary definition of words helps to avoid misunderstanding, two other solutions are possible, even preferable: one is to create new terms specifically for the new concepts, the other is to eliminate words of natural language entirely, and to use letters, as in algebra (Rule XIV). Thus, along with physical science, the nature of the linguistic sign of science has undergone a radical change. The sign is no longer a motivated symbol referring to the infinite signs of Nature, and carrying its own potential for giving new knowledge; the sign is now an arbitrarily conceived sign, pure denotation of a quantity and having only the function of expressing, and not discovering, knowledge.

In the *Regulae*, Descartes has consistently been less preoccupied with a total language than with the individual words of science. At the same time that he was writing the *Regulae* (which is, as far as we can conjecture, around 1628), Descartes expressed his opinion on what a new type of language might be that would conform to the new science, in an interesting letter to Mersenne. In this letter criticizing one of the numerous projects of a universal language of the time, he expressed the wish that such a language might be based on the true Philosophy, which of course rests on the new science, so that it might represent all thought in order and with such clarity and distinction that it would eliminate all possibility for confusion. Such a complete, denotative language, which continues the attempts to define the correct denotation of individual words, would convey all the concepts of true Philosophy, and being coextensive with truth, would be of immense service for thinking: it "would help judgment" so much that even "peasants could judge better the truth of things than the philosophers do now." [6] Ironically, language becomes again an ambiguous tool, utilized both for expressing and for discovering knowledge, as had been the earlier language of the poets (*Cogitationes*): but this time, language would be of service to the new truth rather than the old. Yet, this universal, highly desirable language has no chance of existing except in Paradise, as Descartes concludes in his letter, and philosophers and scientists of the new breed will have to continue the search for truth with less than perfect linguistic tools. That such a language would have to be invented totally anew, consisting therefore of only arbitrary signs, stresses once more the divorce of man from his natural language, and from his natural vision of the world.

Deprived of natural language as an adequate instrument, the mathematician and the philosopher are in a difficult position as regards the search for knowledge; both are in an even more difficult position as regards the propagation and acceptance of the new physics, as there is considerable resistance on the part of a public reluctant to part with a science that codified and confirmed the usual human perspective of the universe. From the internal problem of science, of finding and expressing truth, Descartes soon shifted his interest to the external problem of convincing others of the new physics. This shift, accomplished in *Le Monde,* had, however, great consequences both for Descartes' concept of the new science, and for his use of language. *Le Monde* occupies a crucial position in Cartesian writing in that it marks the introduction of discourse in his production, and as such prepares the way for the later philosophical works.

Although *Le Monde* is more preoccupied with convincing the reader of the new science, this work too contains discussion of language, some of which is placed significantly at the very beginning of the treatise. The doctrine, that we now know well since Saussure, that the sign has a totally arbitrary relation to the thing it indicates, serves to underline the basic difference between our perception (the sign) and our conception of what causes our sensory perception

[6] Letter to Mersenne, November 20, 1629 (Corr. I, 93).

(the thing signified) This position, quite consistent with that of the *Regulae,* and the letter to Mersenne previously quoted, is used here as an example of the gap that may exist between our grasp of things and their true nature. Other examples are given: the fact that there are material bodies that exist although they cannot be felt, such as air. Persuading the reader of these new and radically different views means, however, returning to the domain of the human perspective —which considers the given appearances to resemble the truth of the phenomena—and returning to the use of natural language. The thorny problem of the difference between the physical universe and our perception could be solved, on a scientific basis, only by a scientific study of the physiology of the sense organs, as well as by a much more detailed knowledge of the universe itself. Both these conditions being lacking in the seventeenth century, the scientist such as Galileo or Descartes, who nevertheless wants to reach the public, has only one means to do so, that of language and discourse.

The first words of *Le Monde* are:

Me proposant de traiter ici de la lumière, la première chose dont je veux vous avertir est, qu'il peut y avoir de la différence entre le sentiment que nous en avons ... par l'entremise de nos yeux, et ce qui est dans les objets qui produit en nous ce sentiment. [7]

The speaker ("je") and the listener ("vous") as well as the object and the message ("la première chose" [the first thing]) are present from the very beginning of the treatise indicating the presence of prose that designates itself as discourse, rather than scientific exposition which would omit all references to discursive elements. References to "mon discours" [my discourse] abound, especially in the first five chapters of the cosmogony. Discourse, replacing science as the principal aim of this work, serves as a mediator between the author, science and the subject (the reader). The three principal elements, author-reader-message do not confront each other directly,

[7] "My present aim being to discuss light, the first thing that I want to warn you about is that there may be some difference between the sense perception that we have of light ... by means of our eyes, and what is in the objects that produces this sense perception in us" (AT, XI, 3; chapter 1).

but only through the mediation of discourse. The use of natural language organized in discourse means that the mathematical operations, which are fundamental to science, cannot be used; thus the writer is led to modify the very content of the science that he wants people to accept.

The mechanism of this modification occurs already in the second chapter of *Le Monde,* where Descartes explains: "Lorsqu'elle [la flamme] brûle du bois ... nous pouvons voir à l'œil, qu'elle remue les petites parties de ce bois." [8] This statement contrasts with the earlier one in the first chapter of *Le Monde,* where Descartes emphasized the difference between "what is in the objects" and our perception "by means of our eyes." If our senses were so incapable of informing us on the true nature of phenomena, why appeal here to sensory evidence? And although in the same breath Descartes criticizes the imagining of "qualities" resembling our perception, is he not also asking his reader to believe that the true physical nature of the world resembles a perception of it, both perception and truth being that of particles in motion? Descartes pretends here that the reader can start from certain perceptions (the movement of particles) and can build a correct cosmogony resembling his observations. Of course, the cards are stacked, as the author carefully chooses the perception which, via resemblance, can end up with the desired mechanistic view of the cosmos. Here, in fact, is a return to an earlier scheme that structured the animistic and scholastic sciences, where from man's sense-perception to the truth of the universe there was no radical break, as the conception was imagined to resemble the human perception. In his attempt to bridge the newly instituted and radical discontinuity between man's perception and the universe's true nature, Descartes reverted to an earlier view of man's relation in the world, one based on resemblance, not incompatible with perception and thus acceptable to subjective apprehension. Thus does the effort to persuade the subject through discourse at least partially subvert the science that it was supposed to serve.

---

[8] "When it [the flame] burns wood ... we can see with our eyes that it moves the small particles of this wood" (AT, XI, 7; chapter 2).

Yet, his present structure of man's relation to the cosmos, though based on resemblance to a perception, is not exactly identical to the earlier sciences, as the basis taken is different: now it is the movement of particles, rather than a feeling of heat or light, which is the point of departure. Whereas, before, the basis of science was human perception, indiscriminately:

(1)   perception → conception → nature of the world
       (Essences,
       Qualities)

now a certain conception, selected carefully by Descartes, serves as the starting point:

(2)   perception ← conception → nature of the world
       (motion of
       particles)

The model of the Galilean science, based on the difference between perception and the quantitative conception might be:

(3)   perception/conception → nature of the world

In the course of the first five chapters of *Le Monde,* the two models of science (2) and (3) are present. At times, Descartes repeats his warning that our sense impressions are erroneous (Chapters 4, 5), at other times he appeals to (carefully selected) perceptions (Chapters 2, 3, 5). The discrepancy between the model of science (3) and the form of it modified for the shake of discourse (2) points to a double view of language as well, which, in the science of model (3) was distrusted and redefined or rejected in favor of algebra, and in model (2) is used, on the contrary, to talk about science.

Are the transformation of science and the partial return to perception and resemblance sufficient for Descartes' purpose of convincing the reader? Perhaps not, since he is willing to try the following rhetorical device: "Mais afin que la longueur de ce discours vous soit moins ennuyeuse, j'en veux envelopper une partie dans l'invention d'une Fable." [9] Thus begins the science-fiction of the new Genesis, whereby the reader is asked to imagine a Chaos full of particles set in motion by God, according to the laws of moving bodies, a Chaos built on as few assumptions as possible: and, miraculously, this Chaos transforms itself into something that very closely resembles our world, complete with Sun, planets, Moon, comets, tides, etc.

The purpose of *Le Monde* was to show that *our* world is also explainable by means of the laws of motion governing atoms, and the Qualities, Forms, Spirits and other entities imagined by the scholastics or animists were not required. Can Descartes' fictive world rejoin the existing world? The distinction should be made here between a fiction and a hypothesis, the latter only being capable of emerging into reality at the end. [10] The aim of the Fable of the World is clearly to confirm a certain scientific view of it (a quantitative, mechanistic one), yet its written form is not that of a hypothesis, but of a pure fiction. The ambivalence of *Le Monde*'s Fable, between hypothesis and fiction, between intent and form, is clearly manifested in the letters that Descartes wrote at the same time. On the one hand he is looking for a means to persuade his readers of the truth of his science, "trouver un biais par le moyen duquel je puisse dire la vérité, sans étonner l'imagination de personne, ni choquer les opinions qui sont communément reçues." [11] But in many other letters, one finds statements about the author's "rêveries": for example, "je mêle insensiblement mes rêveries du jour avec celles de la nuit" [12] where the line between rêverie and scientific writing seems to become blurred. Witness also the frequent references to "mon Monde" [my world], which contain the same ambiguity.

[9] "But so that the length of this discourse may not bore you, I wish to clothe part of it in the invention of a Fable" (AT, XI, 31; chapter 5).

[10] For a discussion of the distinction of hypothesis and fiction, based on Vaihinger, see F. Kermode, *The Sense of an Ending* (New York, 1967), pp. 39-40.

[11] "... find a device enabling me to say the truth, without forcing anyone's imagination nor upsetting the opinions that are commonly held." Letter to Mersenne, December 23, 1630 (Corr., I, 183).

[12] "I mingle imperceptibly the dreams of my waking hours with those of the night." Letter to Balzac, April 15, 1631 (Corr., I, 186).

The writer is trapped by his fiction of a similar but other world that can never prove anything about the real one. His use of discourse to overcome psychological resistance to the new science had already occasioned a modification of the scientific model (3); now, after Chapter 6, where the Fable begins, the work is totally removed from science. It is no accident that the Fable of the world accomplished this, for fiction represents discourse at its maximum fulfillment of itself: no longer subordinate to an external goal (of science and explanation of the real world) it can and does function as an autonomous force. Yet the goal of Descartes was to prove something about the real universe, and it is ironic (but completely logical) that, in his attempts to emerge from fiction to reality, he has no other means but the very language that created the fiction in the first place.

As early as the eighth Chapter (the third one of the Fable) Descartes drops a hint: "Ainsi elles [les parties de la matière] ont retenu la forme du troisième élément, & ont servi à composer les Planètes et les Comètes, comme je vous dirai ci-après." [13] "Planets" and "comets" are the first words occurring in the course of the narrative that refer to specific kinds of bodies of our cosmos. By the use of these words, Descartes suggests that his fabled world and ours are the same, and in this case, as in many others, the things will follow after the words. "As I will tell you later": but Descartes has already said it, and we have read it in the inescapable sequence of the text. He cannot maintain his narrative for long at a purely anonymous level, and later in the very same chapter, he informs us that some of these "round bodies" are really the Sun and stars. A similar device is used in his diagrams of the universe, where in a part of the cosmos, a planet conveniently labeled T revolves around S, [14] which particular section is shown later in great detail, with "a Planet marked $\mathbb{C}$" revolving around T; [15] all this before the words themselves are ever mentioned. Although chosen seemingly at random,

[13] "And so they [the particles of matter] have kept the shape of the third element, and have helped to make the Planets and Comets, as I will tell you later" (AT, XI, 52; chapter 8).
[14] AT, XI, 55; chapter 8.
[15] AT, XI, 70; chapter 10.

106

these symbols serve the essential purpose of connecting the two universes, just like the words. Thus natural, conventional language (both words and letter-signs) are pressed into a connotative function to guide the reader back into the known world.

Another very frequent verbal means of connecting the two worlds, one that has more implications, consists in comparing certain actions of this imaginary world to known actions of the real world. The Planets are compared to "une grosse boule composée de plusieurs branches d'arbres;" [16] the laws of motion are illustrated by many examples taken from everyday life, a rotating wheel, wine in a glass, a slingshot, floating bodies on the surface of a river. Relating the movement of celestial bodies to common events ("ainsi que nous voyons tous les jours" [17]) serves a dual purpose: these analogies underline the mechanistic nature of the cosmos, and facilitate the acceptance of this theory, and they also suggest that these everyday events can be accounted for by mechanistic laws, and do not require the invention of spiritual forces or Qualities.

However, words, symbols, and comparisons are not sufficient to dispel the Fable of a similar universe and to bring about the passage to reality. One way of exiting from this blind alley is indicated towards the end of Le Monde:

Or il faut savoir que les hommes de ce nouveau Monde seront de telle nature, que, lorsque leurs yeux seront poussés en cette façon, ils en auront un sentiment tout semblable à celui que nous avons de la Lumière, ainsi que je dirai ci-après plus amplement. [18]

The Genesis of the world has not succeeded (and cannot) in engendering the real world, but it has procreated yet another treatise, that on Man. Fiction has succeeded in perpetuating itself, according to a well-known pattern. [19] However, the Traité de l'Homme [Treatise on

---

[16] "... a big ball made up of several branches" (AT, XI, 67; chapter 10).

[17] "as we see every day" (AT, XI, 57; chapter 9).

[18] "It is necessary to know that the men of this new world will be such that, when their eyes are struck in this way, they will have a sense experience quite similar to our experience of light, as I will tell you later in more detail" (AT, XI, 97; chapter 13).

[19] On the dynamics of discourse that wants to prolong its existence, see T. Todorov, "The discovery of language: Les Liaisons dangereuses and

Man], an equally fictional tale of man's physiology can no more make the jump into reality than *Le Monde,* and, at the end, the reader is left with "ces hommes" [these men], the fictional ones. Although discourse was to be a mere scaffolding to build science the linguistic structure created proves to be enduring, so that the author, paradoxically, has no other means of getting out of the fiction than discourse itself. Since the aim was still to persuade the readers about science, it is little wonder that this work, caught between cross-purposes, remained unfinished.

That Descartes could be led astray by a certain use of language may seem extraordinary since, on the level of conscious theorizing, he was acutely aware of the symbiotic relation between language and science. In both the animistic *Cogitationes* and the mathematical *Regulae,* the emphasis is on the search for a language that might be consistent with the science in question, and the author knows what that language ought to be. The new science, having had to adopt mathematical language, had to reject both man's perceptions of the world, and natural language as a tool of knowledge. The estrangement of man from perception and language created a psychological resistance to the new science, which Descartes sought to overcome by means of persuasive discourse in *Le Monde.* In this work, the mistrust for language has been replaced by a greater trust in it for the purposes of persuasion, i.e. for the construction of a new cosmogony, by words, right in front of the reader, even though the basic mechanistic concept of the universe was obtained through quite different means—precisely through refusal of natural language and sensory perception.

Science was thus subverted by a discourse that led its own life, evolving ever further away from science, in spite of the author's aim. Although *Le Monde* gives little insight into the workings of the cosmos, it does give valuable insight into the workings of discourse, and constitutes the crucial passage from science to discourse in Des-

---

Adolphe," Yale French Studies, No. 45 (1970), pp. 113-126: "There is a fundamental anguish involved in the return to silence by someone who has become conscious of language" (p. 124).

Sylvie Romanowski

cartes' work. [20] Possibly Descartes himself was not completely unaware of the tensions that tore this work apart, and seizing upon the opportunity of Galileo's condemnation, left it unfinished and turned to philosophical writing *(Discourse on Method)*, where discourse could come into its own as an integral part of philosophy.

[20] In the terminology of Paul de Man's recent book, *Blindness and Insight: Essays in the Rhetoric of Contemporary Criticism* (New York, 1971): with Descartes's *Le Monde,* here is another example of an author giving us greater insight (into discourse) while being unaware ("blind") to it and focused on science. An interesting twist is that, in the case of *Le Monde,* the cause of the blindness coincides with the blinded insight—the workings of discourse, which cause the delusion, according to de Man, being also the hidden insight.

Buford Norman

Thought and Language in Pascal

Since the composition of the *Lettres Provinciales* around 1656, Pascal was increasingly aware of the ambiguities of language, of the way it could be twisted to suit a specific purpose, such as Jesuit casuistry. He liked to think of language as "la peinture de la pensée" (Br. 26), [1] but he realized that it had been separated from thought, and from the mental concepts it should ideally represent. The conclusion follows that many things vary and depend on the perspective through which one views a problem, and that this perspective depends on language. Hence Pascal's interest in the thought-language relationship, and his effort to create a style which would bridge the gap between them as much as possible.

This style, which will reach its highest point in the *Pensées*, is developed in the *Provinciales*. Here Pascal took the side of reason against the extreme teachings of the Jesuit casuists, but not of overly logical and cold reasoning, or *raisonnement;* he sought the basic meaning beneath the words, and if he often had to combat his enemies' arguments with arguments of his own, he had better results when he turned to irony, exposing the fallacies of the Jesuits and leading his readers to the conclusion that his own ideas were better suited to the needs of a true Christian (and of the *honnête homme*) than were those of the Jesuits. He did not try too much to prove his own points, but to disprove those of his opponents, rejecting the formal rhetoric of the time, and turning to a more universal means of communication.

The fragments of the *Pensées* are the perfect place to observe this means of communication, precisely because they are fragmentary and "unfinished." In this state they are closer to the thoughts that

---

[1] "The portrait of thought." Quotations from the *Pensées* will be identified by the Brunschvicg numbers, abbreviated Br., but the text will be that of the manuscript.

Buford Norman

were in Pascal's mind when he wrote them, and come closer to a true representation of his ideas than would a polished paragraph.

For example, Br. 412 states the various ideas which were present in his mind, with little elaboration, then joins them together to draw a conclusion, or rather, to present the conclusion to the reader—there is no step-by-step chain of reasoning:

> Guerre intestine de l'homme entre la raison et les passions.
> S'il n'avait que la raison sans passions....
> S'il n'avait que les passions sans raison....
> Mais ayant l'un et l'autre, il ne peut avoir paix avec l'un qu'ayant guerre avec l'autre; aussi il est toujours divisé et contraire à lui-même. [2]

The war between reason and passion is introduced, followed immediately by two possible ways to resolve it; these are stated as briefly as possible, in the form of subordinate clauses, without even bothering to write the conclusion that would come in the principal clause. Then, typically, his mind jumps back to the opposite condition, that of the coexistence of the two, which he has observed to be the true state of things. Peace is introduced and opposed to war to add another element of opposition, and the inescapable conclusion is that of man divided within himself.

There is little originality, theologically and philosophically speaking, in the *Pensées*. What is original, however, is Pascal's "awareness of the possibilities of verbal equivocation, and an even greater keenness at analyzing the sources of ambiguity." [3] His goal was to show how his (or Christianity's) ideas were suited to the human condition and to human needs, and he wanted to refrain from using formal proofs, both because he believed them fallible and because he was directing his thoughts to an audience that would probably not take the time to follow their rigor. Since language was the only means of

---

[2] "War in the innermost recesses of man between reason and the passions.
If he only had reason without the passions...
If he only had the passions without reason...
But, having both one and the other, he can only have peace with the one by being at war with the other; and he is always divided and opposed to himself."

[3] Jan Miel, *Pascal and Theology* (Baltimore, 1969), p. 79.

communication open to him, he used it (in spite of its limitations), but in a novel way that was perfectly suited to his purpose.

Language and Style

Pascal's main practical concern with language in the *Pensées* was to use it as a tool with which to express and communicate his ideas; he saw words as arbitrary signs, languages as "chiffres" (Br. 45), distinct from the things they represent—he complained that Père Noël "ne met point de différence entre définir une chose et assurer son existence." [4] Pascal's method, as we shall see shortly in more detail, consists of joining together various ideas, and his style (i.e., his use of language) is geared to this process. He used language to connect two ideas, having made it clear what he is talking about before he attempts to make such a connection or association. Whether these associations (the *jugements* of the Port-Royal *Logic*, as opposed to *raisonnement*) are positive or negative, they form the base upon which Pascal built his sentences and paragraphs, and constitute one step toward the eventual inferential conclusion.

The link between two ideas is often brusque and always direct, as is the combination of the proposition thus formed with another one already formed and stored in the memory, and sometimes this link is even omitted, so that the two ideas or propositions in question stand in direct contact. In constructing his fragments in this way, Pascal reflects the trend of all users of Indo-European languages toward predication, toward dropping the connectives between subject and predicate, and even of neglecting the subject. This is a very direct use of language, one that concentrates on the specific idea to be emphasized, often to the extent that confusion can arise as to its relationship to the other grammatical parts of the sentence or paragraph.

---

[4] "makes no distinction between defining a thing and asserting its existence." Pascal, *Œuvres complètes* (Paris, 1963), p. 210.

This confusion is limited by Pascal through the use of various types of opposition—he was inclined to believe (Br. 70) that the human brain is constructed so that any signal received there activates its opposite at the same time, and his style reflects this belief. By going beyond the grammatical liaison on the surface to the semantic ties between the actual ideas being considered, Pascal opposes one principal concept to another, through comparison, parallel, progression, series, and other such means in which one element is set directly against another, because they are either similar or different. The end result of this process is a series of ideas tied together through a verb with various positive and negative associations, a series which continues until a complete picture is formed.

For example, in Br. 112, Pascal combines the various nouns which express the opposition of objects and the soul with few connecting parts of speech, contrasting opposites through a parallel construction:

Les choses ont diverses qualités, et l'âme diverses inclinations: car rien n'est simple de ce qui s'offre à l'âme, et l'âme ne s'offre jamais simple à aucun sujet. De là vient qu'on pleure et qu'on rit d'une même chose. [5]

The first part gives similar descriptions of opposite things, and the second sums up the complexity of objects and of the soul by a circular construction:

rien—simple—s'offre—âme
âme—s'offre—simple—rien (aucun sujet.)

The associations and contrasts are made in the simplest form possible, with only the bare essentials in modifiers and connectives. And the conclusion is equally concise: "de là" sums up all that has come before, and the statement about laughing and crying (taken from Montaigne, I, 37) is simply expressed.

---

[5] "Things have various qualities, and the soul various inclinations: for nothing that presents itself to the soul is ever simple, and the soul never presents itself simply to any subject. Which explains how people can laugh and cry about the same thing."

This use of language is a result of Pascal's conception of the role and function of language in man's search for truth, and is an important part of his epistemology and of his conception of human nature and thought. More than a simple system of responses to stimuli, language—to Pascal and many of his contemporaries—was a reflection of thought, or at least it should be. It is more than an instinctive, animalistic reaction; it is what sets man apart from the other creatures, since "toute la dignité de l'homme consiste en la pensée," (Br. 365), [6] and the means through which man tries to express his thought and to communicate it.

Human language is more than a collection of arbitrary rules formulated by grammarians so that all men may speak and write in the same way—beneath this system of communication lies the basis of language, a deeper structure which reflects the basic mental processes. Pascal often criticized the outward deficiencies of everyday language, but instead of rejecting it because of these problems, he went to the root of the matter, and tried to use language in a better way, one that would come closer to its true function as he saw it, that of imitating and expressing thought. [7]

Thought

If one is to understand this relationship between thought and language as Pascal saw it, it is first necessary to look into his ideas about thought itself. Like the language which should be designed to reflect it, thought is a purely human capability, above the level of instinct. This is not to say that it is not an innate ability, for Pascal saw man as born with a capacity for thought, and through this thought, for innovation and invention.

He saw thought as a deep process, neither verbal nor linear, but rather consisting of associations and combinations which aim at re-

---

[6] "All man's dignity consists in thought."
[7] This is quite similar to Shomsky's " 'Deep structures' " (cf. his *Cartesian Linguistics*), and should—though Pascal readily admitted that this was rarely the case—come before language.

ducing the complexity of human experience. There are many different levels of the mental process, the most outward perhaps being that of the surface structure of language, but the essence of thought is more complex and more abstract. In the deepest recesses of the mind, in "cette partie même de moi qui pense ce que je dis, qui fait réflexion sur tout et sur elle-même" (Br. 194), [8] ideas combine in many different ways, and man's most important mental function is to judge which of these combinations should be kept as useful and whether they are positive or negative. In this way man can form a mental picture, without words, of various concepts which result from these combinations of ideas, and conceive of the parts of his existence without the need to fit them with descriptive terms, which limit and distort them. These concepts form and take a definite shape in the mind while they are still being imagined, and they can ultimately be put together with other parts of a person's experience so that they form relatively complete blocks of information. Only then does the need arise to express them in some sort of communicable form, and language enter the picture.

It is this free play of associations and combinations that Pascal and Port-Royal saw as characteristic of human thought, and which they called "jugement." This is what thought really is, and what language should imitate, and such mental processes as formal reasoning *(raisonnement)* and syllogisms are only outside aids to be used when the basic mental operations reach an impasse. Instead of using formal and artificial systems of organizing ideas, Pascal preferred the "digression sur chaque point qui a rapport à la fin, pour la montrer toujours" (Br. 283), [9] the orientation of the various ideas which are combining in the mind toward a specific question or problem. In this way the mind can follow what Pascal considered its natural course, and arrive at a more complete understanding.

Pascal saw thought, then, as operating with ideas and concepts rather than with words, completely independent of language. How-

[8] "This very part of me which thinks what I say, which reflects upon everything and upon itself."
[9] "digression on each point which is related to the end, in order to call attention to it continually."

ever, thought in this sense does not refer to the entire range of human mental capabilities, but only to the most basic—and surest—operation, that of the judgment of the *esprit de finesse.* Pascal said that the *esprit de finesse,* in reaching its conclusions, "le fait tacitement, naturellement, et sans art, car l'expression en passe tous les hommes, et le sentiment n'en appartient qu'à peu d'hommes" (Br. 1). [10] This process, tacit and even mysterious, is completely beyond the reach of human expression, i.e., language, though it nevertheless operates successfully.

This human inability to express the most basic mental operation is the great problem with which Pascal dealt in writing the *Provinciales* and especially the *Pensées*—the complex relationship of thought and the surface structure of language which does not accurately reflect the combinations formed by the judgment. Not only is the human vocabulary inadequate to represent the often complex concepts of the mind, resulting in much confusion as to what is being discussed, but the syntactic structures available to bind the various terms are artificial and awkward, resulting in even greater confusion. In trying to express every detail of the combination being expressed, language is forced to involve superfluous elements of construction which only blur the clarity of the thought being expressed.

Pascal was perfectly aware of these mental and linguistic inadequacies, and kept them in mind whenever he was thinking, speaking, or writing. The considerations, and their influence on his style, are the basis of his method, a method of problem solving that was as closely adapted to the human condition as possible, since the relationship between thought and language is an essential part of this condition. In short, he tried to go beyond the limitations of the grammatical, syntactic surface of language to the deeper, more semantic structure—thought—upon which it is based, and in so doing to imitate the judgment as much as possible.

---

[10] "does it tacitly, naturally, and without any technique, for the expression of them is beyond all men, and the realization of it is within the reach of only a few."

Buford Norman

Thought, Language and Method

Pascal's main principle was to consider everything, to analyze all the aspects of the problem he was considering, and only at the end make some sort of statement about it. The theory of the three orders —facts, ideas, and faith—enabled him to consider the various parts of his existence with their peers and in the proper light, while the *pensée de derrière,* the thought in the back of one's mind, helped him to be aware of all the possibilities at all times. Likewise, through the *renversement du pour au contre,* the reversal of pro and con, he was able to be constantly moving from one side to the other, using the various means of opposition mentioned above to give a careful structure to his ideas. He did not give up in the face of contradiction, but rather welcomed it—"Les deux raisons contraires. Il faut commencer par là" (Br. 567). [11]

Some critics have found confusion in this constant use of opposition and in the great variety of subjects covered, but Pascal's method is not a "confusion sans dessein" (Br. 373); [12] it is rather an ordered mélange in which the different elements are bound together by a series of loose associations. Loose though these associations may be (and, I believe would have been even if Pascal had finished his apology), they are always justified, and they all converge on one final goal, until the reader has been confronted with so many minor, isolated, and informal proofs that, by inference, Pascal's point is made.

This inferential method, also known as inferential logic, [13] was used by Pascal to replace the overly formal and linear types of logic so common in his time, especially among theologians and metaphysicians, an endeavor supported by the *Grammar* and *Logic* of Port-Royal. Following the principle of the "digression sur chaque point," he expressed, in the brief fragments which make up much of the

---

[11] "The two contradictory explanations. One must start there."
[12] "Patternless confusion."
[13] Cf. Cardinal Newman's *Grammar of Assent* (London, 1870).

117

Pensées, the various aspects of a problem which had occurred to him, joining them only through the loose associations mentioned above. Rather than describe them in complex and confusing detail, than establish rigorous arguments, he preferred to present his ideas in the way his mind considered them—the free play of all the possibilities. Just as Wittgenstein decided to do in the *Philosophical Investigations,* Pascal left it up to the reader with a well-formed judgment to make and retain the proper combinations for his own personal use, and to draw his own conclusions.

The problem is that the judgment of many people is not well-formed, and they fail to realize that speech is but an arbitrary set of patterns and rules which, although all men have an innate ability to use it, is based more on the need for a common form of communication than on a way of formulating and studying ideas. Instead of concentrating on their ability to think, they try to fit their available store of ideas into an artificial system of expression, thereby distorting the ideas and separating them from many of their related concepts. They put language before thought, while Pascal saw things in the opposite way—"Pensée fait la grandeur de l'homme" (Br. 346), [14] and man's language (as it is spoken, not as an intellectual phenomenon) is but an offshoot of his society, though a necessary one. Thinking is man's highest goal, and everything else should be centered around it, and around the findings of this thought: since the language Pascal knew failed to reflect this thought, he searched for better ways to adapt it to his ideas.

Pascal's method, then, in addition to being an excellent means of acquiring and communicating knowledge, is also a critique and an indictment of language. The linguistic means with which man expresses his ideas do not, in the opinion of Pascal, reflect the judgment which formed and combined them, and they are incapable of expressing pure thought—the language and logic of words cannot furnish the absolute proof needed for man to establish things with certainty. Only the inferential method, which relies on the illative sense, can attain this certainty in matters such as those with which

[14] "Thought constitutes man's greatness."

Pascal was dealing, and it does not need the complex syntactic systems of human language, but only a simple association between subject and predicate.

In other words, in writing the fragments of the *Pensées,* Pascal had the dual purpose of finding a method that could provide a suitable translation of his ideas, and that would at the same time, through its somewhat unorthodox order, call attention to the basic problem of the huge gap between thought and language. His method permits an author to bare his thought to his readers, so that, instead of artificial rhetoric, one finds ideas relevant to his situation:

Quand on voit le style naturel, on est tout étonné et ravi, car on s'attendait de voir un auteur, et on trouve un homme. (Br. 29) [15]

It is this ability to communicate with his readers as if they had entered into the innermost recesses of his mind, to give the impression that not he, but the reader, is thinking the thoughts expressed in simple words, that creates the validity of Pascal's method, as a method in general, as a means to express his ideas and opinions, and as a way of leading the reader to new ideas of his own. By not proceeding linearly, by not keeping the same subject throughout a sentence, but by jumpling from one idea to another through a series of loose associations, Pascal comes much closer to expressing pure thought in its completeness, especially its associations as explained by the section on judgment in the *Logic*: in the words of one critic, "not a thought, but a mind thinking." [16] Instead of trying to invent a new language, as many scientists of his day wanted to do, he devised a more suitable way of using the existing language through which any lasting—and immediate—message must be expressed.

[15] "When people see a natural style, they are astonished and thrilled, for they expected to find an author, and they find a man."
[16] Morris Croll, *Style, Rhetoric and Rhythm* (Princeton, 1966), p. 210.

Virginia K. Howe

"Les Pensées": Paradox and Signification

Pascalian dialectic employs paradox as a procedure of double negation aiming at the destruction of all worldly values and certainties. The
simultaneous affirmation of contraries is a means of effacing the distinction between the true and the false and thus of rendering impossible the effective identification of perceptible data. Both pure affirmation and pure negation possess some epistemological value, implying
at least the recognized existence of a true and a false. Paradox, as
the statement of a contradiction whose two terms are equally valid,
reveals the possibility of an infinite number of separate and contrary
truths. For Pascal, true knowledge becomes an absolute, a totality
which can only exist by embracing contradiction itself. "No truth is
valid unless the contrary truth is added to it." [1] Epistemologically
as well as metaphysically, man is between two absolutes, between
all and nothingness, which are united only in God. The epistemological impotence of the human and relative finds its expression and
demonstration in Pascalian paradox.

The critical force of the argument thus undertaken is focused at
the level of signification, and the attack is concentrated on three
concepts essential to the structure of meaning whose invalidation
brings about the collapse of the entire system: identification, organization, and gradation. Pascal first explodes the unity of the signifier by recognizing in it a quality of infinite divisibility. The binary
correspondence between signifying unities is put into question by the
proliferation of possible meanings within the signifier itself. The sign,
a conjunction of two elements each identifiable by a certain internal
homogeneity, breaks down when forced beyond the level of generality

---

[1] Lucien Goldmann, *The Hidden God,* trans. Philip Thody (New York,
1964), p. 277.

necessary to its operation. In destroying the identity of the signifier, Pascal affirms at the same time that it is only at this linguistic level of facticious unity that the human mind can function. At the opposite extreme from the repartition "en petitesse", so to speak, exists the cumulative infinity of the general, what Pascal calls the "principles of things". [2] The significative system is suspended between the two infinities of the specific and the generic, as is the human knowledge that depends upon it.

Once the signifying unities are shattered, their effective organization becomes impossible. The divisibility of any meaningful element destroys the representative identity which would allow it to be ranked in a moral or intellectual scale. It participates in all values, containing at once the high and the low in a wealth of internal contradictions. The efficacy of Cartesian enumeration as an intellectual methodology is annulled by the same stroke. It is no longer possible to organize propositions in a scale from the simplest to the most complex: everything is not only relative, but *equally* relative. Any hierarchy built on the inclusion of elements one within another is an arbitrary arrangement of reality.

The final result of the destruction of the signifying unity and the elimination of the qualitative organization of the sign is a complete interchangeability of signifiers in relation to the matter represented. Each signifier contains an infinity of possible and contradictory meanings; it represents everything and nothing. The universe has of itself no order, no structure that can be arranged in a scale or a chain. There remains only an infinite number of equal and interchangeable parts.

The effectiveness, even the necessity of paradox in such a system—or rather anti-system—becomes apparent. It makes possible the presentation of a contradiction whose two terms are equally true, and this is the essence of the Pascalian universe as man can know it. Pascal uses paradox not so much to describe the world as to state the impossibility of such a description. Because any knowledge man

[2] Blaise Pascal, *Pensées,* ed. Léon Brunschvicg (Paris, 1925), fragment 72 (hereafter only the number of the fragment will be given).

can have of the world is contaminated by the traits of his own nature, meaning is rather a human property than a universal one, dependant upon a perceiving subject. It is indeed from the subject, and not from the world, that issue the errors and the limitations of the system of signification as presented by Pascal.

Michel Foucault describes the fundamental change which takes place between the Medieval and the Classical epochs as a dissociation between language and the world. There is no longer a natural order which includes the pre-existence of the sign. Words no longer "belong" to things by the nature of the things themselves, but only begin to represent them with the intervention of the subject. The system of signification is interiorized, establishing itself within human consciousness and knowledge. "In the Classical age, to make use of signs is not, as it was in preceding centuries, to attempt to rediscover beneath them the primitive text of a discourse sustained, and retained, forever.... There can be no sign until there exists a *known* possibility of substitution between two known elements. The sign does not wait in silence for the coming of a man capable of recognizing it: it can be constituted only by an act of knowing."[3] The relationship between man and meaning is one of mutual dependence. The sign exists only through man; but the knowledge that man can have of himself depends upon the same structure of representation that serves him as a tool for all other knowledge. The subject, then, is at the same time source and victim of the insufficiencies of this structure, and may not be separated from it in the dialectic of negation that Pascal undertakes in *Les Pensées*.

The domain of man is between two extremes, that could be characterized in relation to signification as the infinity of divisibility and the infinity of generality. Man's intermediate position is due to the limited extent of his understanding and perception, which makes him incapable of going beyond a certain limit in either direction. As an example of this limit Pascal proposes the arrangement of geometric propositions:

[3] Michel Foucault, *The Order of Things* (London, 1970), pp. 62, 59. Originally published under the title, *Les Mots et les choses* (Paris, 1966).

Mais nous faisons des derniers qui paraissent à la raison comme on fait dans les choses matérielles, où nous appelons un point indivisible celui au-delà duquel nos sens n'aperçoivent plus rien, quoique divisible infiniment et par sa nature. [4]

The smallest unity perceived of imagined is postulated as the smallest possible one. Unable to comprehend the whole of reality, man reasons from the arbitrary point of his own limitation.

Language as well functions in that arbitrary middle region between specificity and generality. Once this region is invaded by the possible decomposition of the signifier, meaning is dispersed and lost. Each unity, whether a particular or a general term, is susceptible to reduction by fragmentation.

Diversité—La théologie est une science, mais en même temps combien est-ce de sciences! Un homme est un suppôt; mais si on l'anatomise, sera-ce la tête, le cœur, l'estomac, les veines, chaque portion de veine, le sang, chaque humeur du sang? Une ville, une campagne de loin est une ville et une campagne; mais à mesure qu'on s'approche, ce sont des maisons, des arbres, des tuiles, des feuilles, des herbes, des fourmis, des jambes de fourmis, à l'infini: tout cela s'enveloppe sous le nom de campagne. [5]

Beyond the presumptive unity of the signifier lies an infinite variety of smaller identities, each in its turn infinitely reducible. Ultimately, the meaning of a word depends upon the conscious subject, because it is he who choses among its innumerable qualities those which will lend themselves to representation.

The subject itself is equally vulnerable to repartition. Confronting a language that offers, in its dissolution, a choice between a diversity of contradictory but equally valid meanings, it is likewise unable

[4] Fr. 72: "But we treat the last which are perceptible to reason as we treat material things when we describe as indivisible a point beyond which our senses perceive nothing more, though it is of its nature infinitely divisible."
[5] Fr. 115: "Diversity—theology is a science, but how many sciences there are! Man is an agent, but if you dissect him, would he be the head, the heart, the stomach, the veins, each vein, each portion of a vein, the blood, each humor of the blood? A city, a countryside from a distance is a city and a countryside; but as you approach, they are houses, trees, shingles, leaves, grass, ants, legs of ant, and so on to infinity: all this is enveloped in the name 'countryside'."

to constitute a stable element. The self is unrecognizable as a homogeneous identity. The Pascalian attack on the integrity of the individual employs the same arguments and produces the same results as that which he makes on the unity of the signifier. These results are especially clear in Bénichou's description of the demolition of the Cornelian hero. Optimistic aristocratic thought before Pascal never denies the plurality of man's nature. Reason and passion may war within him, but he remains conscious of his own internal fluctuation. There is a correspondence between presumed and actual feelings, between motives, actions, and their recognition by the subject. With the aid of this effective self-knowledge, man can, through the rational direction of the will, master his passions and become the only arbiter of his fate. To this consciousness that remains at one with itself, that can manipulate identifiable feelings at will and clearly identify each of its constitutive elements, Pascal opposes a veritable subjective chaos. The different aspects of psychic activity are decomposed to the point where it is impossible to distinguish them from one another. Imagination is confused with judgment, reason with passion. Consciousness is thus subjected to a principle of motivation which surpasses it: it can no longer know itself, being unable to discover any quality that is distinct from the rest. "Pascal ... after having broken the individual down into variable qualities extraneous to his will and judgment, ... asks touchingly, 'Where, then, is this ego?' " [6]

All matter that appears to the subject takes on an infinity of aspects which correspond to an infinity of possible perspectives. Language, means of attaining meaning by the simultaneous operations of identification and representation, cannot describe the true nature of the real without risking a loss of effectiveness. Under these circumstances, paradox becomes the privileged instrument of expression, since it alone can render the internal contradiction of the signifier and make evident the fragmentation of the word without destroying it as a source of meaning. Pascal's procedure is frequently to move from

[6] Paul Bénichou, *Man & Ethics: Studies in French Classicism,* trans. Elizabeth Hughes (Garden City, N. Y., 1971), p. 102, citing Fr. 323. Originally published under the title *Morales du grand siècle* (Paris, 1948).

paradox to fragmentation, using the explanation of his first pro-
nouncement as a means of undermining its principal terms. At other
times the process is reversed, and the argument tends toward a final
contradictory and concentrated enunciation, making of linguistic
decomposition the very model of expression:

Il ne faut pas qu'il ne voie rien du tout; il ne faut pas aussi qu'il en voie
assez pour croire qu'il le possède; mais qu'il en voie assez pour connaître
qu'il l'a perdu; car, pour connaître qu'on a perdu, il faut voir et ne voir
pas ... [7]

The verb "to see" is divided according to the different extents of
sight. The signifier only attains the desired degree of specificity by
surrendering its unity.

Such a surrender makes impossible the idea of order and structure within the system of signs. There is no stable element to serve
as a point of reference for the organization of others, so that any
system based upon the capacity of things to include and complete
each other can only exist by the acceptance of an arbitrary criterion
for judging arbitrarily recognized identities. Cartesian enumeration
takes as its organizing principle the degree of difficulty that a thing
presents for intellectual assimilation, and is then elaborated by movement from the simplest to the most complex. The latter, by a cumulative effect, contains in itself all the steps that led to the final conclusion. This progression touches upon no fixed reality, however, since
each thing may change in aspect and rank according to the perspective of the subject. "The absolute character we recognize in what is
simple concerns not the being of things but rather the manner in
which they can be known. A thing can be absolute according to one
relation yet relative according to others; order can be at once necessary and natural (in relation to thought) and arbitrary (in relation to
things), since, according to the way in which we consider it, the same

---

[7] Fr. 556: "He must not see nothing at all; nor must he see enough to
imagine that it belongs to him; but let him see enough of it to realize what
he has lost; because, in order to know what he has lost, he must see and not
see."

thing may be placed at differing points in our order." [8] The intervention of the subject brings into the proposed order all the intellectual and imaginative errors of man. One thing only leads to another by the will of the subjective imagination, which chooses for consideration one of its diverse aspects and leaves the others aside. The order of logical demonstration is more reversible than rigorous:

Les exemples qu'on prend pour prouver d'autres choses, si on voulait prouver les exemples, on prendrait les autres choses pour en être les exemples; car, comme on croit toujours que la difficulté est à ce qu'on veut prouver, on trouve les exemples plus clairs et aidant à le montrer. Ainsi, quand on veut montrer une chose générale, il faut en donner la règle particulière d'un cas; mais si on veut montrer un cas particulier, il faudra commencer par la règle générale. Car on trouve toujours obscure la chose qu'on veut prouver, et claire celle qu'on emploie à la preuve; car, quand on propose une chose à prouver, d'abord on se remplit de cette imagination qu'elle est donc obscure, et, au contraire, que celle qui la doit prouver est claire, et ainsi on l'entend aisément.[9]

The relationship between the general and the particular, like that between the simple and the complex, is susceptible to total disruption. Any effort of categorization must confront the persistant atomization of things and the explosion of the verbal unity that represents them. Internal diversity prevents the signifier from being arranged along categorical lines, for if some of its aspects do enter into a collectivity, others are more elusive. Each part must be considered as having an independent existence: "La nature a mis toutes ses vérités chacune en soi-même: notre art les renferme les unes dans les autres, mais cela n'est pas naturel; chacune tient sa place." [10]

---

[8] Foucault, *op. cit.*, p. 54.

[9] Fr. 40: "The examples that we choose to prove other things—if we wanted to prove the examples, we should take the other things to furnish the examples; for since we always believe that the difficulty lies in what we want to prove, we find the illustrations clearer and helpful in proving it. Thus, when we want to demonstrate some general proposition, we must cite the rule governing a particular case; but if we want to demonstrate a particular instance, we must begin with the general rule. For we always find that the thing we want to prove is obscure, and that the thing we use as proof is clear; because when we put forward something to be proved, we begin with the assumption that it is obscure and, conversely, that the argument used to prove it is clear, and in that way come to understand it easily."

[10] Fr. 21: "Nature has enclosed each of its truths in itself; our art lies in enclosing them in one another, but that is not natural: each has its prescribed place."

Virginia K. Howe

On the level of language, paradox acts doubly in revealing the plurality of meanings that lie beyong the generalized unity of the word and in selecting from among them a basis for representation. It thus appears as a rhetorical form which reflects a full awareness of its own limitations. Extra-linguistic representation is also presented as the arbitrary recognition of certain significative elements at the expense of others equally in evidence. Any hierarchy based on such a choice has no foundation except the pure will of the subject. In the realm of values, categories dissolve and qualities intermingle. "Nous n'avons ni vrai ni bien qu'en partie, et mêlé de mal et de faux." [11] No emotion can escape moral ambivalence. The futility of an ethical classification of psychological elements corresponds to the impossibility of a similar effort with regard to men. Through their vices, great men are akin to all, "car quelque élevés qu'ils soient, si sont-ils unis aux moindres des hommes par quelque endroit." [12] Thus one of the consequences of Pascalian epistemology, and through which it rejoins Jansenist thought, is the ruin of the aristocratic moral system. Neither men, nor the quality of their feelings, can be hierarchized according to any criterion whatever, for the identity of the criterion as sign has been destroyed. Not only representation, then, but also organization becomes impossible once the consequences of significative dissolution are recognized and carried to their logical result.

The differences between traditional Medieval cosmology and Pascalian cosmology are due to this discreditation of the process of hierarchization. The universe of the Middle Ages and the Renaissance was structured according to the rigorous arrangement of elements that were identifiable and able to be categorized. Classification was added to gradation—gradation between categories and within them at the same time. The categorical order had the form of a chain, whose links made it possible to pass from one to another. Tillyard, in his description of Elizabethan cosmology, describes the universality of the "chain of being" in this way: "The chain stretched from the foot

---

[11] Fr. 385: "We only enjoy partial possession of the true and the good, which are mixed with the bad and the false."
[12] Fr. 103: "for however lofty their position, there is something which creates a bond between them and the least of mortals."

of God's throne to the meanest of inanimate objects. Every speck of creation was a link in the chain, and every link except those at the two extremities was simultaneously bigger and smaller than another: there could be no gap." [13] Pascal brings about the ruin of this order by first admitting that the perspective of the perceiving subject has an absolute power in regard to the quality and the importance of things. Between the great and the small, the noble and the base, the essential and the insignificant, the inconstant mind can distinguish only arbitrarily:

L'imagination grossit les petits objets jusqu'à en remplir notre âme, par une estimation fantastique; et par une insolence téméraire, elle amoindrit les grands jusqu'à sa mesure, comme en parlant de Dieu. [14]

Beside the idea of gradation existed that of progress: the mind, considering in order the elements of the universal hierarchy, could pass from the lowest to the most noble and little by little approach the divine. The relationship to God was, as all else, a matter of degree. For Pascal, the absolute destroys gradation in the domain of the relative, and no combination of elements can constitute a ladder to infinity, for each is equally insufficient:

Qu'importe qu'un homme ait un peu plus d'intelligence des choses? S'il en a il les prend un peu plus haut: n'est-il pas toujours infiniment éloigné du bout, et la durée de notre vie ne l'est-elle pas également infiniment de l'éternité, pour durer dix ans davantage? Dans la vue de ces infinis, tous les finis sont égaux; et je ne vois pas pourquoi asseoir son imagination plutôt sur l'un que sur l'autre. [15]

The natural order is no longer an ascending scale of values leading from the material to the spiritual. The passage from one entity to

[13] E. M. W. Tillyard, *The Elizabethan World Picture* (1943; rpt. New York, n.d.), p. 26.
[14] Fr. 84: "Imagination magnifies tiny objects until, by a fantastic appraisal of their worth, it fills our mind with them; and by its insolent temerity it reduces great things to its own level, as when speaking of God."
[15] Fr. 72: "What does it matter if man has a little better understanding of things? If he has, it simply means that he is a little quicker in grasping them. Is he not always an infinite distance from the end, and is not the span of our life equally tiny in the bosom of eternity, whether or not it lasts another ten years? In the sight of these infinities all finite things are equal; and I do not see why I should fix my imagination on one rather than on the other."

another is no longer a progression, but the simple substitution of one thing for another equal to it.

Here Pascal takes the religious implications of the destruction of the natural hierarchy to their ultimate consequences. Traditional optimistic theology saw a gradation of human conditions in relation to God and to salvation. "Certainly dogma imposed distinct planes— that of grace, that of nature at its highest point, virtue and knowledge, and that of brute nature; in other words, God, Eden, and fallen man." [16] The intermediate plane, that of human greatness, served as a link between the two others. If man still possessed something of his primitive worth, he could that much more easily attain to the level of grace. In the Pascalian system, it is no longer possible to find pure qualities in man, traces of the lost paradise. Since every human gesture is a mixture of changing and contradictory motives, all manifestations of behavior are equal. The only distinction that remains is the immense gulf between man and God, which can only be bridged by divine grace. There is no possible spiritual ascension that depends upon man. In religion as well as in nature and language, progression is reduced to a simple substitution, where movement from one element to another brings neither advantage nor qualitative change.

Interchangeability is the final result of the loss of the power to organize and identify units of meaning. If the sign is a binary union of two elements, one having the power to represent the other and to substitute for it, it cannot be constituted where there exists only an infinity of elements which are equal in relation to signification. Each term of the representative duality holds the possibility of innumerable meanings. A single term can thus be at the same time similar to and different from what it is supposed to represent, depending upon which of its aspects is considered. Ultimately, it is possible to associate any thing with any other. In regard to interchangeability, the subject is at one with the system it has created. Beyond the distinctions of psychological taxonomy lies a whole region of chaos and intermixture. Human actions lose their nature of signifiers in relation to interior reality as the power of reciprocal representation between the motive

---

[16] Bénichou, *op. cit.*, p. 90.

and the act disappears. The same acts can be the issue of several different motives, and the same motive, at different times and in different people, can produce completely dissimilar conduct. The identity between the act and the feeling is destroyed, and its effect is an accumulation of contradictions within the subject. "These contradictions are the final word on human nature, the most profound definition of man; what one ultimately finds in man is a kind of undifferentiated affectivity that can manifest itself in contradictory behavior." [17]

The level of abstraction of the sign and the inconstancy of the mind which conceived it produce together the total incoherence of the subject's projection on the world. It is in attempting to organize perceptual and intellectual data that man participates unconsciously in the effects of interchangeability. Understood reality does not exist as a fixed point from which he would be able to construct an order. It is not the permanent source of a stable referent which would offer itself up to representation by the signifier that man would find for it. The system of meaning only exists inside the consciousness, and cannot attain to the true nature of the real. It shares all human qualities, the errors and the contradictions. Thus a gulf opens up between language, which is of human invention, and the world, which has its true existence outside of the network of meaning that man wants to impose upon it. Man's own nature decides the way in which he attempts to know the world. Together, the subject and language deform reality and reinterpret it according to their own laws of action and representation:

Et ce qui achève notre impuissance à connaître les choses, est qu'elles sont simples en elles-mêmes et que nous sommes composés de deux natures opposées et de divers genre, d'âme et de corps... De là vient que presque tous les philosophes confondent les idées des choses, et parlent des choses corporelles spirituellement et des spirituelles corporellement. Car ils disent hardiment que les corps tendent en bas, qu'ils aspirent a leur centre, qu'ils fuient leur destruction, qu'ils craignent le vide, qu'elle a des inclinations, des sympathies, des antipathies, qui sont toutes choses qui n'appartiennent qu'aux esprits. Et en parlant des esprits, ils les considèrent comme en un lieu, et leur attribuent

[17] Bénichou, *op. cit.*, p. 101.

le mouvement d'une place à une autre, qui sont choses qui n'appartiennent qu'aux corps. Au lieu de recevoir les idées de ces choses pures, nous les teignons de nos qualités, et empreignons de notre être composé toutes les choses simples que nous contemplons. [18]

The sign "internalizes" reality, and in so doing subjects it to interchangeability. The active intellect cannot make of any value the basis of an ascending order, for its action is but a perpetual repetition unproductive of change: "On ne fait que changer de fantaisie; tout ce qui se perfectionne par progrès périt aussi par progrès." [19] Without order, all things are equal, and may serve without distinction as the terms of a sign. The representativity of one thing by another depends on the individual subject. "Et depuis qu'il a perdu le vrai bien, tout également peut lui paraître tel, jusqu'à sa destruction propre." [20]

Interchangeability, indeed, is the final expression of what is consciously admitted in Pascal's use of paradox: that any sign can contain an infinity of meanings, including the most contradictory. This point is reached by the dialectical negation of three powers: those of identification, organization, and choice. It is impossible to recognize the terms of a sign, to isolate them, and to articulate them logically. Meaning, which can function effectively on the level of the relative, becomes thus a non-value in relation to truth. Pascalian paradox is at once an expression and an agent of the annihilation of human signification which occurs when it is placed in the presence of the absolute.

[18] Fr. 72: "And what crowns our incapacity to know things, is that they are simple in themselves and that we are composed of two opposite natures which are different in kind: soul and body.... That is why almost all philosophers confuse the ideas of things, speaking in spiritual terms of material things, and in material terms of spiritual things. For they declare boldly that bodies fall, that they aspire towards their center, that they flee destruction, that they fear the void, that they have inclinations, sympathies, antipathies, which are all attributes belonging to the mind. And in speaking of minds, they treat them as being localized in a particular place, and ascribe to them the faculty of moving from one place to another, which are qualities that belong only to bodies. Instead of perceptions being received in their pure form, they are colored by our own attributes, and we set the stamp of our composite being on all the things which confront us."

[19] Fr. 88: "We do nothing but change our fantasies; everything that is brought to perfection by progress is destroyed by progress."

[20] Fr. 58: "And since he lost the true good, everything can equally appear so to him, even his own destruction."

J. D. Hubert

Myth and Status: Malherbe's Swan Song

As M. Jean Rousset has suggested, [1] the disrepute into which analogical reasoning and its indispensable instrument, the metaphor, had
fallen by the end of the XVIth century, influenced the attitudes of
poets toward their own craft to the point of undermining their self-
confidence as creators; and the emerging conception of language as
a representation of the objective world rather than as an immediate
expression of reality modified the function and aim of poetry. [2]

Because of this transformation, most XVIIth century poets found
themselves in a most awkward situation: as intellectuals, they no
longer could take metaphor seriously, but as practicing poets they
just could not do without. In some respects, they therefore fared no
better than the "poètes maudits" or their successors in so far as the
very act of writing verse becomes tantamount to an avowal of failure
—an admission of the misery, in almost a Pascalian sense, of poetry.
Malherbe's famous comparison between good poets and skillful
bowlers ironically confirms this sceptical attitude toward poetic creation, for efficiency and skill, key concepts during the century of
Henri IV, Richelieu and Colbert, had all of a sudden become the chief
criteria by which to evaluate poets, at the expense of invention and discovery. Malherbe may have rejoiced at the change, lesser rhymesters
may have rebelled, but all had to face the difficult task of reconciling
their performance as poets with their good repute as intellectuals.

Each writer willy nilly had to discover his own solution, or rather
his own pet way of cheating with himself in order to continue using
metaphor and abusing analogy with a fairly clear conscience. Ambivalence of this sort can easily lead to deprecation and especially self-

---

[1] "La poésie baroque au temps de Malherbe: la métaphore," *XVIIe Siècle*,
XXXI (April 1956), pp. 353-70.
[2] Cf. Editor's "Introduction" to this collection.

deprecation. In the uneasy confrontation between the intellectual and the poetic self, the latter usually came out second best. From this tug-of-war emerged, or so it would seem, two stereotypes of the poet, if not created at least propagated by the poets themselves: the "rêveur" and the "poète crotté," stereotypes that hardly exclude one another. The "poète crotté" appeared as a ragged, famished parasite, vainly searching for a patron; the "rêveur" as a foolish, daydreaming excentric, quite out of touch not only with his surroundings, but also with meaningful intellectual pursuits. That major poets such as Saint-Amant and Boileau should have encouraged this kind of characterisation may provide some indication of the low esteem in which they held their own profession. Moreover, Saint-Amant and La Fontaine among others wilfully gave credence to unfavorable images of themselves that had very little to do with the truth: "le bon gros Saint-Amant," preoccupied only with food and drink, "le bonhomme La Fontaine," a lazy, naive and distracted old crony. Needless to say, the former held an important function in the King's navy while the latter usually behaved as a highly sophisticated man of the world. For the sake of contrast, one need only compare such clownish personae to the heroic images projected by Romantic poets such as Byron and Hugo.

This deprecation and depreciation of the poet could even assume a masochistic tinge. The invalid Scarron popularized the self-image of a suffering clown and strove to arouse laughter rather than pity when he referred to the daily tortures he had to endure. His attitude toward poetry appears hardly less destructive, for instance in his unrelenting reduction of the *Aeneid* by means of parody, primarily in order to amuse a fairly sophisticated audience, but more deeply as an expression of derision. And Scarron shows such remarkable skill in setting metaphor against metaphor, analogy against analogy, that he succeeds in attaining a sort of literary nihilism. Saint-Amant, a consummate practitioner of the burlesque mode, had never gone that far, for even in the most hilarious passages he still insists on giving poetry its due at the expense of laughter. Humor, however, was almost

indispensable to Saint-Amant, for it allowed him to wax as metaphorically as any Pléiade poet, while suggesting all along that the spinning
of analogies was no more than a game in which the poet could indulge
without in any way debasing himself as a serious thinker. Précieux
poetry may perhaps lend itself to the same sort of explanation as
the burlesque—a conceptual game that the poet plays while knowing
all along that his audience will never take it seriously. Not surprisingly,
preciosity and the burlesque jointly gave rise to "bouts rimés," a
parlor game.

The foremost poet of the age, La Fontaine, many of whose early
works combined the précieux and burlesque modes, hit upon the
perfect solution for the conflict between poetic creation and intellectual status, simply by writing fables and tales where nobody—
including himself—would ever dream of holding him responsible for
the concatenation of analogies, the multiplicity of personifications
and the unabashed use of metaphor. After all, who would dare ascribe
intellectual responsibility to mute beasts, particularly in dialogues
written for the edification of mere children? This genre, considered
minor, gave La Fontaine all the freedom he required both in versification and in verbalisation. True, the later books of fables do not
make as much use of metaphor as the first six, perhaps because fables
had evolved, through his own efforts, from a minor to a major genre,
thus acquiring all the status of serious poetry. Whatever the case,
animals represent, however metaphorical their language may be,
human behavior, human ways of reasoning, and more often than
not human failure. Not surprisingly, they use language most eloquently
when they have become powerless to act. The lamb's convincing retorts
in "Le Loup et l'Agneau" can serve no practical purpose and are,
as a matter of fact, just about as useless as poetry. The dialogue
between the lamb and the wolf remains purely imaginary, not so
much because animals are dumb, but because the all powerful poet
forces time to have a stop, while in a "real" situation the wolf would
have unhesitatingly pounced on its victim, leaving no room, spatial
or chronological, for speech.

J. D. Hubert

The key figure in the conflict between poetic creation and intellectual status is certainly not La Fontaine, or Scarron, or Saint-Amant, but the first and in some respects the foremost of the classical poets: Malherbe, a rationalist, a stoic, who in his versification strove for perfection. More important still, he has the reputation of having rejected analogical reasoning and, in particular, all metaphorical relationships between the microcosm and the macrocosm. His poetry appears indeed essentially discursive, even if it lends itself to the elucidation of a "higher, hidden order" without ever attaining a perfectly logical coherence. [3]

This preamble might convey the partly false impression that Malherbe uses metaphor mainly for decorative purposes or that he sacrifices ornamentation to clarity or that classical mythology, bereft of all mystery in his verse, serves mainly to heighten an already elevated style. Obviously, Malherbe does not take pagan myths as seriously as did Ronsard. Indeed, the reader has the distinct impression that the myths of the ancient world as they appear in Malherbe's poetry do not reveal any truths about man or the universe and that they have become suggestive literary devices that poets are expected to use, just like rhyme and meter. And one would expect that Malherbe would make far less frequent use of myths or even metaphors than his analogy-loving predecessors or contemporaries.

A cursory reading of odes by some of Malherbe's manneristic contemporaries shows if anything that the opposite is true. Malherbe, the great technician, the eloquent rationalist, relies on metaphor much more than most of his rivals, including the often maligned Nervèze. This holds true not only of an early work such as the baroque Les Larmes de saint Pierre, but also of the later odes, particularly the famous poem written about Louis XIII launching his expedition against La Rochelle. Undoubtedly, Malherbe does not concatenate his multifarious metaphors in the same manner as Ronsard or du Bellay. The earlier poets, intent on maintaining an equilibrium, even

---

[3] Cf. David Lee Rubin, *Higher Hidden Order: Design and Meaning in the Odes of Malherbe* (Chapel Hill, 1972). My discussion of Malherbe's last ode is partly based on Professor Rubin's subtle and convincing interpretation of this poem.

in their most "inspirational" odes, between the inner world of feeling and the outer world of Nature, favor and even require a far tighter structure. As for Malherbe, the more he tightens the verse structure, the less he strives for metaphorical balance, while preserving throughout a semblance of discursive coherence and clarity.

Profusion and looseness in structure do not mean that Malherbe's highly decorative metaphors follows one another haphazardly. On the contrary, they invariably establish or reflect that "higher, hidden order" discovered by David Rubin,—an order much more closely related to social status than, let us say, to the imagined structure of the universe, or, more modestly, man's place in the natural order. Malherbe's preoccupation with status, where political and social considerations play a preponderant part, might even explain why he succeeded so brilliantly in circumstancial verse, a domain where many a poet of comparable merit has failed so miserably. Even in the best known of his devotional poems: "N'espérons plus, mon âme, aux promesses du monde" [Let us rely no longer, my soul, on the world's promises], he can think of no better way of affirming the glory of God and the value of a religious life than by showing the vanity of an existence at court—the shortcomings of status.

All of Malherbe's preoccupations with status, metaphor and myth come to a head in his last great ode where he encourages the King to punish the rebelling citizens of La Rochelle, compared thoughout to diabolical monsters, more pernicious than all the dragons and hydras of antiquity. Unlike many of his contemporaries, Malherbe refrains from describing any battle scenes in this ode concerned mainly, or so it would seem, with warfare. In only one stanza does Malherbe make use of terms suitable to military action, for how else could he describe the horrible conflict between the gods of Olympus and the Titans? That a small dose of realism should appear only in a scene taken from Greek mythology goes far toward revealing Malherbe's true preoccupations as a poet. Moreover, he refers only once to the soldiers who will do the real fighting at La Rochelle. Instead, he makes the king stand for the entire army and transforms him into an avatar of both Hercules and Jupiter. We never glimpse Louis's army joining in mortal combat with the Rochelois or the English; instead, we see a godlike hero slaying infernal monsters.

The king requires, however, the help of Richelieu, quite suitably compared to two members of the Argonaut's perilous expedition to conquer the Golden Fleece: Tiphys the pilot and Lynceus whose piercing gaze could see through walls. Nevertheless, Richelieu remains a prince of the Church who happens to identify his sovereign with God himself and who values his life not for its own sake but because he has given it to Louis. Malherbe implicitly justifies the Cardinal's purely secular devotion by equating God's cause with that of the French king. Throughout the poem the expedition against the protestants of La Rochelle becomes by implication a religious crusade, even though Malherbe never departs from his preoccupation with pagan myths. His constant shifting in this respect conforms to the syncretic practices of the "humanistes dévots," but instead of bolstering Christian saintlines with pagan wisdom and heroism, he has succeeded mainly in assuring the transcendence of literature. Heathen myths intermingle so consistently with allusions to crusading Catholicism and set so perfect a balance that they finally cancel one another out: we can equate the king just as readily with Hercules or Jupiter as with the will of God; and throughout the ode, Malherbe deftly adjusts the scales to suit his poetic purpose.

Numerous allusions convey the impression that the battle for La Rochelle perpetuates the eternal war between Jupiter and the Titans as well as the spiritual conflict between God and Lucifer. Quantitatively at least, this ambiguity dominates the poem to such an extent that the military and political event that Malherbe purports to celebrate recedes into the background. From the very beginning of the ode, Malherbe systematically replaces the actual actors of an historical event with all sorts of mythical beings dreamed up by antiquity. Literally speaking, Malherbe describes a battlefield that would be quite deserted were it not for Cartari and the other compilers of myth books. The poet succeeds in reducing the entire English expeditionary force to a single being: "ce lâche voisin qu'ils sont allé quérir" [The cowardly neighbor the Rochelois have gone to fetch] (line 94). King Louis, by the same token, appears to take on the entire English fleet without the assistance of his army. Thankfully, Neptune, who happens to dislike the British, provides a sufficient number of able seamen by sending the French king his Tritons.

By means of these or similar substitutions and personifications, there emerges, at the expense of the actual events, a purely literary universe, full of gods, titans, devils, as well as an allegorical figure, dear to artists and writers since the dawn of history: the Virgin Goddess of Victory. This overworked figure, academic in the artistic sense of the word, guarantees, by her speech as much as by her attire, the impending triumph of King Louis, much as she had, in the timeless world of mythology, assured Jupiter's successful defense of Olympus. In both predicaments, the beautifully groomed goddess uses the verb "sauver"—saving the King's "Empire" after having saved a (pagan) heaven. By means of this pretty personification of a grim succession of bloody episodes, Malherbe reduces the king of France to a state of passivity and his entire army to a state bordering on nonexistence. As the author had done, indulging in this respect in poetic licence, in previous stanzas, Victory confidently gives direct orders to mighty France: "Si tu veux que je t'aide à sauver ton Empire/Il est temps de marcher" [If you expect me to save your Dominion/The time has come for you to go forward] (l. 67-68). The king of the Gods, however, had hardly played a more active part than Louis:

> A peine cette Vierge eut l'affaire embrassée,
> Qu'aussitôt Jupiter en son Trône remis,
> Vit selon son désir la tempête cessée,
> Et n'eut plus d'ennemis (l. 81-4) [4]

Victory intervenes with so much aplomb that she deprives the King, Richelieu and all their armies of their rightful though still impending

---

[4] Virgin Victory had scarcely taken the situation in hand,
When Jupiter suddenly put back on his throne
Saw that in accordance with his wishes the storm had passed
And was forever rid of his enemies.

J. D. Hubert

triumphs. Indeed, like La Fontaine's vainglorious gnat, a trite conceit takes all the credit, to the eternal benefit of poetry and of Malherbe.

Having rhetorically deflated the King in the very act of praising him, Malherbe can safely assume an apparently humble pose. Because of his great age, he no longer has the physical strength to join the glorious crusade and lose his life in the service of his Majesty. He even goes so far as to eulogize, in purely mythological terms, the best way of departing this world:

> Toutes les autres morts n'ont mérite ni marque:
> Celle-ci porte seule un éclat radieux
> Qui fait revivre l'homme, et le met de la barque
> A la table des Dieux (l. 125-28) [5]

These allusions to Charon's ferry and to the ambrosia-enriched festivities on Mount Olympus elevate or reduce glorious and patriotic demises to the level of literature.

A bit later in the ode, Malherbe's ostentatious regret at his own weakness reaches a suitable mythological climax:

> Ceux à qui la chaleur ne bout plus dans les veines
> En vain dans les combats ont des soins diligents:
> Mars est comme l'Amour: ses travaux et ses peines
> Veulent de jeunes gens (l. 133-36) [6]

In so literary a context, it would hardly be surprising if "veines" referred to poetic veins as well as to physiological ones. In any case, Malherbe all along has made good tactical use of his advanced years and physical weakness.

A more skillfull general than those in Louis' army, he launches his counter-attack in the very next stanza:

---

[5] All other deaths lack merit and distinction:
Only this one shines with a radiance
That gives man a new lease on life, and carries him from the bark
To the table of the Gods.
[6] Those whose ardor no longer boils in their veins
Vainly show their painstaking diligence in battle:
Mars is like Love: his labors and his pains
Are meant for the young.

Je suis vaincu du temps: je cède à ses outrages:
Mon esprit seulement exempt de sa rigueur,
A de quoi témoigner en ses derniers ouvrages
    Sa première vigueur.

Les puissantes faveurs dont Parnasse m'honore,
Non loin de mon berceau commencèrent leurs cours:
Je les possédai jeune; je les possède encore
    A la fin de mes jours (l. 137-44)[7]

Malherbe's last poetic efforts will thus coincide with the King's final triumph over rebellion (cf. First stanza). And as he had at the very beginning of the ode allusively compared Louis to Hercules, he now with still greater subtlety compares himself to that paragon of pagan heroes. Otherwise, why would old Malherbe, in praising his own poetic prowess, mention his cradle and thus run the risk of making his readers titter? Indeed, Hercules had shown miraculous strength in his cradle by strangling the two snakes that Juno had sent to destroy him. No less than Hercules' physical powers, Malherbe's poetic vigor remains intact from the cradle to the grave. And he may well prove to be more Herculean than the King himself, for his timeless triumphs do not require the full support of a goddess, but only the favors of Parnassus.

The last eight lines of the ode show the transfiguration of the poet, similar in some respects to the deification of Hercules:

Le fameux Amphion dont la voix nompareille,
Bâtissant une ville étonna l'Univers,
Quelque bruit qu'il ait eu, n'a point fait de merveille
    Que ne fassent mes vers.

---

[7] I am vanquished by time and retreat before his onslaughts:
Only my mind, sheltered from his rigor,
Has the means to demonstrate in its last efforts
    Its pristine vigor.

The powerful favors Parnassus has granted me,
Not far from the cradle began their course:
I possessed them young; and I possess them still
    At the end of my days.

> Par eux de tes beaux faits la terre sera pleine:
> Et les peuples du Nil, qui les auront ouïs,
> Donneront de l'encens comme ceux de la Seine,
> Aux autels de LOUIS (l. 153-60)[8]

The glory of the youthful king of France coincides with, and derives from, the apotheosis of the aged but marvelously vigorous bard. Thus Malherbe's flattery of Louis XIII finally accrues to his own self-glorification and is returned to him at a high rate of interest in the form of poetic status.

Earlier in the poem he had played a similar rhetorical trick on Richelieu. After describing the prelate as "ce grand oracle," Malherbe reassures his sovereign concerning the superior qualities of his Prime Minister and thus transforms himself into an oracle of far greater power:

> Va, ne diffère plus tes bonnes Destinées:
> Mon Apollon t'assure, et t'engage sa foi,
> Qu'employant ce Tiphys, Syrtes et Cyanées
> Seront havres pour toi (l. 57-8)[9]

As an oracle, great Armand appears somewhat deflated when compared to Apollo, who uses his favorite poet as mouthpiece. And Malherbe takes full advantage of these favorable circumstances in again giving direct orders, albeit poetic, to his sovereign.

Malherbe, however, has still other ways of assuring the triumph of Apollo and his own glorification than the use of mythology as a sort of literary fifth column, capable of taking the entire royal army

---

[8] The famous Amphion whose matchless voice
In building a city astounded the Universe,
Whatever his renown, has never created greater marvels
Than those produced by my verse.

By my verse the world will be filled with your great deeds,
And the natives of the Nile, when they hear of them,
Will bring incense, as do those of the Seine,
To the altars of LOUIS.

[9] Onward, do not delay your goodly Destiny:
My Apollo assures you and gives you his word
That by making use of this Tiphys, Syrtes and Cyaneas
Will be havens for you.

by surprise. Throughout the ode, he had used every possible occasion to transcend, in both time and space, the present historical
moment. For instance, the fortifications erected by the embattled
protestants, like the towers of Babel, or Pelion piled on Ossa, reach
to the heavens, while their trenches go down so deeply that they
bring sunlight to Hades. The expedition against provincial La Rochelle is magnified by allusions to a long succession of conflicts between righteousness and evil, going all the way back to pagan and
biblical stories.

All this leads to the final transcendence of poetry and the poet,
freed, as it were, from both time and space. Analogy, metaphor, and
myth may long since have ceased to be suitable pathways to truth;
but, at least in this ode, they afforded a most efficacious device for
an old and impoverished "rêveur" to put himself a cut above the
highest dignitaries in the land and provide him with at least the illusion of having attained high estate. Nothing could be truer in this
connection than Théophile's statement: "Malherbe a très bien fait,
mais il a fait pour lui," which loosely translated and interpreted
means: Malherbe did very well for himself, poetically.

Herbert De Ley

Two Modes of Thought in "L'Astrée"

In the first sentence of his long novel, Honoré d'Urfé suggests metaphorically that his text will present a considerable variety of objects, personages, customs, and events. The plot will unfold, he writes, in "a country named Forez, which although very small contains all that is rarest in the rest of Gaul..." He adds that Forez, "being divided into plains and mountains, both are so fertile and situated in so temperate a climate, that the soil there is capable of everything the plowman may desire." [1] Thus, although the novel's pastoral personages by definition cultivate the simple life, the microcosm of Forez also has room for queens and princesses, for nymphs and knights in armor, for city dwellers and druidic priests and soothsayers. The borders of the province are open, and passing travellers tell stories of distant places. Life is long in Forez, moreover, and nymphs and shepherds have lived other lives under different circumstances. Some have themselves travelled or been educated outside the province and have spoken with people well informed on late imperial Roman politics, druidic theology, or life in early London or among the Visigoths, all of which subjects find their way into Honoré d'Urfé's text.

Perhaps most striking of all, although the intellectual alternatives available to shepherds living in Forez in the fifth century A.D. might reasonably be limited to Christian and pagan religious beliefs, perhaps mixed with superstition and platonic and other classical philosophy, in point of fact L'Astrée also owes something to science and invention as understood in early seventeenth century France. One recurring

---

[1] Ed. H. Vaganay (Lyon: Masson, 1925), I, 9. Henceforth in text. Translations by author.

personage of the novel is the unscrupulous Climante, a kind of amateur scientist who uses a series of bizarre, Rube Goldberg-like machinery to further his evil schemes. In volume one the nymph Léonide, lodged in that typical decor of the picaresque or realist novel, the country inn, overhears Climante describe in detail the scientific trick he used to deceive Léonide and some of her friends when they recently visited his false soothsayer's temple. Climante explains:

In front of the mirror, there was a plank on which Hecate was painted. This plank had the whole lower end sheathed in steel, and, as you know, it was suspended only by a few horsehairs, so fine that in the half darkness of the place no one could possibly notice them. When one pulled them away, the plank fell, and with all its weight struck a stone hard enough so that it almost never failed to strike a spark. At that same spot I had placed a mixture of sulphur and saltpeter that caught in such a way when sparks touched it, that a flame suddenly billowed up, and scarcely anyone could help but be dumbfounded—all of which I had invented to make people believe it was some kind of divinity or magic... (I, 158)

Climante returns with similar magic tricks in subsequent volumes (cf. IV, 28-29, etc.)—in every case opposing the doubtful magic of scientific knowledge to the true magic of Adamas, the druids, and their friends.

In general, just as druidic mysticism curiously coexists with do-it-yourself science in the novel, the thoughts and deliberations of Honoré d'Urfé's personages manifest a variety of intellectual assumptions. Indeed, in debating moral, scientific, and religious questions, shepherds, shepherdesses, druids, and princes use at least two sharply contrasting methods of arriving at their various conclusions. For this reason, rather than implying a unified set of basic assumptions concerning the limits of human knowledge, the novel presents an essentially heterogeneous epistemology. The problems posed by such epistemological assumptions, of course, have the most far-reaching consequences for the worldview of the novel as a whole. Moreover, to the extent that *L'Astrée* may be suggestive of the evolution of French literary conceptions in the seventeenth century, its epistemology may throw light on both preceding and succeeding literary works, as the following analysis will suggest. [2]

The contrasts in *L'Astrée* can perhaps best be illustrated by analysing two texts, appearing in the first and second volumes respectively. The first text is one of the pastoral work's numerous shepherds' debates—in this case between the notoriously inconstant lover, Hylas, and the constant or nearly "perfect" lover, Tyrcis. As might perhaps be expected, their half-humorous discussion concerns primarily the merits of their respective approaches:

"And how do you know," answered Hylas, "that I am not in love?"

"I know it," said Tyrcis, "by your never-ending changes of heart."

"We are," he said, "of very different opinions, for I have always believed that any worker perfected his skill, the more often he exercised his profession."

"That's true," answered Tyrcis, "when you follow the rules of the art, but when one does otherwise, he is more like those who, when they take a wrong turn, go farther from the path the longer they walk. And that is why, just like a rolling stone that never gathers moss but only filth and dirt, your frivolity may gain you shame, but never love. You must know, Hylas, that the wounds of love are such that they can never be cured."

"God save me," said Hylas, "from such wounds as those."

"You're right," replied Tyrcis. "For if every time you were wounded by a new beauty, you had received an incurable wound, I don't know if there would be a single healthy spot anywhere on your body. But also, you're deprived of those pleasures and happiness that Love gives to true lovers—and gives miraculously (as in all his other actions) by the very wound he makes. So that if the tongue could well express what the heart cannot wholly feel, and if you were permitted to hear the secrets of this god, I doubt you would hesitate to renounce your infidelity." (I, 28-29)

The remarkably different second text appears in *L'Astrée*'s second volume, first published in 1610. In it, the nymph Léonide gives her verdict on a lovers' quarrel presented to her and her fellow nymphs for judgement. After the three principals have told the rather complicated story of their relationships, she is asked to decide whether

[2] Parts of this article were delivered as a paper at Storrs, Connecticut, 1969. Thanks for comments to Jean Paris and others. Excerpted from a work in preparation on epistemological assumptions in seventeenth-century French literature.

the shepherdess Célidée should prefer the young Calidon or her older suitor Thamire:

"Judgement of the Nymph Léonide"

Three things are before us concerning the quarrel of Célidée, Thamire, and Calidon: first, love; second, duty, and last, offenses. In the first, we take note of three great affections; in the second, three great obligations, and in the last, three great injuries. From the cradle, Célidée has loved Thamire; Thamire came to love Célidée when already advanced in age, and Calidon loved her from his youth. Célidée was obligated by the virtuous affection of Thamire, just as Thamire was to the memory of Calidon's father, and Calidon to the good offices of Thamire. And finally Célidée was greatly offended by Thamire when he tried to cede her to Calidon; Calidon did no less offense to Thamire and Célidée: to Thamire by refusing him the same courtesy he had received from him, and to Célidée, by pursuing her against her will, so that she lost the person she loved.

All these things debated at length and carefully considered, we have recognized that, just as the things which nature makes are more nearly perfect than those produced by art, so love that comes from inclination is greater and more admirable than that which comes from intention or obligation. Moreover, the obligations which we incur in our own person being greater than those we honor out of consideration for others, it is certain that a benefit creates a greater obligation than a remembrance. And finally if offense mixed with ingratitude is more grievous than that which merely offends us, no one will deny that he who commits both is more worthy of punishment. Now we know that Thamire's love proceeds from inclination, since ordinarily those that do are reciprocated, and that loving Célidée he was loved in return, which was not the case for Calidon, whose infertile affection produced nothing but pain and scorn.

... ...

This is why, in the first instance, we order that Calidon's love give way to that of Thamire, that Thamire's obligation be judged less than Calidon's, and Calidon's offense greater than Thamire's. And as regards Thamire and Célidée, we declare that Célidée is more obligated to Thamire, but that Thamire has more offended her, since he loved her so nobly and raised her so carefully, that she would be ungrateful if she did not recognize her obligation. But the offense he caused was no small one, since to the disadvantage of his own affection, he decided to satisfy his supposed obligations to Calidon. And yet, because there are no offenses which cannot be overcome by someone who loves deeply, we order, with the concurrence of all those who have heard this case with us, that the love of Célidée shall overcome the offense she has received from Thamire, and that the love Thamire shall bring her in the future shall surpass in exchange that which Célidée has shown him up to now. For such is our judgement. (II, 72-73)

While these two texts display certain similarities, their most striking difference is no doubt in their respective approaches to the problems with which they attempt to deal. In the first text, having registered a difference of opinion with Tyrcis, Hylas draws an analogy between lovers who improve their technique through practice and workers who improve the more often they exercise their profession. Tyrcis responds with a second analogy: Those who practice incorrectly do not improve with time, because they are like those who, having once taken a wrong turn, get farther from their destination the longer they walk. The beginning of Tyrcis' next sentence, "And that is why," suggests a causal relationship between what preceeds and what follows. In this case however, what follows is a second analogy, a proverb as venerable in French as in English: A rolling stone gathers no moss. Extending the proverb's meaning, Tyrcis evokes a stone rolling "continually" and states that not only will it gather no moss, but will instead be covered with filth and dirt. At the same time, he alters slightly the proverb's traditional significance: frivolity never gains love, only shame. A little farther on, Tyrcis and Hylas both play on the possible physical effects of the poetic "wounds of love." Hylas prefers not to be wounded; Tyrcis agrees he is right, since "If every time you were wounded by a new beauty, you had received an incurable wound, I don't know if there would be a single healthy spot anywhere on your body."

Thus both Hylas' and Tyrcis' style of debate proceeds from variations on proverbial and poetical analogies. Unsupported by any other kind of justification, their remarks must depend exclusively on whatever merit lies in the idea that inconstant lovers actually are like rolling stones, or that the wounds of love actually do hurt, or that even platonic lovers can hope, like apprentice artisans, to improve with practice. Taken at face value then, these assertions imply that rolling stones and inconstant lovers, wounds of love and real wounds, and the like, are in some sense connected, and thus that the structure of the real world in some measure consists of relationships not unlike the correspondences of Baudelaire. Taken as a whole, *L'Astrée* presents a considerable quantity and variety of such affirmations. With

147

the result that one of the epistemological systems present here and in a great many passages of the novel is an essentially poetic or pantheistic one.

For this reason, these and the similar analogies in Honoré d'Urfé's masterpiece relate a part of the author's worldview to a current of thought running back through his own earlier works as well as such disparate spirits as Saint François de Sales, Pierre Charron, the young Malherbe, and Philippe Desportes, among others. Among the very large body of comments on the subject in authors of the period, this current perhaps finds its most eloquent expression in Montaigne. The latter writes in his *Apologie de Raymond Sebond,* for example, that "it would be incredible if the whole [world] machine bore no marks of the hand of this great architect, and if there were no image in the things of this world relating in some way to the worker who formed and built them. God has left in his works the character of his divinity, and only our own imbecillity prevents us from recognizing it. As He Himself says to us, His invisible actions are manifested by visible ones.... For this world is a most holy temple, into which man is allowed entrance to contemplate statues—not those chiselled by mortal hands, but those made visible by divine thought..." In a later addition to his text, Montaigne further asks himself rhetorically: "Haven't I seen in Plato this divine sentence, that nature is nothing but an enigmatic poetry?... Certainly philosophy is merely an adulterated poetry. Where do these ancient authors get their authorities, if not from the poets? And the first ones were poets themselves and treated it according to their art." And whereas a modern reader might suppose that poets are at best something like philosophers who are vague and not sufficiently rigorous, Montaigne surprisingly expresses the opposite idea—concluding that "Plato is only a poet gone incoherent." [3]

In this way, Hylas' and Tyrcis' mode of thought benefits from the weight of a late sixteenth century philosophical tradition, as well as from the strength and apparent clarity of folk wisdom and poetic

---

[3] *Essais,* ed. A. Thibaudet (Paris, 1950), pp. 490-491, 600-601. ["Platon n'est qu'un poëte descousu."]

convention. At the same time however, it implies certain difficulties and weaknesses. For if one essential statement to be made about lovers is that they resemble workers, lost people, or rolling stones, there may exist no general rule to prove that they are not also like sick people, the victims of tyrants, or persons with deep taproots planted in their hearts—all of which additional comparisons are adduced by Hylas and Tyrcis in the pages following the text quoted above. Under such a system, each metaphor must be examined on its merits. There may thus exist no general understanding of the extent to which one may be argued or extended. Nor any general method of explaining the relationship between various analogies presented. Hylas and Tyrcis may thus possess no general method of discovering possible relationships between rolling stones and taproots, between workers and the victims of tyrants, between the lost and the sick, other than what still further analogies may suggest.

In *L'Astrée* as a whole, as indeed in French literature generally between 1580 and 1607 or later, human thought is most often portrayed as a sea of conflicting thoughts, emotions, and desires. As Charron puts it, the human mind is "a pit of obscurity full of hollows and dungeons, a labyrinth, a confused and twisting cavity ... " So that in the end one may well fear, in Tyrcis' words, that the tongue may be unable to express precisely that which "the heart cannot wholly feel." [4]

For Léonide, rendering judgement in volume two of *L'Astrée*, truth is something other than rolling stones, incurable wounds, or taproots. Her judgement is a fairly long one, and as such it sacrifices much of the spontaneity and apparently direct, Dionysian wisdom of Hylas and Tyrcis. As Léonide herself remarks, she draws her conclusions only when "All these things" have been "debated at length and carefully considered." At the same time however, her longer discourse nevertheless resolves itself into the repetition of a rather simple schematic procedure—a kind of algorithm of sentiment.

[4] *De la sagesse* (Paris, 1789), I, 165.

Attempting to discover whether Célidée should love Calidon or
Thamire, she immediately formulates the problem in terms of three
fundamental criteria of analysis: "Three things are before us," she
declares, "first, love; second, duty, and last, offenses." To lovers
who have loved as much as Hylas or waited in vain for solutions as
long as Céladon, such a formulation might appear excessively for-
malistic or simplistic. Léonide implies as much herself when she
enunciates the principle that "the things which nature makes are
more nearly perfect than those produced by art," at the same time
recognizing the inherent superiority of spontaneous love over senti-
ments based on such intellectual constructs as intention or obligation.
On the other hand, Léonide's categories have the advantage of ready
application, since she in fact sees three examples of each category
in the quarrel before her: "In the first, we take note of three great
affections; in the second, three great obligations, and in the last
three great injuries."

In her second paragraph, Léonide enunciates principles permitting
her and her hearers to arrange loves, obligations, and offenses along
scales of value. Montaigne's and Charron's view that universal difference and universal resemblance make meaningful categorization
difficult or impossible is implicitly rejected. As the example quoted
above suggests, Léonide considers different loves not as ingenious
mixtures of nature but as straightforward phenomena to be graded
in essentially quantitative fashion. Her other statements of principle
also imply quantitative differences between varying examples of
obligation and offense. Thus she suggests that "the obligation which
we incur in our own person being greater than those we honor out
of consideration for others, it is certain that a benefit creates a greater
obligation than remembrance." And that "if offense mixed with ingratitude is more grievous than that which merely offends us, no
one will deny that he who commits both is more worthy of punishment."

These and similar quantifying principles are applied to the
examples in Léonide's second, third, and fourth paragraphs. She
observes that "we know that Thamire's love proceeds from inclina-

tion, since ordinarily those that do are reciprocated, and that loving Célidée he was loved in return ... " And so on, until each of her three personages has been placed on a scale of value with respect to each category. Having dealt with the issues in this manner, Léonide is then ready to eliminate the lesser loves, duties, and injuries in favor of the greater. Like king Tulle in Corneille's *Horace,* she concludes that one obligation shall give way to another. Léonide saves the most difficult problem for the last part of her decision, until like so many kings and others in the great tradition of Cornelian theatre, she ends her judgement with the command that one personage love another: "We order ... that the love of Célidée shall overcome the offense she has received from Thamire, and that the love Thamire shall bring her in the future shall surpass in exchange that which Célidée has shown him up to now."

Examples of such sublime confidence in schemes of classification as a means of resolving problems are relatively difficult to discover among French authors in the thirty years immediately preceding publication of the second volume of *L'Astrée.* Léonide's approach, of course, has less to do with the irregularly organized essays of Montaigne or the dissertations of Charron than with the far more schematic style of the *Discours de la Méthode.* In particular, whereas Montaigne, Charron, Hylas, and Tyrcis are unable to limit the number of factors which will enter into their analyses, Léonide's method leads her, like Descartes, to "include nothing more in my judgements than that which to my mind stood out so clearly and so distinctly that there was no reason to doubt it." She is resigned to certain arbitrary qualities of her categories, apparently believing like Descartes that "In the beginning, it is better to use only those which present themselves spontaneously to our senses and which we cannot ignore ... rather than to seek out rarer and more subtle ones ... " Whereas Montaigne, Charron, Hylas, and Tyrcis encounter difficulty in identifying the relative importance of factors in concrete situations, Léonide is supremely confident that she can evaluate occurrences in terms of salient factors. Like Descartes, she is able to "divide each one of the difficulties I would examine in as many sections as it could be ... [and] conduct my thoughts in order, beginning with the simplest and most easily accessible matters, and climbing little by little, as if by steps, up to knowledge of the most complex ones." [5] Such methodology, of course, is not limited to any small number of passages, works, or authors in the period. Just as Montaigne's, Hylas' and Tyrcis' epistemological assumptions underly a very large number of texts in the period running forward from 1580, assumptions common to Léonide and Descartes are present in a great many texts published in France after 1607.

As analysis of both the preceding texts suggests, in *L'Astrée* as a whole there is not only alternation between their two modes of thought, but also a certain measure of exchange between them. In this way, for example, Hylas' and Tyrcis' debate contains one reference to the "rules of the art" which might permit the participants to overcome the limitations of purely analogically based thinking. Similarly, one of the general principles adduced in the second text, namely that "just as the things which nature makes are more nearly perfect than those produced by art, so love that comes from inclination is greater and more admirable than that which comes from intention or obligation," is itself an otherwise unsupported analogical view.

Curiously enough, although Léonide's reasoning seeks to avoid complication by identifying a few presumably salient factors, in the heterogeneous pages of *L'Astrée* her assumptions appear essentially as one further type of ratiocination added to the first. As such they tend to complicate rather than simplify the novel. As might be expected, the difficulty of reconciling two epistemological modes renders more difficult the moral dilemmas posed in Honoré d'Urfé's plot and numerous sub-plots. Inevitably, the exploration of the possibilities of multiple assumptions lengthens and enriches considerably the work's meandering course. As one personage remarks, speaking of only a part of the plot, "Time was conquered, difficulties or even impossibilities disdained, absences overcome, paternal angers scorned, his rigors, his crualties, even his disdains endured, over so long a

---

[5] In *Œuvres*, ed. A. Bridoux (Paris, 1953), pp. 137-138, 169.

time that I don't know anyone who could have done it, but Céladon" (I, 32). Until the point when, in a kind of final synthesis of the two modes, Céladon succeeds in reconciling his moral principles with his more analogically based aspirations—winning back Astrée and restoring the function of the Fountain of the Truth of Love at the novel's conclusion.

Thus in a larger context, as a meeting ground and synthesis of two remarkably difference modes of sixteenth and seventeenth-century thought—both with broad implications for the moral life and world-view of the novel's personages, as well as considerable resonance among contemporary authors, *L'Astrée* may also confirm in some respects such quasi-structural theories of the period as those of Michel Foucault. For like the almost exactly contemporary *Don Quixote* as analysed in *Les Mots et les Choses, L'Astrée*'s heterogeneous epistemological assumptions may be interpreted as transitional between two literary *epistemes*. At the same time however, *L'Astrée* and its successors confirm the reservations of Professor Foucault's critics in at least one important respect. For rather than discontinuously following and replacing one another as he suggests, *L'Astrée*'s two modes of thought coexist in most if not all French literary works of the next several decades. In many of these as in *L'Astrée*, moreover, the salient epistemological issue is the possible synthesis of the two modes. Appearing almost precisely at the mid-point of the baroque age of literature in France, the development of this issue parallels that of the classical literary aesthetic. Perhaps more than it confirms Michel Foucault's concept of intellectual discontinuity therefore, analysis of *L'Astrée* and its epistemological resonances may confirm Henri Peyre's recent remarkable redefinition of classicism as a "momentary harmony between the faculty of understanding and the faculty of feeling" in seventeenth-century France. [6]

---

[6] *Qu'est-ce que le Classicisme?*, rev. ed. (Paris, 1965), p. 262.

Beverly S. Ridgely

Racan and the Old and New Astronomies

Although Honorat de Bueil, seigneur de Racan (1589-1670), is today little read and less studied, in his time he was generally judged the most naturally gifted of Malherbe's disciples, and this despite a reputation for ignorance, laziness, and lack of commitment to poetry that he neither disputed nor discouraged. [1] A faithful if occasionally unrigorous or careless *Malherbien* in matters of prosody, language, and poetic form and devices, Racan was very unlike his master, and most other French poets of the day, in assigning to the heavens and the celestial bodies, particularly the stars, a frequent and often prominent role in his poems. Moreover, he was one of the very few French seventeenth-century poets who show any awareness of living during what we now consider an age of revolution in man's thinking about the universe and his place in it. Racan thus offers what I believe is a unique combination of characteristics—fidelity to Malherbe as concerns the art or, better, skill of poetry-making, a penchant for astronomical and astrological material, and some knowledge of at least the dispute over heliocentrism—a combination that makes his work of great interest to any one seeking to understand the impact of the old and new astronomies on poetic imagination, content, and form in France.

---

[1] Louis Arnould has done the only important scholarly and critical work on Racan in the twentieth century. His *Un Gentilhomme de lettres au XVII*e *siècle: Honorat de Bueil, seigneur de Racan* (Paris, 1901) remains the best general study, and he published excellent editions of portions of Racan's work, *Poésies lyriques* (Paris, 1930), and *Les Bergeries* (Paris, 1937). For the poet's many paraphrases of Psalms, and for all his prose writings, the only relatively modern edition is his *Œuvres complètes,* ed. T. et A. de Latour, 2 vols. (Paris, 1857).

In my text, references to Racan's poems are to Arnould's edition of the *Poésies* unless otherwise indicated, and those to prose works are to the Latour edition.

Beverly S. Ridgely

As a result, we could use Racan's complete poems for a purpose that would be impossible with the work of Théophile de Viau, Saint-Amant, or any other contemporary French poet whom I know: that is, to construct a *Sphaera* of current doctrines, assumptions, and myths about the heavens, incomplete and undetailed, to be sure, but comparable to what Du Bartas and other sixteenth-century versifiers provide in full measure in their learned poems. We cannot of course attempt such a compilation in this short essay. Our intent is rather to consider Racan as a poet who used a rational, thoroughly modern form and language yet, despite some familiarity with the new astronomy, included only old, often outdated concepts about the heavens. To illustrate and understand this curious but, in an important sense, natural practice, we shall single out Racan's predilection for one such notion, that the spirits of the blessed "dwell above" and "walk upon" the stars, and analyze its use and significance in one of his finest poems, the "Consolation à Monseigneur de Bellegarde, sur la mort de Monsieur de Termes son frère."

We can no doubt never learn the extent of Racan's knowledge of the astronomical revolution or, more importantly, whether he felt anything of what we now consider its profoundly unsettling consequences and implications. Our only indications that he knew of it at all are two prose passages in which he speaks briefly of heliocentrism, each time to an informed audience. In 1635, for his "Harangue" to the new-born Académie Française, Racan had the inspiration of delivering a eulogy of ignorance, and this to Chapelain, Conrart, and others among the most learned men of the age. The fact that the *directeur* of the Académie actually read the "Harangue," in Racan's absence from Paris, adds piquancy to the occasion and the text. With good grace and considerable wit, the poet accepts and proceeds to make the most of his reputed laziness and ignorance. In particular, he admits to charges of unfamiliarity and even unconcern with philosophical and scientific matters. Then, neatly reversing his field, he sets out to debunk the allegedly great progress in all fields of learning, by listing, *à la Montaigne,* errors and follies then plaguing the sciences. Included is what Racan considers a premature concern with plotting the movements of the planets and stars before there is any proof as to which world system, geocentric or heliocentric, represents reality: "auparavant que d'estre d'accord avec Galilée, si ce sont eux [les cieux] ou la terre qui tourne, si elle n'est point une des estoilles, si le soleil leur porte la lumière, ou s'il attend sans se mouvoir dans le centre de l'univers, comme un roy dans son throsne, que ses sujets la viennent prendre de luy" (Latour, I, 241.). [2] Wherever Racan may have picked up these details, scanty and in part inaccurate, yet including Copernicus's celebrated comparison between sun and monarch, he clearly knew at least the essentials of the two competing theories.

In 1656 Racan wrote a letter to Chapelain that not only reveals a greater familiarity with the overriding astronomical issue of the time but also provides our only evidence of his opinion in the matter. This letter is especially interesting for the poet's reminiscences about his days in the school for pages at the court of Henri IV. As in the "Harangue," he takes the tack of self-disparagement, playing up his ignorance as a pupil and ineptitude as a page with good humor and sly wit. When discussing the rudimentary instruction in mathematics he had received fifty years and more earlier, Racan readily justifies the dislike he then felt for astronomy: "J'en trouvois les démonstrations trop peu assurées" ["I found its demonstrations too unsure"] (Latour, I, 335). Even now, in mid-century, the continued lack of sensory or experimental evidence made any decision between the geocentric and heliocentric systems unwise if not impossible. This was also the attitude of Mersenne, Pascal, and other French men of learning far more competent than Racan to judge this question yet who, out of scientific prudence, could and would not take sides. Even so, the poet does express a preference to his friend Chapelain: "si j'avois à prendre party, ce seroit plustost du costé de Copernic et de Galilée que de celuy de Ptolomée et de Sacrobosco, et croirois que

_____

[2] "before agreeing with Galileo, whether the heavens or the earth turn, whether the earth is not one of the stars, whether the sun brings them light or rather waits motionless in the center of the universe, like a king on his throne, for its subjects to come and get light from it."

la terre tourne plustost que le soleil" (Latour, I, 335).[3] However, under no compulsion to choose, he will not, for two reasons that exemplify the major areas of disagreement with heliocentrism at the time.

On the one hand, there remained physical obstacles to movement by the earth such as had been debated since the fourteenth century when Jean Buridan and Nicole Oresme began serious examinations of that possibility. Thus, Racan affirms his willingness to accept the idea, "si l'on me pouvoit faire comprendre comment cet air, que l'on dit qui suit ce mouvement rapide de la terre, peut estre capable de changer celuy d'un corps solide et pesant, et de faire tomber une bale de plomb, que l'on auroit jettée en l'air, plus d'un quart de lieue loin d'où elle devroit tomber perpendiculairement si la terre tournoit en vingt-quatre heures. Je ne vois point d'exemple de cela, et ces grands vents qui ont emporté nos maisons la semaine passée n'estoyent pas seulement capables d'emporter dix pas une bale de pistolet" (Latour, I, 335).[4] For all its *naïveté* in modern eyes, this kind of argument still concerned not only poets but also Galileo, Mersenne, and other men of learning in seventeenth-century Europe. Also like many contemporaries, Racan had religious scruples about the moving earth as physical reality: "elles [ces nouvelles opinions] choquent quelques passages de l'Ecriture sainte" ["these new opinions offend some passages of Holy Scripture"] (Latour, I, 335). Doubtless the poet felt no need to spell out for Chapelain what he had in mind, the miracle of Joshua and other Biblical texts that, literally interpreted, eliminated heliocentrism as the true system of the world for many sixteenth and seventeenth-century minds. In any event, Racan had both physical and religious reasons for suspending his judgment between the old

---

[3] "if I had to take sides, it would rather be with Copernicus and Galileo than with Ptolemy and Sacrobosco, and I would believe that the earth is turning rather than the sun."

[4] "if I could be made to understand how the air, that they say follows this rapid movement of the earth, can be capable of changing the movement of a solid, heavy body, and cause a lead ball, thrown into the air, to fall more than a quarter of a league distant from where it ought to fall straight down, if the earth did rotate in twenty-four hours. I see no instance of that at all, and those strong winds that carried away our houses last week were not even capable of carrying a pistol bullet ten paces."

and new theories about the earth's position and its stability or mobility.

As regards other important aspects of the new astronomy, we have less detailed and clear evidence of Racan's knowledge, much more his personal opinion. Concerning, for example, speculations about the indefinite or infinite extent of the universe in space, he, like other French seventeenth-century poets, says very little. His work naturally contains stock phrases like "universelle rondeur" and "au bout de l'univers" ["universal roundness," "to the end of the universe"], but in using such clichés, he may well not have been consciously affirming the doctrine of finitude. And there are passages like the following, from his ode in praise of Anne of Austria, written in mid-century, in which, characteristically, he introduces cosmological material that powerfully expands his source, Psalm VIII:

> Seul Dieu de qui le nom est partout glorieux,
> Dont la grandeur remplit et la lumière éclaire
> L'espace imaginaire
> Des viudes infinis qui sont dessus les Cieux. (Arnould, p. 284) [5]

Yet even these lines extend the Empyrean rather than the physical universe beyond the one world of our solar system. And nowhere, in poetry or in prose, does Racan express any reaction to what many contemporaries were beginning to realize was a totally new situation for man, in a universe without center or limit. He had, however, heard of another significant development, the "new stars" or novae of the late sixteenth and early seventeenth centuries, study of which helped greatly to destroy the time—honored distinction between the supralunary and sublunary regions. Racan's only reference to this phenomenon, again in his "Harangue" to the Académie, expresses the unshaken conviction, whether grounded in old science or religion or both, that "La terre ne produit point de nouvelles fleurs, ny le ciel ne (sic.) nouvelles estoilles" ["The earth produces no new flowers,

---

[5] "One God whose name is everywhere glorious, / Whose grandeur fills and whose light illumines / The imaginary space / Of the infinite voids above the heavens."

nor heaven any new stars"] (Latour, I, 247). Thus, for Racan as for other French poets of his day, the absolute separation between the elemental and celestial parts of the world remained a dramatic way to contrast and also explain man's perhaps miserable but transitory existence on earth, and the eternal bliss awaiting him in heaven. As we shall see, this is the basic assumption of the "Consolation à Bellegarde".

From the slim evidence just summarized, it is clear that Racan's knowledge of the astronomical revolution of his time was slight indeed —although, we should emphasize, greater than that revealed by Malherbe, Théophile, or most other French seventeenth-century poets. Racan seems to have reacted only to the quarrel over the stability or mobility of the earth, and to have misunderstood or simply been unconscious of findings and speculations that we, with three centuries of hindsight, regard as deeply unsettling, such as comets as well as "new stars" situated far beyond the moon, the nature of the Milky Way and of the lunar surface, the doctrines of infinity and a plurality of worlds, and the rest. If we now ask how this limited awareness of the new astronomy affected Racan's poetry-making, the answer is equally clear as regards subject matter: despite his penchant for material relating to the heavens his poems make no reference to any new astronomical development. Racan evidently considered even matters with which he had some familiarity, the moving earth, say, or "new stars," unsuitable for the poetry he wanted to write and the readers he wished to please. And although such an attitude may be surprising at first glance, it is actually perfectly logical and natural. Racan wrote at a time when, in sharp reaction to sixteenth-century principles, practices, and tastes, French poets and readers found learned poetry in the manner of Du Bartas or even of Ronsard's *Hymnes* too specialized and didactic to be pleasing. Therefore the paradox of a French seventeenth-century poet who, like Racan, knew something about the new astronomy yet kept silent about it in his poems is only apparent. In a very real sense, in short, it was because Racan shared the dominant attitudes of his day toward the subject matter of poetry and the role of the poet that his own poems assume and often depict the relatively small, closed, anthropocentric universe and the celestial phenomena and influences that had long been familiar to savants and laymen alike, and that no reader could find overly technical, obscure, or upsetting.

If we consider next the how rather than the what of astronomy in the poetry of Racan, his manner of presentation rather than his material, we are faced with another contradiction, perhaps even more striking than the first. The structure, prosody, and language of his work are eminently Malherbian, that is, resolutely modern and marking a break with the Pléiade and its followers as complete in these respects as in those involving learned poetry and the poet as teacher of scientific or philosophical truths. And yet, we must wonder, how can this new poetic mold successfully hold and convey the old myths and notions about the pre-Copernican heavens? Did the poet feel any incompatibility between such content and his way of presenting it? Is this contradiction real or apparent? To illuminate if not resolve such questions, let us examine a specific example of Racan's handling of a favorite celestial theme.

Throughout his career, the poet played numerous variations upon the originally pagan myth that the spirits of the elect abide in eternal bliss above or upon the stars.[6] It was in the equally ancient genre or form of the consolatory poem that he made most effective use of this means of making celestial glory concrete and comprehensible. In 1621 Racan and his cousin and protector, the duc de Bellegarde, participated in the expedition led by Louis XIII to subdue the rebellious Huguenots in southwestern France, and were present when Bellegarde's younger brother, the marquis de Termes, died of wounds received during the siege of Clairac. The three men had long been good friends, and Racan had addressed to Termes his ode "sur la venue du printemps" and had also been paying poetic court to the

[6] See, e.g., the apotheosis of Henri IV, in his "Ode au Roy," in which the late monarch is pictured "walking upon the stars" (Arnould, p. 33). Racan also used this theme to make graphic, indeed physical the place of God and the Virgin Mary in heaven (e.g., Latour, II, 138, and Arnould, p. 8, respectively). And on at least one occasion it served him in a comic context: in lyrics composed for a ballet, the poet has a Matamore figure proclaim, "Les Astres effroyez tremblerent sous mes pas" (Arnould, p. 202). ["In fear the celestial bodies trembled beneath my steps."]

marquise de Termes. These circumstances and relationships must have made the composition of the "Consolation à Bellegarde" a far more immediate, personal experience for Racan than is often the case with such pieces.

The poem consists of nine *sizains,* in dodecasyllables, with each stanza comprising two *rimes plates* followed by four *rimes croisées.* Every structural element exemplifies the careful planning and fitting, the symmetry and solidity, that are the hallmark of the Malherbian revolution as concerns the architecture of a poem. Thus, the pattern of masculine and feminine rhymes alternates regularly between stanzas, each caesura is strongly marked, and every three lines there are syntactic breaks or pauses. Even the overall form of the poem reinforces the impression of calculation and control by the poet. Its shape is perfectly circular: the five central stanzas, concerned with the situation of Termes in heaven, are enclosed by two at the start and two at the end that deal with the state of mind of Bellegarde on earth. In effect, the "Consolation à Bellegarde" has the same shape as the equally man-designed and man-centered little universe that Racan's work portrays, and in which most men then believed they lived.

Addressing Bellegarde as the close personal friend that he was ("Roger", "tu"), Racan opens his poem with the directness, almost abruptness, that are also characteristic of the various types of lyric poetry written by Malherbe and his school. Straight-away the poet establishes a martial mood appropriate both to the circumstances of Terme's death and to the battle between the forces of despair and fortitude now joined within Bellegarde. Indeed, fate has just launched its heaviest strike ("coup") against the stronghold of Bellegarde's valor ("vertu"), and the issue is still in doubt. Language and metaphor combine to create the impression of a duel between perfectly matched adversaries:

> Chacun avecque doute attend l'evenement
> D'un combat où l'on voit une extréme constance
> S'opposer aux assauts d'un extréme tourment. (Arnould, p. 209) [7]

[7] "Everyone, in doubt, awaits the result / Of a combat in which they see extreme constancy / Oppose the assaults of extreme torment."

In his second stanza, Racan suddenly changes the atmosphere by adopting the moralizing stance and preachy tone that are all too familiar in consolational writing. Moderate your grief, he commands Bellegarde, remiding him of two conventional truths. The first is a standard Stoic remedy in such situations: tears are understandable and even excusable in low-born and unpracticed souls, but emphatically not in a hero who has been tested by trials and misfortunes. Racan's second admonition is more appropriate to the occasion and central to the development of a poem that takes for granted man's dominion over his emotions, his mortality, and even his world. How can you be so inconsistent, the poet asks, as to lament your brother's winning the very reward that you, yourself also a soldier and a Christian, desire and indeed seek?

This revelation of the cause of Bellegarde's grief—the reader, however, still knows none of the particulars of Termes's death and will learn very little—provides a smooth transition to the five stanzas devoted to the deceased's new estate. Racan briefly eulogizes Termes's pursuit of military *gloire* and his dedication to *vertu* in time of peace as well as war. But the poet's interest quickly focuses upon Termes's deep religious faith and its reward. This theme appears at the end of the third stanza: "Cependant que le sort l'arrestoit sur la terre, / Tous ses vœux ne tendoient qu'à retourner aux Cieux" (Arnould, p. 210). [8] In turn, this triple antithesis, highly condensed and symmetrical, serves as another skillful transition. It carries us to the climax of the poem, the immortality enjoyed by the Christian whose spirit has quit the central but lowly and mortal earth and journeyed to what men had long assumed was the perfect and immutable realm above the firmament. In dying, the Christian warrior Termes has thus gained eternal life, which was his heart's desire all along and the ultimate triumph for one who had, in Racan's forceful image, "become sated" with every prize and honor that mortal existence offers. In another of the fusions of pagan and Christian that appear frequently in sixteenth- and seventeenth-century works, the poet affirms that "Les

---

[8] "While fate held him fast to earth, / All his desires were directed solely at returning to the Heavens."

Dieux l'ont retiré des mortelles alarmes" ["The Gods have withdrawn him from deadly alarms" (Arnould, p. 210). This being so, Bellegarde's tears and lamentations are not only unmanly and contradictory but, even more, all that can detract from the bliss enjoyed by his brother.

Racan now undertakes to make the nature of that bliss clear and concrete. At the mid-point or, more properly, the pinnacle of his poem, he paints a grandiose vision of the earth and heavens from the privileged viewpoint of the blessed dead. And in depicting Termes's new situation and activities, he places both stars and earth in a markedly inferior position:

> Il voit ce que l'Olimpe a de plus merveilleux,
> Il y voit à ses piés ces flambeaux orgueilleux,
> Qui tournent à leur gré la Fortune et sa roüe:
> Et voit comme fourmis marcher nos legions,
> Dans ce petit amas de poussiere et de boüe,
> Dont nostre vanité fait tant de regions. (Arnould, p. 211)[9]

Racan has selected and arranged every element of this stanza so as to give Termes truly titanic stature now that he has moved into the pre-Copernican macrocosm. At the same time, the strongly pictorial emphasis encourages the reader to see the same things as Termes, but in his own way. That is, by not specifying or detailing the wonders of pagan Olympus—strangely at home in an ostensibly Christian poem because the theme and atmosphere are very Virgilian—Racan obliges each of us to imagine them for himself. And he gains added participation or complicity by presenting the stars in their astrological role, perhaps their most familiar function for seventeenth-century minds. The matter-of-fact way in which Racan asserts astral control over man's mortal destiny appears frequently in his work and seems to reflect his personal belief. [10] But whether conviction or convention, he

---

[9] "He sees what is most wonderful in Olympus, / There he sees at his feet those proud torches, / Which turn as they please Fortune and its wheel: / And [he] sees as ants our legions marching, / In this little heap of dust and mud, / Of which our vanity makes so many regions."

[10] Racan apparently considered celestial influences an important part of God's design for man (see, e.g., Arnould, p. 23). Interestingly, however, he differed from most contemporaries in denying that man can predict their

163

here expresses the alleged influence of the heavenly bodies upon human life in strikingly concrete and visual terms. Personification of the stars and planets reinforces the pictorial effect, calling up for the reader visions of haughty gods or monarchs spinning the great wheel of fate. Of course the fortunate Termes has now risen above the stars and their control, just as he has overcome the vicissitudes of earth.

In the second half of this climactic stanza, as the deceased looks down upon the earth, much farther below him than any celestial body, Racan introduces another familiar philosophical and religious theme, the very different light in which those dwelling above the firmament view the ambitions and accomplishments of those still living here below. It is undeterminable and really unimportant whether the poet borrowed the notion from Malherbe, as seems most likely, [11] or from Montaigne, Seneca, Pliny, or some one else again. What does matter is his success in compressing and highlighting this commonplace, thanks above all to his choice and placement of appropriate visual antitheses. In line four of the stanza, the words at the caesura and at the rhyme stand in sharp and picturesque contrast: what Termes's eyes discern as ants, terrestrials continue to regard as legions. And the implication of the simile is even more humbling: as we earthmen are to ants, so the titan Termes is to us. The last two lines of the stanza are opposed as units: Termes now sees in true perspective, as but a small pile of dirt, what proud but myopic men persist in carving up among themselves. Surely the hackneyed device of antithesis has rarely been used as effectively as by Racan in this stanza summarizing one of man's most enduring myths or dreams about the afterlife.

The poet now refocuses our attention upon the heavens and the in every way superior situation of the blessed dead. His sixth stanza is built upon still another commonplace of French sixteenth- and seventeenth-century poetry, the metamorphosis of the honored one into a star. This means of praising either the living—say, a beloved

effects, and in his "Harangue" to the Académie he included a strong condemnation of judicial astrology as an infringement on divine prerogatives (Latour, I, 242).

[11] For a discussion of possible sources, see Arnould, pp. 211-12, n. 1.

lady as a sun—or the dead was the only kind of creation in the heavens acceptable to those who, like Racan, continued to believe in the physical and metaphysical distinction between the regions above and below the moon. Even more, the supposition of the physically immutable heavens enables the poet to pay the supreme compliment to Termes, who has nonetheless increased their perfection. And Racan can then speak in an exclamatory, exultant tone that impels the reader to rejoice with him at the deceased's great good fortune, and also to envision a truly dazzling scene:

> Quelle magnificence aux hommes inconnuë,
> A tesmoigné là haut l'aise de sa venuë!
> Que de feux eternels naissoient dessous ses pas!
> Qu'il augmenta du Ciel la clarté coustumiere,
> Et que ce grand flambeau qu'on admire icy bas,
> Aupres de ce bel Astre avoit peu de lumiere!
>
> (Arnould, pp. 212-13)[12]

This accumulation of words designating both fire and light and also bright, flaming objects creates an effect of all-encompassing brilliance that has few if any equals in French poetry. One pictures an immense display of fireworks honoring the new arrival, but set off in a strangely reversed direction, for these stars and planets shine forth below Termes. Moreover, they are "eternels" and thus not to be mistaken for newly created, physical entities, for in Racan's poetic universe, created for man, centered upon his planet, and comprehensible to his reason, only men and women can become new stars. In such circumstances, the seventeenth-century reader, familiar with the idealized physical and spiritual premises upon which the poem rests, understood and probably expected the poet's last bit of hyperbole, the dimming of the real sun before the human sun that has assumed its rightful place in heaven.

After the brilliant apotheosis of the Christian hero, the seventh stanza of the "Consolation à Bellegarde," the last devoted to Termes,

---

[12] "What magnificence unknown to men, / Bore witness up there to the joy at his [Termes's] arrival! / How many eternal fires blazed forth beneath his feet! / How much he increased the usual brilliance of Heaven, / And how weak the light of the great torch we admire here below, / In comparison with that of this beautiful Star!"

is inevitably an anticlimax. Twice more Racan stresses the deceased's position of towering physical and spiritual superiority: Termes can now hardly deign to lower his eyes upon the tiny, base earth and its trivial preoccupations, located, as Racan impresses upon us for the third time, far below his feet. The poet also continues to present a presumably Christian heaven in the guise of pagan Olympus. Thus, the gods are vying with one another to pour nectar for the honored newcomer, all, that is, but two, for Bellona and Mars are off waging war on earth, intending to punish "Les auteurs de sa mort sur les rives du Tar" ["The authors of his death upon the banks of the Tarn"] (Arnould, p. 213).

This vague and imprecise reference is all that Racan tells his readers concerning how and where Termes had died. It is also the last transitional element in the tight and logical construction of the poem. The poet alludes once more to Termes's triumph and its rewards—"puisque ses travaux ont treuvé leur azile" ["since his travails have found their refuge"] (Arnould, p. 213)—and then returns his attention to the grieving Bellegarde. Immediately the moralizing tone and imperative mood of the second stanza reappear, in another command to the latter to cease his useless lamentation. The following line, "Dont l'injuste longueur traverse tes plaisirs" ["Whose unjust duration thwarts your pleasures"] (Arnould, p. 213), exemplifies the inattention or unconcern of which Racan is at times guilty: in such close proximity to "*tra*vaux" and "*treu*vé" of the first line of the stanza, "*tra*verse" strikes a decidedly cacophonous note. The second half of this, the eighth, stanza is more successful. The only rhetorical question of the poem forcefully restates Racan's basic admonition and at the same time major consolation to Bellegarde:

> Croy-tu que joüissant d'une paix si profonde,
> Il voulust à present que selon tes desirs
> Le Ciel le renvoyast aux miseres du monde?
>
> (Arnould, pp. 213-14) [13]

[13] "Do you believe that, enjoying so profound a peace, / He now would want Heaven, acceding to your wishes, / To send him back to the miseries of the world?"

Viewed so rationally and unemotionally, Bellegarde's grief must indeed seem both illogical and selfish, at least to readers who are outsiders.

The concluding stanza of the "Consolation à Bellegarde" is its most Malherbian in both themes and symmetrical structure. The first half consists of three one-line truisms that together summarize the fleeting nature of terrestrial happiness and fame and also the rule of fate over our lives. To the end, the poet continues to stress the distinction between earth and heavens. Thus, in his first commonplace, "Le bon-heur d'icy bas se passe en un moment" ["Happiness here below passes in a moment"] (Arnould, p. 214), the focal word, "ici-bas", epitomizes the place and status of the earth in the world-system that the poem assumes and utilizes. Moreover, Racan specifies that only on earth does fate hold absolute sway. A reader today may find the third cliché, "Par luy [le sort] ce grand Cesar n'est plus rien que fumee" ["By fate's decree this great Caesar is now but smoke"] (Arnould, p. 214), the least interesting of the lot. Yet Bellegarde and other seventeenth-century readers in the know must have appreciated its double meaning, for the deceased was in fact named César-Auguste de Saint-Lary.

Lest any one be discouraged by these assertions of the unhappy aspects of man's lot, Racan balances and completes his conclusion with another three-line unit that sounds a note of limited but positive uplift. After reminding Bellegarde that Termes has undergone a total metamorphosis, the poet offers a last counsel, reaffirming the dichotomy of mortality and immortality which is as basic to the Christian view of man as that between earth and heavens is to the pre-telescopic system of the world: "Au lieu de sa despouille aime sa renommee" ["Instead of his remains love his renown"] (Arnould, p. 214). The closing line, "C'est surquoy le destin n'aura point de pouvoir" ["That is what destiny will be powerless against"] (Arnould, p. 214), is probably as "consoling" to Termes's family as anything could be. More importantly, it serves both a thematic and a structural function in the poem and is thus another example of Racan's careful planning and control. Within the last stanza, the final line corrects or at least qualifies the second of Racan's truisms: fate does not, after all, totally rule human life on earth, for it cannot adversely affect such fame as Termes has won. Simultaneously, in the poem as a whole, this concluding line brings the development full circle. Racan, we recall, had begun by personifying fate and its all-out attack against Bellegarde. Now, at the very end, the poet assures us that while fate controls everything physical in our lives, Bellegarde, and, by extension, any reader similarly afflicted, can win spiritual triumph over its worst assaults. Thus, Termes's renown will be as undying even on the corruptible earth as his soul in its new abode above the immutable stars. And, by implication, Bellegarde too can confidently look forward to the same kind of double immortality.

In its content as in its execution, Racan's "Consolation à Bellegarde" emerges as a hymn to man's triumph over his physical mortality and to his spiritual dominion over the universe itself. Everything in the poem, from its implicit assumption of a finite world that man's mind has devised and placed around his earth and its explicit assurance of his victory over grief and even death, to its regular prosody and symetrical rhythmic patterns, its block-by-block construction, and its rounded shape—everything presupposes and also illustrates human understanding and manipulation. And although unquestionably one of Racan's finest works, the poem is like all the rest both in exemplifying this tight control and in supposing this "little world made cunningly," centered upon and concerned with man.

One cannot but wonder how it could have been otherwise, and not just because, early in the seventeenth century, most French men of letters and readers came to dislike learned poetry and to reject the poet's function as seer and teacher of great philosophical and scientific truths. One must wonder, in other words, how the kind of poetry-making advocated, practiced, and eventually imposed by Malherbe and his followers, emphasizing solid architecture and logical progression and utilizing moral and ideological commonplaces, rigid prosody, and clear, abstract language, could have handled, much more welcomed, material relating to the new universe, which had neither center nor shape, which the human mind could no longer grasp, and

Beverly S. Ridgely

in which man seemed to have lost his place, his rights of possession, and his unique reason for being. Viewed in this light, the presence of the old universe in the new poetic form and idiom used by Racan and most French poets of his times does not seem a surprise or paradox after all. On the contrary, we may now better understand why those poets do not discuss or react to the new astronomy in their work, even when, like Racan, they clearly knew something about it. Each of us must of course decide for himself whether it is inconsistent and contradictory or natural and fitting that a poetry so modern, rational and scientific continued to present a world system so old-fashioned, anthropocentric, and mythic. Either way, however, we should remember Racan as one of the few French seventeenth-century poets to whom the old heavens gave moments of true inspiration, probably of personal delight, and no doubt of comfort, that all was still right with the creation, with man's close involvement in it, and with his spiritual dominion over it.

David Lee Rubin

Consciousness and the External World in a Caprice by Saint-Amant

First published in the second part of his *Oeuvres* (1643), "Le Mauvais Logement" (*The Bad Billet*) has been traced by biographers to the poet's real or supposed presence in parts of Italy and Southern France during military campaigns mounted in the early 1630's by Louis XIII and Richelieu. [1] In motif, style, and plan, the poem recalls the satires of Berni: that is, it diminishes its banal subject by an apparently random accumulation of concrete details, as disgusting as they are ridiculous. Consequently, critics using the paraphrase method have found the poem both formless and themeless. [2] But close inspection of style and structure—particularly the relationship between imagery, ideas, and dramatic situation—discloses not only the poem's inner coherence, but above all, its intellectual suggestiveness. [3] This suggestiveness, as the following interpretation will show, is most strongly felt in the relations established by the poet between the speaker's consciousness and the external world.

The poem deals with the rather one-sided conflict between the speaker, quartered for the night at a commandeered inn, and the bats,

---

[1] Saint-Amant, *Oeuvres,* ed. Jean Lagny (Paris, 1967). All references to Saint-Amant—indicated by line numbers in the body of the article—are to this edition.

[2] See, for example, Françoise Gourier, *Etude des oeuvres poétiques de Saint-Amant* (Paris, 1961), p. 141; and Richard Mazzara, "Saint-Amant and the Italian Bernesque Poets," *French Review* 32 (1965), 241. Alone among recent commentators, William Roberts has asserted that "the universe of 'Le Mauvais Logement' possesses a certain valid harmony and a certain valid consistency." See his important study, "The Malo Allogio Motif in Saint-Amant," *Studi Francesi* 27 (September-December 1965), 465-471.

[3] For a fuller account of the method employed in this essay, see my study, *Higher, Hidden Order: Design and Meaning in the Odes of Malherbe,* University of North Carolina Studies in Romance Languages and Literatures 117 (Chapel Hill, 1972).

birds, and goblins sheltered there on a permanent basis. Frightened and confused, the speaker passes abruptly from complaints to unrelated and often hallucinatory narrations, from narrations to descriptions of new phenomena, and then repeats the process. The attacks of constantly increasing harshness culminate in homosexual rape. Unable to understand the experiences his mind and body undergo, the speaker withdraws until dawn disperses his assailants and reveille calls him to action.

"Et la Nuit si longue m'y semble / Que je croy qu'elle ait entrepris / D'en joindre douze ensemble" [And the night seems so long to me there / that I think it has undertaken to join twelve together] (vv. 8-10): along this overextended continuum of psychological time, the speaker will suffer the first attack. The aggressor is the setting itself. Though singular and of limited dimensions, the inn quarters subhuman and supernatural beings almost without limit: "la Vermine" (v. 4), "mille oyseaux de Nuit" [a thousand night birds] (v. 34), "un essaim de maudits Cousins" [a swarm of accursed mosquitoes] (v. 41), "cent Rats" [a hundred rats] (v. 51), "une trouppe de Farfadets" [a band of hobgoblins] (v. 61), and "un Incube" (v. 93). To these are added disagreeable or positively noxious furniture and outfittings: "un chien de grabat" [a contemptible little bed] (v. 1), "un infame lit de plume" [a disgraceful featherbed] (v. 2), and "une vilaine Couverture" [a sordid blanket] (v. 15). Finally, there are "cent chimeres hideuses" [a hundred hideous visions] (v. 83). In sum, nothing less than an epitome of the nonhuman world attacks the speaker's body and mind.

The plan of attack calls for two strikes. The first, designed to weaken the victim's defenses, consists in exerting irresistible pressure from every direction. Laterally, the tactic is to bind or enclose for restriction of movement. The "grabat" (v. 1) is a small bed, and thus almost certainly cramped. "Vilaine" (v. 15), the blanket is not only sordid, but, according to a seventeenth-century play on words, tight. Because of the hobgoblins' antics, the speaker's sight is "fascinée" (v. 65), that is, either bewitched or bound, or both. Vertically the procedure is to keep the victim in a defenseless and, if possible, a humiliating posture. He is and remains throughout the poem "gisté" (v. 1), passively laid out. His featherbed is "infame" (v. 2), not only disgraceful in itself, but debasing to whoever uses it. In such a state, the victim is prepared for the second and most aggressive phase of the campaign: intimate contact. Now, among other things, "la Vermine me combat" [the vermin makes war on me] (v. 4). Some of the attackers puncture the speaker: the barn owls' and bats' "cris sont autant de playes / A l'oreille qui les entend" [cries are just so many wounds / to the ear which hears them] (vv. 36-37). Others seek to consume him. One of the mosquitoes "sur ma main donne en Sangsuë" [attacks my hand like a leech] (v. 45). Later, the rat colony "s'en vient ronger en tout festin / Les entrailles de ma paillasse" [returns to gnaw the guts of my straw mattress just for a treat] (vv. 59-60). This augurs ill for the speaker's own entrails if the rats are as hungry as they are "d'insolence animez" [stirred up by petulance] (v. 51). Still others pursue a different end. The sordid blanket "s'offre à me baiser" [proposes to kiss me] (v. 17), and is so maddened by desire that, to complete its mission, "elle suplante les linceuls / Qui se sauvent dans la ruelle" [it ousts the sheets / which escape into the space between the bed and the wall] (vv. 21-22). Later, bats and barn owls swoop down "jusqu'où mon corps s'estend / Et le muguettent comme une ombre" [to where my body is stretched out / and woo it like a shadow] (vv. 39-40). Thus, beyond damaging and pillaging the victim, the fauna and the eerily animated outfittings seek to possess his body, and even his soul. To escape intact from this situation seems impossible: willy-nilly the speaker may yield up a relic, like his predecessor in the same bed, who left the sheets "teins d'apostume" [stained with pus] (v. 3).

Two images sum up the speaker's situation with utmost vividness. The first appears in his own analogy: "et comme un Oyson à la broche / Je me tourne de tous costez" [and like a gosling on the spit / I turn on all sides] (vv. 13-14). Penetrated and locked into place, he seems condemned to engage in movement which is not only repetitive, but above all suicidal, for it hastens his arrival at the state desired

David Lee Rubin

by those who seek to consume him. The second image occurs near the end of the poem where the speaker reports that as he drifts off to sleep "Un Incube... me créve" [an Incubus splits me open] (v. 93). Held down fast, he is violated by a male demon, that is: totally immobilized, humiliated and possessed.

Against these attacks, the speaker is unable to mount an effective defense. He sinks into brutish, inarticulate rage: the noise made by the mosquitoes "me fait renasquer en moy-mesme" [makes me snort to myself] (v. 43). A futile effort to counterattack leads to dehumanization: beleaguered by the night birds themselves, "je les poursuy, je les attrappe, / Et sans m'espargner le museau / Pour les y tuër je me frappe" [I chase them, I catch them / and without sparing my own snout / I hit myself to kill them there] (vv. 48-50). Finally, his physical and mental soldiery are one by one rendered immobile, subverted, neutralized, captured, or dispersed in panic. After the hobgoblins have bewitched or bound his eyesight, "mon oüye est subornée" [my hearing is induced to perjure itself] (v. 66). The hobgoblins frustrate the speaker's effort to shield his eyes from their monkeyshines: they elicit a fear which "par un effet malicieux / Change en bezicles mes paupieres" [through a wicked act, / changes my eyelids into lenses] (vv. 79-80). Because of the hundred hideous visions, "ma trop credule fantaisie / .... est si vivement saisie / Qu'elle mesme se fait horreur" [my too gullible imagination is so sharply grasped / that it horrifies itself] (vv. 85-87). And finally, "ma cervelle est hors de soy" [my brain is beside (literally, outside of) itself] (v. 67). The speaker seems doomed to defeat, even destruction.

Nevertheless he survives unvanquished. To ascertain the reason requires further consideration of two key categories: space and quantity. In respect to both, the victim and his assailants are exact opposites. The assailants—as indicated above—are multiple, while the victim is single. Yet, if the dimensions of the inn—which aids and abets the attack—are extremely restricted, the speaker's limbs, senses, and faculties succumb one by one to outside bedevilment, his consciousness, reduced to a minimum, becomes suddenly calm and—

while entertaining thoughts of sleep (v. 91-92)—even defiant. Having accepted the temporary loss of almost all physical and most of his nonstrategic mental terrain, this minimal consciousness seems to retreat to a point virtually inaccessible to pressure or penetration. There, while awaiting future developments, it suffers nothing but a slight jolt when body and imagination are rent by their final assailant, an Incubus.

With the particulars of this attack now in focus, certain symbols become transparent. The maneuvers take place "au clair de la Lune qui luit / D'une lueur morne et blafarde" [in the moonlight which shines / with a sad, pale glimmer] (vv. 31-2). The moon's presence correlates with—but does not necessarily cause—many of the substances and qualities, passions and states that obtain during the attack. Traditionally linked with the supernatural, the moon is here associated with a perversely long night, the presence of hobgoblins, and the appearance of a demon. Moreover, the speaker's passivity, his coerced femininity, as well as the affliction of his fancy and reason, all have a strong lunar resonance. Secondly, the speaker reports that throughout the night of wrath "je conte tous les coups de Cloche" [I count all the peals of the bell] (v. 12). These mechanically produced sounds emphasize not only the night's endlessness, but also the assault of the nonhuman world upon the speaker's body and mind. Like the gosling simile, these features play roles on the poem's literal plane, while synthesizing important aspects of its thematic structure.

As the Incubus attacks, the whole company of assailants "s'émerveillent / D'estre quasi surpris du jour; / Ils font gille à son arrivée" [are astounded / to be almost trapped by the day; / they flee at its arrival] (vv. 96-98). That a brilliant light enters the room and disperses the speaker's enemies suggests far more than the end of his discomfort and the resumption of waking activities. Indeed, it foreshadows a complete reversal of relations between the victim and his tormentors.

Aside from the biographical evidence recounted in the introduction, three textual details point to a link between the speaker and a campaigning army. First, he has spent the night in traveler's lodgings, and at dawn is awakened by the "diane du tambour" [the drum's reveille] (v. 99). Second, it is the time of year for military operations, "la saison des raisins" [grape season] (v. 43), late summer or early fall. Finally, the speaker's vocabulary is redolent of the martial mentality and experience: no fewer than seventeen words contained in the narrative refer to the phases, effects, or equipment of combat.

Identified with an army waging war, the speaker is almost certainly implicated in border skirmishes and incursions, battles for control of key positions and dispersals of enemy troops. In this context, his nocturnal sufferings—the peripheral attacks and counterattacks; the bites, noise, and other forms of penetration; the struggle to retain control of senses and faculties; and finally, the retreat of his consciousness—appear as a reversed and scaled down image of the daytime operations with which he is associated. This state of affairs is neatly summed up in a pair of figurative substitutions: by day, the entire contained entity (the army) commits aggression against the entire container (the territory where the inn is located); by night, however, a part of the container (the inn) afflicts a part of the contained entity (the speaker).

This symmetry is reinforced by a second pair of symbols. Whereas the nocturnal engagement took place under the sign of Diana and to the accompaniment of a clocktower bell, the day's operations are announced by the "diane du tambour" which is sounded as "l'Aube est levée" [the sun is up] (v. 100). In contrast with the lugubrious bell, the drum commands the hearer to rise and seize the day, assisting directly or indirectly in the conquest of a territory which only moments ago sought to conquer him. Similarly, the sun, which traditionally represents masculinity, rationality, and the propensity to action, is a model for whoever answers the summons of the drum.

The sense of the parallel between the explicit night and the implicit day maneuvers emerges from scattered remarks about the setting itself. There, the speaker states, "je passe les plus tristes heures / Qui dans les mortelles Demeures / Puissent affliger les Esprits" [I spend

175

the most melancholy hours / which can afflict souls in a mortal dwelling] (vv. 5-7). The stress on "mortelles" intimates that the only place worse than the inn would be an immortal dwelling where souls suffer. The gosling simile, already discussed in another context, portrays the speaker's forced suspension over fire. The natural and supernatural fauna of the inn have unmistakeable traits: the mosquitoes are "maudits" [accursed] (v. 41); the hobgoblins are "Diables-Cadets" [young devils] (v. 64) and disport themselves in "infernales nigeries" [hellish trifles] (v. 73); and finally all are "Demons" (v. 96). The setting, then, is an earthly Hell, where the speaker suffers in the image of the acts no doubt committed by the army with which he is connected.

Thematically, then, the poem centers on two facets of man's relationship to the external world. Mutually covetous and antagonistic, each strives to invade and possess the other, but with uncertain success. All that can be attained is peripheral or secondary; the essence remains elusive. Analogous to physical possession is mental possession, or knowledge and understanding. It is in this domain that the poem achieves its deepest irony. At best the speaker displays only an imperfect grasp of events. While he uses military terms to describe his night experience, he never overtly compares them to war. Thus what seems to reveal understanding may only be a nascent insight or a symptom of professional deformation. Nor is there a positive sign that he takes the daytime actions into account or sees their relation to his nocturnal sufferings. As a result, his words, comparing the inn to Hell and the pests to demons, rank as mere expletives. It is the reader who, at three removes from the events, must find the coherent, meaningful pattern hidden by the poet in the speaker's language and unreliable narration.

Man and the world remain physically inaccessible to each other, despite many and varied interpenetrations; likewise, the apprehension of order in the relationship between the two is difficult of attainment. The latter varies inversely with the nearness of consciousness to experience and the readiness of mind to impose its own relatively adequate structures on the evidence of the senses. Distance, then, is

David Lee Rubin

a mixed blessing in the domain of uncriticized experience as well as a prerequisite to knowledge, whether scientific or poetic. [4]

<hr>

[4] That the themes and theses of "Le Mauvais Logement" parallel certain preoccupations of the new science is not surprising. During the period between the conception and publication of this poem, Saint-Amant became conversant with the theories of Galileo and Campanella. A direct reference to current debates on astronomy occurs in his "Epistre à Monsieur le baron de Melay," also contained in the 1643 volume. For a full discussion of this and related matters, see Beverly S. Ridgely's important article, "Saint-Amant and 'The New Astronomy'," *Modern Language Review* 53 (1958), 26-37.

Jacqueline Van Baelen

Reality and Illusion in "L'Autre Monde": the Narrative Voyage

While *L'Autre Monde* has been studied primarily for the philosophical and scientific ideas it expresses in fictional form, it might be well to remember that it is also a very amusing and fantastic adventure novel concerning the experiences of its hero Dyrcona, both on earth and during his voyages to the moon and sun which occupy the major portion of the novel. Although the principal action of the novel takes place during these voyages, it may be useful to look more closely at the "earth" passages and at the way in which they are incorporated into the structure of the novel.

If we consider *L'Autre Monde* as a novel in two parts, each corresponding to one of the voyages, it seems clear that the earth passages were intended to frame the voyages and give unity and completeness to the novel by using a circular structure. This is indeed the case for the voyage to the moon; with the voyage to the sun, however, the return to earth is missing and the final passages show us Dyrcona conversing with Campanella on the nature of images and the way in which they are created. In terms of the structure of the novel, therefore, the earth passages can be considered as a normative point of reference for the voyages and can be equated with the commonplace reality of Dyrcona's world.

These passages, however, offer more than a useful yardstick to evaluate Dyrcona's adventures. We find in them a discussion, however brief, on the nature of art and the artist, for Dyrcona not only travels to hitherto unknown worlds, but decides to share his experiences and visions by writing about them. Thus, he encounters all the problems of the writer developing his work and, subsequently, as the object of criticism and ridicule. It may be said, therefore, that the earth passages also offer an exploratory voyage and commentary on the nature of art that parallels the voyages and observations of Dyrcona on the moon and sun.

There are four earth passages of varying length and importance in *L'Autre Monde*; three are to be found in the *Etats et Empires de la Lune* and the fourth serves as a link between the two parts of the novel. We shall examine them separately as they present different problems, both in terms of the structure of the novel and of the perspective they offer us on the nature of art and the role of the artist.

In the opening chapter of *Les Etats et Empires de la Lune,* reality consists of Dyrcona and his friends walking home on a moonlit night, feeling rather jovial and regaling themselves with comical fantasies on the nature of the moon:

> The moon was full, the sky was clear and nine o'clock had struck when, coming back from Clamart, near Paris (where M. de Cuigny the younger who owns it, had entertained me and several of my friends, the various thoughts that this saffron ball aroused in us, kept us amused along the road. So, with eyes fixed on this great heavenly body, one would take it to be one of Heaven's skylights through which the glory of the blessed could be glimpsed; another, believing ancient tales, thought that Bacchus was quite possibly running a tavern in the sky and that he had hung the full moon as its signpost; yet another insisted that it was the board on which Diana pressed Apollo's collars; another, that it might well be the sun himself who, having taken off his rays one night, was peering through a hole to see what was going on in the world when he was not there.
>
> As for me, said I, I would like to add my comments to yours, and without wasting time on fanciful word games with which you try to make time go faster, I would like to state that I believe the moon to be a world like ours for which our world is a moon.
>
> Some of my companions greeted my statement with a burst of laughter. [1]

The parody of religious and mythological motifs is sufficiently obvious not to merit further discussion. What is surprising, however, is the laughter evoked by Dyrcona's statement which certainly seems no more ludicrous than the burlesque images conjured up by his companions, and yet, he becomes the object of ridicule when he persists

---

[1] Cyrano de Bergerac, *Oeuvres,* ed. Georges Ribemont-Dessaignes (Paris, 1957), pp. 49-50. Translations of the text are my own and page references in subsequent quotations refer to the edition cited above.

in his notion. A quick analysis of the passage will show that Cyrano presents two points of view on imagination and its functions and on the artist or painter of images.

By poking fun slyly at mythological figures, and somewhat ir-reverently at religious beliefs, Dyrcona's friends emphasize the separa-tion between the world of reality (a clear moonlit night, jovial friends wending their way home), and that of illusion (Bacchus the tavern-keeper, Diana the laundress). Moreover, their fantasies are limited and quite specific: each is a small comical tableau depicting a familiar scene, complete in itself. No philosophical or metaphysical questions are raised. For Dyrcona's friends, their fantasies are a gratuitous product of their imagination with no aims or consequences, other than the hilarious deflation of imaginary creatures. Theirs is a momentary act of wit requiring no further thought or comment.

By positing the moon as a mirror world for the earth, however, Dyrcona injects a disturbing element in an otherwise harmless and silly discussion. For, if his assumption is to be considered at all, then the moon is no longer that silent, distant globe, clearly separated from earth and its activities. Lines and perspectives become blurred and merge, and the thought arises that if the moon is indeed a mirror image of the earth, then it is equally possible that, wending their way home on a clear earthlit night, a group of jovial friends will glance up at the earth and make comments about it in terms not too dis-similar from those of Dyrcona's friends. The novelty and implicit danger in Dyrcona's statement lies in its implications for both art and the artist, for imagination is no longer to be used exclusively to create entertaining fantasies devoid of serious intent nor is it to be limited in its scope. By presenting the moon as a mirror world, Dyrcona opens up the entire realm of human experience to the artist's scrutiny and suggests that fantasy and illusion can become sources of knowledge as valid as reality.

Consequently, as a new Prometheus, Dyrcona will set out on his journey in order to eventually bring back to his friends, the knowledge that he has acquired. His first attempt, however, is an abortive one and he finds himself in Canada. The entire Canadian episode is important, not only for the various philosophical discussions between Dyrcona and the Viceroy, but also because it points out quite dramatically that the real world of the colonies can seem as unreal and fantastic as any imaginary world, depending on one's knowledge, perspective and expectations. The natives who first encounter Dyrcona flee in fear because his appearance and behavior seem peculiar; Dyrcona is equally disoriented and surprised to find himself in a land both familiar and strange, where even a common language can lead to misunderstandings, as happens in his first encounter with the company of French soldiers. Throughout his discussions with the Viceroy, Dyrcona insists on the need for tolerance and open mindedness as a means of acquiring knowledge, even though he is himself considered a suspicious figure. Dyrcona's sojourn in Canada serves a dual purpose in the development of the novel, for in terms of the structure, it is a transitional episode which foreshadows the problems that he will encounter on the moon and subsequently, on earth; in terms of Dyrcona's original statement, the episode lends weight to the notion of an inhabited moon by pointing out that the real world is both strange and imaginary so long as it is unknown and undiscovered.

Dyrcona's successful departure and his various adventures on the moon finally come to an end, and he returns to earth, landing in Italy. This passage, the shortest one in *L'Autre Monde,* merely serves the conventional purpose of getting our hero back to earth and thence, to France, as quickly as possible. The short passage in which Dyrcona is attacked by dogs because he still carries the moon's aura about him once again pokes fun at superstitions but also prefigures Dyrcona's reception by critics in France. Here, he will get rid of the dogs by letting the sun purify him just as later, he will escape persecution and imprisonment by going to the sun.

The most important passage, however, is the lengthy opening chapter of *Les Etats et Empires du Soleil* which links both parts of *L'Autre Monde.* Dyrcona finds his friends, recounts his adventures and is prevailed upon to set them down on paper as *Les Etats et*

Empires de la Lune. He has become notorious and Cyrano gives us
an amusing and rather biting description of Dyrcona's literary success:

> Among those who read my book were many ignorant people who only
> leafed through it. But in order to appear as intelligent as their friends, they
> would applaud like them and even go so far as to clap their hands at every
> word for fear of making a mistake, and overcome with joy, they would cry
> out: "how marvelous!" at the passages they did not understand. But, supersti-
> tion masquerading as remorse whose teeth are only too sharp in a foolish man,
> so gnawed at their hearts that they preferred giving up being philosophers
> (which ill suited them), to having to account for this on Judgement Day.
>
> So now we had the other side of the coin with people fighting to be the
> first to recant. The book they had so prized was really nothing more than a
> potpourri of ridiculous stories, disconnected fragments and fairy tales fit only
> to put a child to sleep, and those who had not even opened the book con-
> demned the Author to light a candle to Saint-Mathurin.
>
> This division of opinion between the clever and the foolish merely increased
> the book's reputation. Shortly thereafter, manuscript copies were selling under
> the counter; everyone who was anyone, from the nobility down to the priests,
> bought the book: women even took sides and the quarrel went so far as to
> divide the city into two groups, the lunar and anti-lunar factions. (p. 149)

Dyrcona's popularity is short-lived and he quickly discovers that
he has become a controversial and suspicious figure, accused of
sorcery and diabolical magic practices. He realizes that his host M. de
Colignac is in a precarious position and he decides to seek refuge
with the Marquis de Cussan. Accordingly, he packs his belongings
and sets out on a journey he will not complete for he is ambushed
along the way and then, imprisoned in Toulouse. Cyrano gives a
detailed account of prison conditions and of Dyrcona's treatment at
the hands of his jailers which is sufficiently gruesome to make the
reader realize that by comparison, Dyrcona was treated more humane-
ly on the moon. Eventually, after failing in his first attempt to escape,
Dyrcona will succeed and journey to the sun.

While this lengthy passage does contain a caustic indictment of
justice and a satire on superstition, its main interest lies in Cyrano's
account of the way in which Dyrcona's adventures are received by
his countrymen. Here again, Cyrano blurs the lines separating reality

and illusion in order to give us a clearer perspective on Dyrcona's situation which reflects rather faithfully that of Cyrano and his friends. *L'Autre Monde* is after all, a novel about an author writing about his adventures. The fiction created by Cyrano is the reality or truth described by Dyrcona; we have, in a sense, a *novel within a novel* in which fictional reality (the earth passages) seems to mirror historical reality much as the moon seems to mirror the earth.

Cyrano's technique is not merely a useful device, for in the passages we have been discussing, he implicitly raises questions concerning the nature of art and artistic truth, concerning the nature of imagination and the artist's role as a *maker* of images. The two voyages are not only fanciful and amusing tales through which Cyrano can expound his philosophical ideas,[2] but also an *art poétique* in which the earth passages offer theories on the nature of art and on the artist's situation for which the voyages are examples or illustrations.

Cyrano's views on art and on the artist closely parallel his intuitions on philosophical and scientific problems. Rejecting traditional concepts, he advocates complete freedom in content and form. He elevates the role of fiction to a serious art, capable of imparting knowledge and of transforming man's perception of his world; it is perhaps not insignificant that he should have chosen the novel, the most formless and least regulated genre in seventeenth-century France, to express his ideas.

But what of the novel itself? The circular structure that works so well in the first part fails in the second part and we are left dangling with Dyrcona and Campanella discoursing on the nature of images. The ending is ambiguous and yet, perhaps the only viable ending. To bring Dyrcona back to earth is either to end his adventures or to repeat them *ad infinitum*. Instead, he leaves us with a description of a universe composed of images which can be directly imprinted on the soul; the novel opened with a discussion on the nature of images

---

[2] For a discussion of Cyrano's philosophical ideas, see Erica Harth, *Cyrano de Bergerac and the Polemics of Modernity*, (New York, 1970).

and Dyrcona has travelled from the sublunar world to the supralunar world of ideas and ideals. He has shed materiality and has escaped reality, but in so doing, he has also failed as Prometheus, for he has not been able to transform his world any more than Cyrano was able to change his.

Jacques Neefs

Cyrano: "Des Miracles de Rivière"

Sir,

With my stomach lying on a river's edge and my back
stretched out under the branches of a willow which is gazing
at itself in the waters, I shall recreate with trees the story
of Narcissus. One hundred poplars are throwing one hundred
other poplars into the waters, and these watery beings are
so horror-struck by this fall that they yet tremble each day,
moved by a wind that touches them not. I fancy that the
night has blackened all things, and that the sun is plunging
them into the water for a bath. But what can one say of
this liquid mirror, of this little upside-down world which
puts oak trees beneath moss and Heaven lower than the
oaks? Are these not among those virgins of time long past
transformed into trees who are throwing themselves head
over heels into this river as they despair at having their
chastity once again violated by Apollo's kisses? Or is it
not Apollo himself who hanged them by the feet, offended
that they should have dared to protect the coolness against
him? Today fish stroll in the woods, and entire forests appear in the midst of the waters without becoming wet. One
old elm, in particular, would make you laugh, for it has
rather draped itself across to the other bank so that its
reflection, taking quite the same pose, would form a hook
for the fish with its trunk and its reflection. The waters are
not unappreciative of the visit these willows pay it. The
river has bored right through the universe, lest the mud of
its bed soil their boughs, and, not content with having made
crystal out of mire, it spanned the Heavens and the Stars
down below so it could not be said that those who had
come to see it had lost the day-light they left for it. Now
we can lower our eyes to the Sky and day, weak though
it be at four o'clock, can now boast that it nevertheless
has the strength to cast Heaven into an abyss. But let us
admire the domain the lower reaches of the soul exercise
over the higher ones; after having discovered that this
whole wonder is only a trick of the senses, I can still not

185

stop my eyes from mistaking at least this imaginary Firmament for a vast lake on which the earth is floating. A nightingale, gazing at himself in the water from his perch in a tree, believes he has fallen into the river. He is at the top of an oak and yet fears drowning. But then, after dispelling his fear by feeling his feet and using his eyes again, and taking his self-portrait to be only another rival to fight, he warbles and chirps like him [and the other nightingale, too, chirps and warbles silently]—but so convincingly that one almost fancies he is both singing and yet not uttering a single word, so as to answer his enemy and at the same time not to violate the laws of the country he inhabits, whose citizens are mute. The perch, the dorado, and the trout which see him know not if it is a fish garbed in feathers or a bird despoiled of its body; they gather about, eyeing him as a monster; and the pike (that tyrant of rivers), in his jealousy at meeting a stranger on his throne, seeks him as he finds him, touches him and yet cannot feel him, pursues him in the midst of himself, and marvels at having passed so many times through him without wounding him. As for myself, I am so bedazzled that I am obliged to leave this picture. I beg you to refrain from censuring it, as it is difficult to opine concerning a shadow; for if my raptures should acquire a reputation for being greatly enlightened, it is not inconceivable that this picture's light should be found to be modest, having been taken down in the shade. And then, what other detail could I add to the description of this colored image except that it is a nothing you can see, a spiritual chameleon, a darkness which darkness itself causes to expire, a trial for the eyes and the mind, a lack of light which light itself brings into plain view, in short that it is a slave which is lacking no more from matter than is from the end of my letters, your Servant,

de B. [1]

The play of reflections is a known phenomenon. The early years of the 17th century manipulated the device enough for us to be used to it

[1] The French text of this letter will be found at the end of the present article. I have utilized the text of the Paris manuscript, BN, nouv. acq. fr. 4557, f. 173. The 1970 Garnier-Flammarion edition of *L'Autre Monde* quotes this letter, with one interesting omission (the passage indicated between square brackets). Indeed, the imperceptible transition between the real (?) nightingale and the reflected nightingale is thereby made even trickier. I should also add that this study arose from my surprise at this passage, which was made all the more unusual by the omission.

without being bored. [2] As a protraction of analogy, the interplay of reflections recreates the familiar in such a way that differences and quantitative characteristics cannot yet be distinguished, and it hinders the possibility of defining the objects involved, bathing them in a perception which is committed to illusion. However, this letter is characterized by a good deal more than extraordinary virtuosity.

Cyrano's letters on illusion are numerous (in particular his "Description de l'aqueduc ou la fontaine d'Arcueil" or the play on the river idea in his letter "Le Printemps," or in the description of Paradise in *L'Autre Monde*), but the attraction of these letters lies primarily in the fact that they always take the given theme to its limits, demonstrating in the end the omnipotence of writing, and the astonishing process of desire which it brings into being. As with other writers of the baroque (especially Saint Amant or Le Moyne), the present is the obligatory tense for writing, as it makes possible the presence of the desired image, and any text of this sort must be hypotypotic; to "somehow place before one's eyes" (to use Fontanier's definition of hypotyposis) "the colored image," the impossible image, a text must not only present a copy of the illusory effect but also produce the very work of illusion. Considered in this light, then, this letter is exemplary, with its continued present and sustained temporal proximity ("today," "now"), both of which orient a reading of the text toward the untenable and the intolerable (that which cannot reasonably be suggested but also that which cannot be endured), to the point where writing disintegrates: "as for myself, I am so bedazzled that I am obliged to leave this picture." The "picture" being more what the letter has just conjured up before our (the readers') eyes than just any scene reproduced. Cyrano, however, goes on: "... what other detail could I add to the description of this colored image except that it is a nothing you can see, a spiritual chameleon, a darkness which darkness itself causes to expire, a trial for the eyes and the

---

[2] Jean Rousset's investigations in this whole area are seminal. He has examined in depth the phenomena of dissociation, the power of the imaginary, deceptive appearances, and the criticism of illusion, particularly in his essay "Reflets dans l'eau," to be found in *L'Intérieur et l'Extérieur* (Paris, 1968), pp. 195 *ff.*

mind, a lack of light which light itself brings into plain view." Having arrived at the limits of the illusory process (the process is deliberate and explicitly stated at the beginning of the letter by Cyrano's affirmation of his aim: "...I shall recreate with trees the story of Narcissus"), the writer must still define what his writing has just attempted to grasp. This need to define is quickly incorporated into the "picture": "...but what can one say of this liquid mirror, of this little upside-down world..."

As it progresses toward this definition, the puns based on shadow and light point up the unusually divisive function of writing in Cyrano: "...it is difficult to opine concerning a *shadow* [*ombre*]; for if my raptures should acquire a reputation for being greatly *enlightened* [*éclairés*], it is not inconceivable that this picture's *light* [*lumière*] should be found to be modest, having been taken down in the *shade* [*ombre*]." The chiasmus is built on the metaphoric use of "enlightened" and "light" (the metaphor's "vehicle" [3] is, of course, borrowed from the description of dawn, the coming out into daylight and the look of the water being cleverly implied at the same time), but in order to separate as effectively as possible two meanings of the word "shadow," the first instance means an "appearance" or a "semblance" and the second refers to the initial position of the writer-observation, which is itself already divided and dividing, *in the shade* of a tree: "with my stomach lying on a river's edge and my back stretched out under the branches of a willow which is gazing at itself in the waters..." We may then interpret this rather indirect process as being the progression of the writing, going off into arabesques and tracing parallel lines, continually breaking apart and coming together again. With his "stomach lying on a river's bank" on the one hand, and his "back stretched out under the branches of a willow" on the other, Cyrano is writing at the very point where division splits his body, the spot where separate and ordinarily exclusive terms come together (the willow tree *gazes at itself* in the river). He himself becomes a mere

---

[3] If we distinguish carefully between "tenor" and "vehicle," according to Richards' terminology.

surface of conjunction and disjunction, a writing plane pure and simple.

The definition of the image-in-reflection only brings that much closer together those ambiguities that made the "picture" possible and sets forth its paradoxical logic, juxtaposing and combining as it does the terms and their divisions into five segments of increasing length: "a nothing you can see" and "a spiritual chameleon" actualize the alternative between the visible (palpable) and the spiritual, and the juxtaposition of the two definitions is already described as a "trial [*procès*] for the eyes and the mind." This isolates the two other segments in their parallel positions: "a darkness which darkness itself causes to expire" and "a lack of light which light itself brings into plain view." But why do we have this game to define exactly the paradoxal image, to define the production of the imaginary itself? [4]

The fact is that only one definition does not suffice, for in a single word and in a discreet utterance one can not completely state the paradoxical immediacy whose precise duty must be the articulation of divarications and contrasts. That which is absence (the negative meaning of "*rien*" already dominant in the 17th century) on the surface of reason is something (the positive meaning of "*rien*" still current in the 17th century) on the surface of the visible, of the perceptible. But *at the same time* it is absence itself ("*le rien*") which is made visible because it is an object ("*un rien*") capable of indefinite modification within the mind, because it can only take on the form and appearance of those things with which it finds itself contiguous (whence the chameleon or reflecting surface phenomenon). The same

---

[4] I differ here with Jean Rousset (*op. cit.*, p. 210) in believing that Cyrano does not make a genuine criticism of imagination. If expressions such as "the dominion the lower reaches of the soul exercise over the higher ones" and "this whole wonder is only a trick of the senses" suggest a severe criticism of imagination, I would suggest that it is also important to note a certain irony and read positively "let us admire" and "wonder," and above all such phrases as "I can still not stop my eyes" or "I beg you to refrain from censuring it, as it is difficult to opine concerning a shadow." Cyrano exhibits the character and the power of the imagination at the same time as he appears to indulge in a reasoned critique. Here again, Cyrano can write only *simultaneously* for and against imagination in much the same way as he writes elsewhere (albeit in two separate letters) for and against sorcerers. This is not any relativistic shillyshallying, only a desire to hold the contradictory in its own contradiction.

logic links the two other segments of the definition. That which is night or lack of light on the surface of reason (or of existence, *cf.* "shadow") expires or appears ("comes into plain view"—*"vient au jour"*—the writing here saturates the use of words) with night or with day's light (a visible, tangible surface). The collusion of terms here is astonishingly effective for juxtaposing and dividing, not to link opposites but to make the division of meanings and terms *work* and progress. And there is much more here than in a riddle text, where one must find the Name around which the definitions revolve, either by allusion to certain properties or representations of the object which is the riddle's aim, or by games using other words as intermediaries (*cf.* "sleep" in the "riddle on sleep": "I... am having done... what a little boy does to his wooden shoe when he whips it"). In the riddle, the missing term is gradually crystallized out of those categories and paradigms to which it can belong. Here the term is defined by its *simultaneous* membership in different orders and it is just the possibility of any distinction between parallel series of any spread into distinct paradigms (day/night; eyes/reason; being/nonbeing) which is grasped in the form of the object/fantasm (the being of the reflection in its elusiveness and not the thing reflected or the reflection of a thing), which must belong to both series without being more of one than of the other. With the convergence of all his definitions and the carefully set up tug-of-war with metaphors, Cyrano points to what we may call the *"différentiant,"* [5] that ambiguous term by which those categories that we place in contrasting and meaningful relationships are made to operate (and thereby made possible).

Syllepsis, or Nonexclusive Disjunction

Using this multiple definition as a starting point, we should return to the letter and to Cyrano. Indeed, we may now better understand the extraordinary method which contributes to the intricate interplay

[5] *Cf.* Gilles Deleuze, *La Logique du sens* (Paris, 1969), p. 66. The reader will easily recognize these observations' debt to Deleuze's analyses of Lewis Carrolls' paradoxes.

Jacques Neefs

of parts. From the beginning of the letter, there is of course a setting up in relationships of heterogeneous elements and the disturbance which arises thereby: in this case, air and water "a hundred poplars (air) are throwing [*précipitent*] into the river (in the etymological sense of "to throw in head first") a hundred other poplars (water); and these watery beings (water) are so horror-struck by their fall that they yet tremble every day from the wind (air) which touches them not." The chiasmus here reflects itself. [6] The subsequent "episodes" are developed from the same confusion—the old elm tree and especially the nightingale, whose status as a creature of the air predisposed him to some unusual feat. But on top of this confusion of elements, of itself a commonplace arising from a disorder in analogy, is a well-articulated usage of syllepsis: [7] *e.g.* "tremble," which belongs *at the same time* to the paradigm of terror ("are so horror-struck . . .") and to the paradigm of the physical phenomenon (" . . . by a wind") ("which touches them not" turns the paradox around and locks the sentence into its unsettled effect). Likewise, in the interpretation which follows the sentence we have just examined ("I fancy . . ."), "blackened" belongs both to that body of expressions pertaining to night and, with "is plunging them in the water for a bath," to that of dirt, And, what is more, the long mythological interpretation is also constructed on a syllepsis, an implicit one this time. We should first of all notice the astonishing over-determination in the use of the mythological chain, which in this sort of text is rarely as rich: the allusion to Daphne, the daughter of the river-god Peneus, is a commonplace, but it acquires individual force through its contiguity with the liquid surface, and above all it permits a mythologism for the coming of dawn: " . . . having their chastity once again violated by Apollo's kisses" (Apollo being the sun god). Finally, the two jux-

[6] The same occurs classically in baroque poetry: "fish (water) stroll in the woods (air), and entire forests (air) appear in the midst of the waters (water) without becoming wet," with the last three words pointing up the paradox.

[7] "Those mixed tropes which are called syllepses consist of taking a single word in two different senses simultaneously, one meaning being literal or supposedly so, but at least *proper*, and the other being figurative or supposedly so, even if it indeed is not always so." (Fontanier, *Les Figures du discours* [Paris, 1968], p. 105).

191

taposed interpretations ("are these not..." or "was it not") show how general the split is. The interpretations are produced by the highly organizing figure of the chiasmus (the virgins [Daphne]-Apollo/Apollo-the virgins ["they," "them"]) and are split apart by the double localizing reference: the phrase "who are throwing themselves head over heels" has as its presumed reference point the ground from which the observer views the scene (plunging from the air into the water); the phrase "(Apollo) hanged them by the feet" puts us in the dimension of fictional space (hanging from the ceiling of the water), and we may guess at the ambiguous term hidden in the two clauses or between them. This term, the driving force behind the juxtaposition, is none other than the syllepsis "shadow," which the conclusion of the letter develops most fully on both planes of meaning. The tree-nymphs become shadows (reflections, spectres, illusion) because they dared to make shade ("protect the coolness against [the sun]"). This last point will not seem all that debatable if we consider the workings of entire episodes in the *Voyage dans la lune,* those impressive narrative apparatuses which are deployed to justify, explain, and take literally either implicit or explicit proverbial expressions (*cf.* "a land where larks fall from the sky fully roasted," and the episode of "friendly cannibalism," [*cannibalisme amical*] to use Maurice Blanchot's expression). [8]

What is of interest to us in this usage of syllepsis is its capacity to expand in equal series: all subordination of the proper and the figurative consequently appears as totally unsuitable, inasmuch as it is on the contrary a question of multiplying paradigms around the point-sign, the divisive word which is its meeting place and division. Fontanier's treatise, that delayed and self-appointed echo of the classical ethos, dismisses syllepsis as being a "frigid misuse of the mind,"

---

[8] *Cf.* Maurice Blanchot's article on Cyrano de Bergerac in *Tableau de la littérature française de Rutebeuf à Descartes* (Paris, 1962): "*L'Autre Monde* gives one the impression of a world in which words seek out their own meaning; without any clash, these words appear to be innocently and falsely surprised to be ahead of or behind their meanings" (p. 561). This race for meaning, with all the splits it implies, is undoubtedly the most remarkable element in Cyrano and what makes his writing one perpetual excess.

a "ridiculous exaggeration," [9] an aberration in reason and taste. But Cyrano ridicules this indignation by the generalized splitting with which he follows the syllepsis everywhere. It is only at this point, he tells us, that there exists a productive force of the imaginary, of writing, causing as it does disparate series and separate waves of words to pass by a single point while at the same time keeping the disjunction firmly implanted.

In so doing, Cyrano goes very much beyond the fight over metaphor which had so divided the beginning of the 17th century. If, in fact, as Jean Rousset has shown, [10] the "relative dying out of the metaphor" in the 17th century is due to the repression of analogical thought by post-Galilean science, then Cyrano shifts the whole question around by showing yet another possibility of thought. At stake is not the formulation of metaphors which wrap up analogous areas in a unity or which blur boundaries to maintain a viewpoint composed of similitudes; nor is it a question of expanding the number of optical tricks into generalized anamorphoses in order to see "one object in another," [11] to state ultimately that everything is in everything and thereby proclam universal unity. On the contrary, disjunction needs to be lived and pursued to the breaking point: "I am so bedazzled." In opposition to defining by differences and identities and by those exclusive syntheses which will order his century, Cyrano underlines the productive, inclusive and non-limiting use of disjunctive syntheses: "a disjunction which remains disjunctive, and yet affirms the terms disjoined, affirms them regardless of all the distance separating them, without limiting the one by the other nor excluding the one from the other—this is perhaps the most sophisticated paradox." [12] Cyrano postulates the generalization of the schizoid position. This is what is profoundly subversive in Cyrano and scandalous in his century (and later centuries, besides). Roland Barthes has noted that a paradigm is very moralistic: "to each thing its season, let us

[9] Fontanier, op. cit., p. 107.
[10] Cf. Jean Rousset's "La Querelle de la métaphore" in L'Intérieur et l'extérieur, p. 57 ff.
[11] Cf. Jean Rousset, op. cit., p. 68.
[12] Gilles Deleuze and Felix Guattari, Capitalisme et schizophrénie: l'Anti-Oedipe (Paris, 1972), p. 90

not mix things up . . . and that this is the way meaning, that dispenser of law, clarity and security, will be established." [13] Cyrano's writing exists precisely to blur meaning, not to say "one thing for another" but "always two things at once"—never mixed together, but held very far apart from very close by, around a single element which effectively halts any and all superpositioning or identification. [14]

In this connection, the dissymetry in the paradoxical play, "if it is a fish garbed in feathers or a bird despoiled of its body" is remarkable. Baroque analogies take a statement by the spot where it is exactly reversible: "one wonders whether the bird is swimming or the fish is flying." [15] Cyrano is interested not in the confusion of opposites but in the definition of the paradoxical position. The nightingale is indeed a "monster," a body *and* a portrait, [16] but it is a body without identity (a fish covered with feathers) and a portrait without a body (a bird despoiled of its body). The laws of water and sky are juxtaposed in the nightingale without being confused (the bird sings and must be silent *all at the same time*) and if it is out of its element in the water, the reason is simply that it is not there. This then is the meaning of the stunning capture script which leads to the limits of the thinkable, a genuine performance of the object/fantasm, whose essence is to be real without substance, whose function it is always to be out of place and to be merely a floating effect—a true u-topia.

It seems hardly necessary to add that the subversive function of this paradoxical real quality is suggested by some curiously novel

[13] Roland Barthes, *Sade, Fourier, Loyola* (Paris, 1972), p. 155.

[14] The study of analogical figures should probably be re-approached from a point of view different than that of similitude. Theory on what makes up this duplicity is strangely lacking. In the extended formula for the analogical figure, which may be enunciated as "my love burns like a flame" (*cf.* Gérard Genette's excellent table "La Rhétorique restrainte" in *Figures III* [Paris, 1972], p. 130), what is most interesting is the *reason* for the comparison (the "ground" in Richards' terminology). The reason may be implicit (for example, in a simple metaphor, "my flame"), but this reason is always present as a divisive figure, as the paradoxical point of these inclusive and nonlimiting syntheses which are analogical figures.

[15] Habert de Cerisy, quoted by Jean Rousset, *Anthologie de la poésie baroque* (Paris, 1961), I, p. 245.

[16] The whole problem of the body and the portrait is explicitly presented here: the old elm tree forms "a hook for the fish with the trunk and its reflection."

Jacques Neefs

phrases: "we can now lower our eyes to the sky," "throw the heavens into abysses," and "the pike (that tyrant of rivers), in his jealousy at finding a stranger on his throne." Indeed, to the tyrant and the hierarchy of a throne, to the high position of the sky, is always opposed the affirmative existence of disjunction, which overthrows orders, topples scales and disrupts—as a foreign element.

Transversality

We may properly conclude these remarks with a glance toward the traveler from Earth to the Moon. Indeed, the Narrator of *L'Autre Monde* is in exactly the same position as the paradoxical object—he is out of place on Earth and he is out of place on the Moon. In order to position spaces (epistemological, political, social, and moral) in disjunction without exclusion, one must travel through them without pause at the fastest possible speed in a nondecomposable space. Then we "do not cease wandering, we change person as well as sex, and leaving becomes as simple as birth and death." [17] The narrator might be a man on Earth or a bird on the Moon, but he is also a bird on the Earth (he flies toward the Moon) and a man on the Moon (he maintains the earthly discourse). He may be male on Earth and female on the Moon. This does not mean he is a hermaphrodite, which is a unitary notion from analogical and alchemical thought. Quite the opposite is true: the most important thing is always to be at the greatest distance from oneself, adrift in a sea which washes away sex and identity (*cf.* the Canadian episode and the France— New France relationship). Cyrano is supremely indifferent to any unity of the subject and reveals that productivity of thought processes which the Cartesian revolution would relegate to the order of the rational subject.

The paradoxical position is nowhere better defined than in the description of the passage (onto the moon): "I found myself sud-

[17] Deleuze and Guattari, *op. cit.,* p. 101.

195

denly falling, with my feet up, without having somersaulted at all." [18]
What changes is the verb: I rise in relation to the Earth, but I fall,
"suddenly," in relation to the Moon. The position of the body-object
does not change ("without having somersaulted at all"), it merely
comes to the intersection of two series, it belongs in one form to one
and in another form to the other. This appearance, however, is always
contradictory in relation to the series in which it is operating, and
the narrator is overcome by a passion for exclusion. He, too, can
only be a stranger, out of place, for he is the utopia which permits
the seriality of spaces, theories and epistemologies. [19]

The narrator's body always lends an ear to all discourses—it does
in fact have two and this is precisely where everything is disturbed
and where everything functions. For the other ear is already prepared
for the Other discourse, in the same way that I, with my feet on the
Earth, am already prepared for the Other world, towards which my
head is already falling. Thus Cyrano, with his rapid, furtive flights,
passes through all transversals; [20] for the frenzied "schizo's walk"
leads him as nearly as possible to a point of coincidence with the
production of the real—and it is with this perspective in mind that
we should read *Les Etats et empires du soleil,* which are by definition
never-ending.

Translated by Charles S. Fineman

---

[18] *Voyage dans la lune* (Garnier-Flammarion), p. 41.

[19] The cohabitation of contradictory reports has been frequently noted,
particularly in the long lunar conversations. But, far from being a confusion
in Cyrano's scientific thought supposed as caught between two "épistémés," the
one incompletely forgotten and the other incompletely accepted, this juxtaposition situates us at the very center of production of discursive formations.

[20] It would be interesting to situate Cyrano in relation to that dimension
of transversality described by Felix Guattari as being "the opposite and
complementary dimension to the generative structures of pyramidal hierarchisa-
tion" (*Psychanalyse et transversalité* [Paris, 1972], p. 84).

Jacques Neefs

DES MIRACLES DE RIVIERE

Monsieur,

Le ventre couché sur le gazon d'une rivière, et le dos étendu sous les branches d'un saule qui se mire dedans, je vais renouveler aux arbres l'histoire de Narcise; cent peupliers précipitent dans l'onde cent autres peupliers: et ces aquatiques ont été tellement épouvantés de leur chute, qu'ils tremblent encore tous les jours, du vent qui ne les touche pas. Je m'imagine que la nuit ayant noirci toutes les choses, le soleil les plonge dans l'eau pour les laver; mais que dire de ce miroir fluide, de ce petit monde renversé, qui place les chênes au-dessous de la mousse, et le Ciel plus bas que les chênes? Ne sont-ce point de ces vierges de jadis métamorphosées en arbres, qui désespérées de sentir encore violer leur pudeur par les baisers d'Apollon, se précipitent dans ce fleuve la tête en bas? Ou n'est-ce point qu'Apollon lui-même, offensé qu'elles aient osé protéger contre lui la fraîcheur, les aient ainsi pendues par les pieds? Aujourd'hui le poisson se promène dans les bois, et des forêts entières sont au milieu des eaux sans se mouiller; un vieil orme, entre autres, vous ferait rire, qui s'est quasi couché jusque dessus l'autre bord, afin que son image prenant la même posture, il fît de son corps et de son portrait un hameçon pour la pêche. L'onde n'est pas ingrate de la visite que ces saules lui rendent; elle a percé l'univers à jour, de peur que la vase de son lit ne souillât leurs rameaux, et non contente d'avoir formé du cristal avec de la bourbe, elle a voûté des Cieux et des Astres par dessous, afin qu'on ne pût dire que ceux qui l'étaient venus voir eussent perdu le jour qu'ils avaient quitté pour elle. Maintenant nous pouvons baisser les yeux au Ciel, et par elle le jour se peut vanter que tout faible qu'il est à quatre heures, il a pourtant la force de précipiter le Ciel dans des abîmes. Mais admirez l'empire que la basse région de l'âme exerce sur la haute; après avoir découvert que tout ce miracle n'est qu'une imposture des sens, je ne puis encore empêcher ma vue de prendre au moins ce Firmament imaginaire pour un grand lac sur qui la terre flotte. Le rossignol, qui du haut d'une branche se regarde dedans, croit être tombé dans la rivière: il est au sommet d'un chêne, et si il a peur de se noyer; mais lorsqu'après s'être affermi de l'œil et des pieds, il a dissipé sa frayeur, son portrait ne lui paraissant plus qu'un rival à combattre, il gazouille, il éclate, il s'égosille,

(et cet autre rossignol, sans rompre le silence s'égosille)
comme lui; mais si vraisemblablement qu'on se figure presque qu'il chante, et ne dit mot tout ensemble, pour répondre
en même temps à son ennemi, et pour n'enfreindre pas les
lois du pays qu'il habite, dont le peuple est muet; la perche,
la dorade, et la truite qui le voient, ne savent si c'est un
moisson vêtu de plumes, ou si c'est un oiseau dépouillé de
son corps; elles s'amassent autour de lui, le considèrent
comme un monstre; et le brochet (ce tyran des rivières),
jaloux de rencontrer un étranger sur son trône, le cherche en
le trouvant, le touche et ne le peut sentir, court après lui
au milieu de lui-même, et s'étonne de l'avoir tant de fois
traversé sans le blesser. Moi-même, j'en demeure tellement
consterné que je suis contraint de quitter ce tableau. Je vous
prie de suspendre sa condamnation, puisqu'il est malaisé de
juger d'une ombre; car quand mes enthousiasmes auraient
la réputation d'être fort éclairés, il n'est pas impossible que la
lumière de celui-ci soit petite, ayant été prise à l'ombre;
et puis, quelle autre chose pourrais-je ajouter à la description de cette image enluminée, sinon que c'est un rien
visible, un caméléon spirituel, une nuit que la nuit fait
mourir, un procès des yeux et de la raison, une privation
de clarté, que la clarté met au jour: enfin que c'est un es-
clave qui ne manque non plus à la matière qu'à la fin de
mes lettres, votre Serviteur,

de B.

Maurice Laugaa

Cyrano: Sound and Language

Completely absorbed in a language of which he is both cause and effect, the author establishes in certain segments of his discourse theoretical regions in which language is conceived as object. These mirrors, these mechanisms in Cyrano's utopian narrative cross fire, cross paths. Since Maurice Blanchot, the narrative function of metaphors has been recognized. But less well-known, in the context of theater, are the "vers équivoques" [ambiguous lines], the "vers qui cachent un autre sens" [lines concealing another meaning], with which Agrippine reveals the ruse of a plan to which the subject falls victim, in that murder of the signifier which duplicates the death of Germanicus.[1] Finally, the hypothesis and representation of other languages in the *Etats et Empires de la lune et du soleil* open up another scene in the narrative.[2] This use of language poses the question of metalanguage to the text itself, even as it questions the possibility of such a metalanguage. It engages the subject and its figures (author, narrator, reader) in a process of transformations and shifts which the signified of the travel narrative simultaneously sustains and reactivates, but without permitting the sign and its referent to be sorted into two heterogeneous (noncommunicating) areas.

We will limit our scope here to the observation of how Cyrano's narrative[3] represents and produces its origin by duplicating the enunciation of the Other language with an enunciation upon the Other

---

[1] Savinien Cyrano de Bergerac, *La Mort d'Agrippine veuve de Germanicus, tragédie* (Paris, 1654). See, III. 2 and 4; IV. 3.

[2] All references are to the following edition: Cyrano de Bergerac, *Histoire comique des Etat et Empire de la Lune et du Soleil,* texte établi et présenté par Claude Mettra et Jean Suyeux (Paris, 1962).

[3] More precisely, here, the *Soleil.* Nonetheless, the *Lune* makes its presence felt in two ways: it is mentioned by the narrator of the *Soleil;* it functions, less evidently, according to the same model.

of language; of how the narrator produces, besides the construction (or reemployment) of codes—matrix language on the sun, lunar idioms—a more fluid, more disseminated matter, whose differences prevent us from positing their identity at the outset. *Bruit* (noise, sound, pure sound), in Cyrano's narrative, may be taken as that raw material of discourse whose articulations will repeat, represent a genesis.

In order to "situate" the hypothesis, an exhaustive list of the uses of the word has been compiled using the sentence as its context. [4] This chart should be completed with a list of other series: shouts, whinnies, uproars, outbursts. [5] The reading we propose here of these signs scattered throughout the text of the *Soleil* only breaks the ground for a generalized reading of the Alternations and Alterations which occur in numerous examples in the rest of his work. [6]

Though fragmentary, this reading is nonetheless subordinated to the limits posed by the nature of the questioning itself. What, indeed, is to be made of a procedure which tends to set apart a few sentences in a corpus, whose only common feature happens to be a particular word? Fearing that he might distort the meaning of that word by removing it from its immediate context, the critic assumes that the limits of the sentence are sufficiently stable to allow an abstraction of the larger context. But a legitimate question still remains as to whether the reader has the right to confuse the identity of the signifier with that of its meaning. While phonetically [bryi] remains the same, the semantic and syntactical variations of *bruit* forbid us from insisting upon the priority of sameness over difference so as to place the latter in a previously closed set.

[4] See this list at the end of the present article. All translations are from the Aldington translation mentioned in note 7.

[5] Cf. also the use of the verb *bruire:* pp. 195 and 215; and of the adjective *bruissant:* p. 240.

[6] In the *Lune,* of course, but also in the letters: see, particularly, the *Satire contre Soucidas* [*Dassoucy*]: "Quand je vous contemple si décharné, je m'imagine que vos nerfs sont assez secs et assez préparés pour exciter, en vous remuant, ce bruit que vous appelez langage...." In Cyrano de Bergerac, *Voyage dans la lune* [suivi de *Lettres diverses*], éd. Maurice Laugaa (Paris, 1970), p. 158. "When I look at you so emaciated as you are, I imagine your nerves to be dry and ready enough for me to provoke, by shaking you, the noise you call language...." (trans. T. J. R.).

Maurice Laugaa

We shall not attempt an answer here by reference to the tenets of any particular theory of discourse or narrative, but will only try to consider under which conditions we might conceive of the possibility of a meaningful examination of the sign *bruit,* knowing this to be in some degree a utopian desire in that it pretends to set aside all consideration of positivities and probabilities.

The following, then, represent the conditions of our examination: 1) We hold the two preliminary questions above to be unresolvable, though by the same token necessary; 2) We must expose the definition of *bruit* to a twofold interrogation: what is to be made, in a theory of referent and sign, of a noun *(bruit)* which marks an ambiguity of signification, such that we are witness to the dynamics of a sign cancelling itself in the opacity of a nonsignifying reference? And what is to be made of the status and positions of the enunciation's subject in the fulfilling of a meaning?

Depending on the spatial representation in which we place the definition of meaning, we will obtain different values: an arrangement of usages in the columns of a dictionary gives rise to a twofold transformation of meaning:

—discontinuities are accentuated
—the spatiality of the chart slurs over the hypothesis of an expansion of meaning.

But both dictionary and user register an *acte de parole:* its rooting/ uprooting in the shout *(cri)* and pure sound *(bruit)* and its musical and gestural continuities presuppose less the preexistence of a repertoire or code than they do the continual construction of an expanding space. And this spatial expansion is closely related to the *acte de parole.* The piling-up of meanings within the signifying envelope is only a metaphor. The production of sound and its reception, the intertwining of speech and nonspeech, imply that at a precise point of a discursive chain, the force of the context upon the word produces a meaning whose differentiation is to be understood as a simulacrum of the differential play in the sound/speech relationship.

This expansion of meaning within a defined space can be read in Cyrano's text through a system of equivalences and metaphors.

We will begin by referring to the episode of the speaking trees (where passages 11 and 12 come in). The way in which the sequences are linked is significant: the narrator, 1) allows himself to fall asleep, 2) is awakened with a start "par un bruit incertain de voix confuses" [by an indistinct noise of confused voices], 3) succeeds in identifying "le murmure" which surrounds him, for the trees are speaking Greek. During a first period, the narrator intercepts the remarks that are being exchanged without his own presence having been noticed. In a second, several voices mingle together, "qui disaient qu'assurément elles sentaient un homme" [(which said) that assuredly they perceived a man]. An exchange of information next ensues in which the narrator confirms that there is indeed a man present and in which he asks to know the source of the voices so as to identify his interlocutors. This is followed in turn by the story concerning the transfer of Dodona's oak trees to the sun by the intermediary of an eagle which had eaten and regurgitated acorns. But communication, once established, is not exhausted by the commentary on its own possibility and its own existence. It tends to represent itself as the mediator of a knowledge which the narrator may not grasp directly:

encore que vous nous entendiez parler une langue humaine, ce n'est pas à dire que les autres arbres s'expliquent de même; il n'y a rien que nous autres chênes, issus de la forêt de Dodone, qui parlions comme vous; car pour les autres végétants, voici leur façon de s'exprimer. N'avez-vous point pris garde à ce vent doux et subtil, qui ne manque jamais de respirer à l'orée des bois? C'est l'haleine de leur parole; et ce petit murmure ou ce bruit délicat dont ils rompent le sacré silence de leur solitude, c'est proprement leur langage. Mais encore que le bruit des forêts semble toujours le même, il est toutefois si différent, que chaque espèce de végétant garde le sien particulier, en sorte que le bouleau ne parle pas comme l'érable, ni le hêtre comme le cerisier (pp. 223-24). [7]

[7] "But although you hear us speak a human language, it does not mean that other trees express themselves in the same way; only those oaks issued from the forest of Dodona speak as you do. As to other plants, this is how they express themselves: have you ever noticed that fine gentle breeze which never fails to breathe on the outskirts of woods? That is the breathe of their speech, and the little murmur or the delicate noise by which they break the

Maurice Laugaa

The equivalence *BRUIT*/LANGUAGE is formulated here at the conclusion of a testing in which the subject plays its part. The sensitivity of the narrator to the "voices," his recognition of the Other as interlocutor, creates the conditions of a discourse of the Other in which this last establishes, on the basis of a third party, the equation *BRUIT*/LANGUAGE. The preceding exchange cannot, then, be reduced to the giving of a formula. Speech does not tend towards the accomplishment of its conclusion. It extends indefinitely the field of enunciation. But this is also because the subject of speech, in silence and sleep, unravels the already present portion of the possible relationship in the confusion of voices. [8] By means of a necessary return to the reader ("soyez attentif, car je crois parler, en vous parlant, à tout le genre humain" [9]), the narrator indicates incidentally that the place of the Other is empty and remains indefinitely to be occupied.

The other values of the word *bruit* represent, in various ways, the pull towards an identity which fails to be reached. Such is the case of all the propositions in which the contiguity *bruit/parole, bruit/cris, bruit/mots* (passages 5, 6, and 7) implies within the opposition and resolution of differences, the see-sawing of sameness (see also, 13). This is also the case for the metaphorical relationships between the unheard and the heard, where the solar sounds are defined as an absence whose place is occupied by the narrator, in this sliding movement of writing, by whose means the master of metaphor plays with a fiction to evoke the reality of elementary sounds (passages 15,

---

silence of their solitude is actually their language. But although the sound of forests always seems the same, it is really so different that every kind of plant has its own; the birch does not speak like the maple, nor the beech like the cherry tree." *Voyages to the Moon and Sun,* trans. Richard Aldington (London, [c. 1923?]), p. 264.

[8] Sleep here does not only fulfill a function of discontinuity [*rupture*] in the narration. It represents at once an absorbing by the subject of the "*fraîcheur*" and the "*solitude,*" and (despite the narrative's fall into verisimilitude: for the narrator wakes up) a contiguity between repose, interval, and interpretation of noises.

[9] "... be attentive therefore, since when I speak to you I imagine I am speaking to the whole human race." Speech of the "arboreal voice" (Aldington trans., p. 265).

16, 17, and 20. Passages 2 and 5 function according to a closely similar model).

From this point of departure we might indicate areas in Cyrano's text corresponding to distinct phases in the *bruit*/language conversion process. The narrative would be taken as constructed, partially, on the basis of a de-construction of an initial formula: *JE PARLE : DU BRUIT*. By deciphering simultaneously the scope of *bruit* and the scope of language one would obtain for each of the places (terrestrial prisons; sojourn among the little men; among the birds; among the trees) a different musical phrase, and one articulated upon this very difference.

The sounds of the earth (passages 1-8), in their various values, are sounds of war. The Other always announces himself as a threat. Inscribed in the interval between two voyages, they result really from the author's initiative: [10] the *bruit* "false news" provokes the publication of the *Etats et Empires de la lune* (passage 1), which in turn provokes the *bruit* "reputation" (passage 2) (author/sorcerer), and which then provokes imprisonment, pursuit and their noises of panic (passages 4-8). In this way, the noise of others is provocation to travel; but this provocation originates in the evocation by the subject of an initial voyage. The anonymous crowd, crossing and confounding the lines of circulation in an immense space, is in confrontation to the pure trajectory of experience. The bolting in of noise and its unbolting (the keys are an ambiguous signal of a change of place: see passages 4 and 8) form the basis of the subject of the phantasm. The subject of the narrative is not an identity, which an academic definition would confirm: it is this potential of forces and transits whose encounter with a (dis-)oriented field leads not to the production of a true verbal series *(parole)* but to the auto-destruction of its messages, and can only engender listeners whom it forthwith betrays. In other words, all syntagms, all sentences in which the word *bruit* is one of the components, cannot be interpreted outside the meaning

---

[10] It would be appropriate here to examine the distortions caused by writing, as mnemonic technique and figure, upon a representation of sound, echo, oral narrative and ... noise.

imposed by the subject of the discourse: the narrator, whether retracing his solar adventures or relating his earthly misadventures in transit between two voyages, does not absent himself from his project as he notes the variations of volumes of sonority. This constitutional relationship between what is enunciated and the act of enunciation must be taken in a very precise, even restrictive, way: advancing one level, the representation of discourse intends to be understood as an operation upon sonorous material, which places in question any radical rupture between discourse and nondiscourse, and which constitutes the very subject of this process. *Against mere noise, I speak; from this mere noise I attain speech.*

The episode of the speaking trees may be taken inversely to correspond to the formulation: *noise speaks to me,* by the supposition of a regular permutation of the complements: *noise speaks to me, of myself (Je)/of noise,* and indeed of subjects: *I speak of noise which speaks to me.*

The two other episodes of the *Soleil* which exploit the relationship narrator/*bruit,* i. e. the battle between the remora and the salamander, and the description of the streams of the Five Senses and of the Three Rivers, [11] may be taken as illustrating two other types of transformation:

1. The elementary opacity is reformed. Noise, however, rediscovers its values as signal, it organizes the progression; while, on the other hand, invoking metaphor (see above), it involves the "present" reader by so doing in a decoding of meaning.

2. Campanella's discourse, intermingled with the narrator's sleep, expresses the relationship between Hearing and Memory, and concludes with this denial: "la plus grande part des philosophes ne parlent pas avec la langue; mais quand ils veulent communiquer leur pensée, ils se purgent par les élans de leur fantaisie d'une sombre vapeur..." (p. 261). [12]

[11] Since the last example (sentence 20) fits, no doubt, into another series (missing); it is included, all the same, in the series *bruit*/metaphor.

[12] "The greater part of the philosophers do not even speak with their tongue but, when they desire to communicate their thought, they purge

These two episodes may be considered as stating the relationship of subject and sign according to two complementary modalities: on the one hand, in order to give verbal form to *bruit,* I must go beyond language, I must record the material experience of thunder and hot iron; on the other, the repetition of sound and speech must disappear before the transparency and the writing of meaning: "quand il (the philosopher) parle en soi-même, on remarque clairement les espèces, c'est-à-dire les caractères de chaque chose qu'il médite, qui s'imprimant ou se soulevant, viennent présenter aux yeux de celui qui regarde, non pas un discours articulé, mais une histoire en tableau de toutes ses pensées" (p. 262). [13]

Between earthly noises and solar noises is interpolated the meeting with the man of the "little World," who speaks an unheard of language which is yet completely intelligible to the narrator (pp. 170ff.). The Other language, contrary to the lunar idioms, which can be mastered by a foreigner after an apprenticeship, offers the paradox of being closer to the subject than is his "mother" tongue without ceasing —despite this—to maintain the subject in all his difference: indeed, each individual understands the other, but each speaks *his* language. This attempt to displace and pin down difference, without absorbing it in the task of memorization, permits us to account for a detail which is in itself meaningless. The meeting with "le petit homme tout nu assis sur une pierre" [little man entirely naked sitting on a stone] (p. 170) coincides in the text with a gap in memory: "je ne me souviens pas si je lui parlai le premier, ou si ce fut lui qui m'interrogea" [I do not remember if I spoke the first or if he questioned me]. This gap is the site of a continuous slurring of the subjects as masters of discourse. To be sure, the mastery of the Other is confirmed by the superiority of knowledge, but speech present itself as the anticipation of an eventual reflection upon the subjects of the nondifferentiation of

themselves by a sally of their fantasy of a dark vapour..." (Aldington trans., p. 302).

[13] "When he [the philosopher] speaks to himself the elements, that is to say, the character of everything he is meditating upon, are clearly seen either impressed or in relief, presenting before the eyes of the onlooker not an articulated speech, but a pictured story of his thoughts" (Aldington trans., p. 303).

names and things, of men and beasts. The matrix language represents the limit case within the system noise/language. The experience of the Other as a passage through pure sound is annulled. It is all the more interesting that Cyrano's text should partially contradict the rules it establishes. A little further on in fact, the narrator begs the king of the little men to tell the story of the nightingale:

"Ma foi! me dit-il, excuse une personne qui se sent déjà hors d'haleine. Comme dans un corps étroit, j'ai les poumons serrés, et la voix par conséquent si déliée, que je suis contraint de me peiner beaucoup pour me faire ouïr, le rossignol trouvera bon de parler lui-même de soi-même. Qu'il chante donc si bon lui semble! Au moins nous aurons le plaisir d'écouter son histoire en musique." Je lui répliquai que je n'avais point encore assez d'habitude au langage d'oiseau; que véritablement un certain philosophe que j'avais rencontré en montant au soleil, m'avait bien donné quelques principes généraux pour entendre celui des brutes; mais qu'ils ne suffisaient pas pour entendre généralement tous les mots, ni pour être touché de toutes les délicatesses qui se rencontrent dans une aventure telle que devait être celle-là (p. 187). [14]

This ambiguity—which could be interpreted as a weakness in narrative technique—marks in fact the necessity of reestablishing difference within sameness, and time as a condition for a possibility of meaning. All discourse of the Other conceals a measure of pure sound; all "reflected" discourse requires its third person.

The new language, defined by its difference from other languages and by the internal play of its own differences, [15] in the leap from

[14] " 'By my faith, you must excuse a person who is already out of breath. I have crowded lungs in a little body and my voice is consequently so weak that I am forced to strain to make myself heard. I hope the nightingale will speak for himself. Let him sing if he wishes, and we shall at least have the pleasure of hearing his story in music.' I replied that I was not yet sufficiently practised in the language of birds; that, indeed, a certain philosopher whom I had met on my way to the Sun had given me some general principles to understand that of the beasts, but that they were not enough to understand all words in general, nor enough for me to be moved by all the delicate points which would be met with in an adventure such as this must be" (Aldington trans., p. 226).

[15] One should come back, here, to the *Lune,* so as to examine the difference between the lunar languages and to show how other moments of the narrative reveal the meeting of languages. Thus the meeting with the "vieillard olivâtre" [old man, yellow as an olive], in New France, in which the final remark concerning the common language underlines the ever-open possibility of non-communication. The other language is immediately deciphered as a non-language.

nonknowledge to knowledge, neutralizes its reverse side, the root of difference that is to say, a time for the subject of a knowledge based upon a twofold relationship with others (my language as noise for the Other/ the Other's language as noise for me). Noise, as a reserve of differences, displays the differentiation of its subjects as the possibility of a difference of languages and their articulation. While the subject studying the Other language enters into the play of intervals which throws him off center, the time of *bruit,* eliminating identification of language and of the subject with his language, represents this time of Otherness as the subject of differentiation.

I would like to note, in conclusion, though this would be the matter of another text, that upon this mounting and descending scale between "here" and "elsewhere," the narrator's return is not equivalent to the return "here" of Other languages; [16] these are lacking where the narrating subject presents himself to us as the (forbidden) locus of this differentiation.

Translated by Marla Kaplan

List of occurrences of the word "bruit"

Earth

1. "Mais, bons dieux! il n'est donc pas vrai le bruit qui courut que vous aviez été brûlé en Canada, dans ce grand feu d'artifice duquel vous fûtes l'inventeur?" (p. 130) "But, Good Gods! it is not true then [as rumour had it] that you were burned in Canada in the great firework display you had invented?" (pp. 167-68)

2. "J'apprehende que le bruit dont ils ont éclaté ne soit le tonnerre de la foudre qui s'ébranle pour choir" (p. 134). "I apprehend that the noise they broke out with is the thunder of the storm set in motion before falling" (pp. 171-72).

3. "Tout le monde, attiré par ce bruit, prenait prétexte de venir voir le seigneur pour voir le sorcier" (p. 135). "Everyone, attracted by these

16 Il one does not take into account—but one must—the return of proper names, in the *Lune.*

rumours, found some pretext for visiting the Seigneur to see the sorcerer" (p. 173).

4. "Je vainquis là pourtant toute la dureté de deux heures très difficiles, quand le bruit d'une grosse de clefs, jointe à celui des verrous de ma porte, me réveilla de l'attention que je prêtais à mes douleurs" (p. 145). "Nevertheless I overcame there the duration of two very difficult hours when the noise of twelve dozen keys added to that of the bolts on my door drew me from the consideration of my miseries" (p. 183).

5. "Enfin ma peur subornant ma raison, chaque homme me semblait un archer; chaque parole, *arrêtez,* et chaque bruit, l'insupportable croassement des verrous de ma prison passée" (p. 150). "At last my fear debauched my reason and I imagined every man was an archer, every word "arrest" and every noise the unendurable creaking of the bolts in my late prison" (p. 188).

6. "A peine étais-je là, que j'entendis les cris de cette enrouée populace longtemps avant le bruit de leurs pieds" (p. 152). "I had scarcely done this when I heard the noise of this hoarse-throated populace long before the sound of their feet" (p. 190).

7. "Comme ces charitables médecins s'occupaient à guérir l'hydropisie de ma bourse, un grand bruit s'éleva, toute la place retentit de ces mots: *tue! tue!* et en même temps je vis briller des épées" (p. 153). "While these charitable physicians were occupied in curing the dropsy of my purse, a great clamour arose; the whole square echoed with the words "Kill, kill!" and at the same time I saw the glitter of swords" (p. 191).

8. "A sept heures sonnantes, le bruit d'un trousseau de clefs donna le signal de la retraite" (p. 154). "As seven o'clock struck, the noise of a bunch of keys gave the signal for bed" (p. 192).

Sun

9. "Ainsi étendu à l'ombre de ces arbres, je me sentais inviter au sommeil par la douce fraîcheur et le silence de la solitude, quand un bruit incertain de voix confuses qu'il me semblait entendre voltiger autour de moi, me réveilla en sursaut" (p. 220). "Stretched out thus under the shadow of the trees I felt invited to sleep by the soft coolness and the silence of solitude, when an indistinct noise of confused voices, which I seemed to hear fluttering about me, woke me with a start" (p. 261).

10. "Ces paroles achevées, je n'entendis plus le moindre bruit" (p. 222). "After these words I did not hear the least sound" (p. 262).

11. "C'est l'haleinte de leur parole; et ce petit murmure ou ce bruit délicat dont ils rompent le sacré silence de leur solitude, c'est proprement leur langage" (p. 223). "That is the breath of their speech, and the little murmur or the delicate noise by which they break the silence of their solitude is actually their language" (p. 264).

12. "Mais encore que le bruit des forêts semble toujours le même, il est toutefois si différent que chaque espèce de végétant garde le sien particulier" (p. 223). "But although the sound of forests always seems the same, it is really so different that every kind of plant has its own" (p. 264).

Fight of the remora and salamander

13. "Cette voix allait je pense entamer un autre discours; mais le bruit d'une grande alarme qui survint l'empêcha" (p. 239). "I think the voice was going to begin another discourse; but it was prevented by the noise of a loud alarm" (p. 279).

14. "Comme je me vis au bout de mes raisons, enfin le désir de connaître la cause d'un événement si extraordinaire m'invita de marcher vers le lieu d'où le bruit semblait s'épandre" (p. 240). "I was unable to find reasons for this and my desire of knowing the cause of so extraordinary an event urged me to walk towards the place whence the noise seemed to come" (p. 280).

15. "Chaque heurt qu'elles se donnaient, engendrait un coup de tonnerre, comme il arrive dans les mondes d'ici autour, où la rencontre d'une nue chaude avec une froide excite le même bruit" (p. 244). "Each blow they exchanged caused a clap of thunder, as it happens in the worlds about where the meeting of a warm with a cold cloud excites the same noise" (p. 284).

16 and 17. "Nous connûmes bien le philosophe et moi, qu'à force de choir et se relever tant de fois, elle s'était fatiguée; car ces éclats de tonnerre, auparavant si effroyables, qu'enfantait le choc dont elle heurtait son ennemie, n'étaient plus que le bruit sourd de ces petits coups qui marquent la fin d'une tempête, et ce bruit sourd amorti peu à peu, dégénéra en un frémissement semblable à celui d'un fer rouge plongé dans de l'eau froide" (p. 244). "The philosopher and I could easily see it was tired from falling and rising up again so often; for the thunder-claps created by the shock as it struck its enemy, which were before so terrible, were now only the dull sound of those small rumbles which mark the end of a storm; and this dull sound, diminishing little by little, degenerated into a hissing like that of a red-hot iron plunged into cold water" (p. 285).

Campanella

18. "Celle de l'ouïe est pareillement double; elle tourne en s'insinuant comme un dédale, et l'on doit retenir au plus creux des concavités de sa couche un écho de tout le bruit qui résonne alentour" (p. 255). "Hearing is similarly double, it turns in as many windings as a maze and in the most hollow concaves of its bed can be heard an echo of every noise which sounds about it" (p. 296).

19. "L'eau de ce fleuve [*la Mémoire*] paraît gluante, et roule avec beaucoup de bruit" (p. 256). "The water of this river seems viscous and flows noisily" (p. 297).

20. "Ce ne fut pas toutefois encore tout; incontinent après un bruit aigre et criard, semblable au son d'une poulie qui tournerait avec rapidité, vint frapper nos oreilles, et tout au même temps nous vîmes choir à nos pieds une cage" (p. 262). "But this was not all; immediatelly afterwards a sharp squealing noise, like the sound of a pulley turning rapidly, struck our ears and at the same time we saw a cage fall at our feet" (p. 303).

Erica Harth

Classical Innateness

The existence of a human nature (<*natus*) is one of the fundamental assumptions of French classical literature; Descartes's innate (<*in-natus*) ideas are a conceptualization of this assumption. What was considered to be innate in the seventeenth century—be it character or idea— is an area fraught with contradiction. The dualism from which the notion of innateness would seem to be inseparable is both a locus for the contradictions and a historical juncture: *res cogitans* and "human nature" provide at once a rationalization for the status quo and the rationality of a new era.

The challenge posed by Alceste in Molière's *Misanthrope* is to destroy the myth of a character that is fixed and inherent; he would marry Célimène in order to *change* her, to purge her of the "vices du temps." Significantly, of course, he fails in the attempt, but the tension produced by the opposing attitudes toward "humanity" of Alceste and Philinte reflect a profound unease surrounding the concept of a human nature at this time. For Philinte, it is biologically given, as his comparison of humans to animals would indicate:

> These faults of which you so complain
> Are part of human nature, I maintain,
> And it's no more a matter for disgust
> That men are knavish, selfish and unjust,
> Than that the vulture dines upon the dead,
> And wolves are furious, and apes ill-bred. (I, i)[1]

La Bruyère echoes this attitude, which has become, some twenty years later, clearly prescriptive: "Let us not be angry with men when we see them cruel, ungrateful, unjust, proud, egotists, and forgetful of others;

[1] Molière, *The Misanthrope and Tartuffe*, trans. Richard Wilbur (New York, 1965).

they are made so; it is their nature; we might just as well quarrel with a stone for falling to the ground, or with a fire when the flames ascend" (Of Mankind, 1). [2] In a period when the traditional prerogatives of *naissance* were being severely undermined by the venality of offices, when the revocation of the Edict of Nantes provoked renewed chafing at a monarchy based on hereditary divine right, La Bruyère's words have a distinctly reactionary ring. Evils which are seen as part of "nature" itself—biological or even inanimate—are obviously not changeable.

Descartes had ostensibly taken great pains to separate the biological from the specifically human. Man deprived of his soul would be indistinguishable from the automata that are beasts, according to the Cartesian schema. Language, insofar as it proceeds from *res cogitans,* is logically the external mark of distinction. However, Chomsky points out that Descartes's dualism is preserved in his concept of language: the "creative principle" which governs the formation of deep structures would correspond to the mind, the "mechanical principle" regulating surface structures, to the body. [3] The creative principle is closely allied to innate ideas in Cartesian thinking. An elucidation of the latter term will serve to explain the connection between the two.

Although some confusion may arise on this point, it would seem that even in Descartes the phrase "innate ideas" includes both the faculty of thought and certain substantive ideas "imprinted on our souls" by God. [4] The Port-Royal *Logique* suggests that both "faculté" and "idées" are innate: "Suppose it is not denied that we have an idea of existence and an idea of thought. Then I ask through what senses have these ideas entered? ... it must be admitted that the ideas of existence and of thought do not in any fashion have their origin in the senses. Moreover, it must be conceded that the mind can

---

[2] References are to La Bruyère, *Characters,* trans. Henri Van Laun (London, 1963).

[3] Noam Chomsky, *Cartesian Linguistics: A Chapter in the History of Rationalist Thought* (New York and London, 1966), pp. 5-6.

[4] Cf. Geneviève Lewis, *Le Problème de l'inconscient et le cartésianisme* (Paris, 1950), pp. 79-84.

form these ideas independently." [5] The creative principle is evidently a function of the innate faculty. Descartes associates the two in the fifth part of the *Discours de la méthode,* where it is apparent that of the creative and mechanical language principles only the latter can account for any sounds animals might utter whereas both are utilized by humans. Similarly, he argues, animal actions are regulated by a mechanical principle alone, human actions by *reason,* a "universal instrument." [6] The creative principle, like the faculty of thought, or "reason," is an instrument for concept formation, in particular for the formation of those abstract structures that determine the semantic interpretation of a sentence. [7]

These illustrations show that Cartesian dualism both maintains a continuity with animality and sets up a radical distinction. The mechanical functions in both beasts and humans, but to the latter alone belong the faculty of thought and the creative language principle. The "nature" of each is determined by mechanism and reason respectively—if animals *are* automata the *essence* of man is reason—but both partake of the mechanical. In this sense we may speak of a "biological innateness." "Ideas" (faculty and substance) are as innate to man the animal as mechanism is to animals. In other words, Descartes succeeded in separating not necessarily the human from the biological but rather the human *animal* from the animal. In strict Cartesian thinking, it is not reason which distinguishes man, but dualism.

A biologically grounded dualism and the concept of biological innateness have profound implications for the French classical Weltanschauung. That which is viewed as innate by the authors of this period is invariably a duality. Thus, according to one of La Rochefoucauld's Maximes: "On every man at birth Nature seems to set limits for both virtue and vice" (189). [8]

---

[5] Antoine Arnauld [and Pierre Nicole], *The Art of Thinking: Port Royal Logic.* Trans. James Dickoff and Patricia James (Indianapolis, 1964), p. 37.

[6] René Descartes, *A Discourse on Method and Selected Writings,* trans. John Veitch (New York and London, 1951), pp. 48-49.

[7] See Chomsky, p. 33.

[8] References are to La Rochefoucauld, *Maxims,* trans. Louis Kronenberger (New York, 1959).

Erica Harth

That the duality may derive from a theology of original sin is relevant to our discussion insofar as the notions of grace and corruption serve to determine a dualistic human nature considered as biologically given. We can discern, for example, a double movement informing the *Maximes*. If on the one hand La Rochefoucauld reduces all *vertus* to pure "intérêt"—"Virtues are swallowed up by self-interest as rivers are lost in the sea" (171)—he also points to the *degeneration* into vices of what were originally *vertus*: "Vices help make up virtues as poisons do medicines. Discreetly tinctured and blended, they become a means of combatting life's ills" (182). In the present state of corruption all virtues are no more than cleverly disguised vices, but the vices in turn have "poisoned" an original purity (the Biblical overtones are unmistakable). The result is an inherent dual character to which "fortune" is but incidental: "Fortune brings out virtues and vices as light does objects" (380).

If in Pascal a dualistic human nature exemplifies some of the fundamental paradoxes besetting Western man, a similarly derived dualism in La Bruyère has become so rigid as to create an atmosphere stifling in its dogmatic assertiveness. Unhappiness, according to the author of the *Caractères,* is basic to the human condition, and any misfortune whatsoever must be accepted as part of our nature: "Men seem born to misfortune, pain, and poverty, and as few escape this, and as every kind of calamity seems to befall them, they ought to be prepared for every misfortune" (Of Mankind, 23). Despite the Jansenist doctrine of predestination he adopts, Pascal, curiously enough, does not leave us with the impression we have in the *Caractères* of a human nature so fixed as to render futile any attempt at change. The dialectic of the *Pensées,* on the contrary, allows for a radical reappraisal of political and social institutions in the light of those absolute values which have been lost in the fall from a state of grace. And whereas Pascal's God must be sought with anguish, the positive pole of La Bruyère's dualism is as firmly established as the negative. His principle of happiness does not reside in the lost paradise hovering over the *Pensées,* nor is it arrived at by the subtleties of an ontological proof. It is just *there,* like a biological fact of nature, and his statement

215

of faith smacks of complacency: "I feel that there is a God, and I do not feel there is none; this is sufficient for me, and all other arguments seem to me superfluous: I therefore conclude that He exists, and this conclusion is inherent to my nature" (Of Free-thinkers, 15). In La Bruyère, the area circumscribed by the innate seems to expand to ever greater proportions; each *caractère* is born such: "Foolishness is a criterion of a blockhead, vanity of an ass, and impertinence of an impertinent man" (Of Opinions, 47)....

Pascal's dialectic was exceptional, La Bruyère's outlook typical. The classical concept of inherent character traits, epitomized in the *Caractères,* serves a political purpose. A social hierarchy in imminent danger of crumbling can be rationalized by the notion that its members are fitted by nature for their respective places. Thus Jacques Savary, supposedly the apologist for a rising bourgeoisie, in fact sets limits on the mobility of this class by restricting its activities to a sphere deemed its own. Sons of *bourgeois,* for example, who are sent to *collèges* will come to disdain business enterprise by their association with the sons of noblemen who have traditionally spurned these occupations. But even among those destined by their class to be merchants or tradesmen only the ones who display a natural penchant for such roles should be encouraged: "Inclination is the first thing to be considered in children in order to make them succeed in the occupation of Trade: it does not depend on the parents, but on a natural disposition found in them."...[9] Like la Bruyère's *sot,* Savary's merchant is inborn. Class is sanctioned by Nature.

Cartesian dualism with its correlative innateness finds its way into a Great Chain of Being which eventually includes the social hierarchy to be defended. In Bossuet's version of the Chain, the central link is formed by man, whose spiritual-corporeal nature relates him at once to the superior region of the divine and the inferior region of the animal.[10] But if it is *res cogitans* which links man to God, it is an easy step from there to declare that the nobler the human being

[9] Jacques Savary, *Le parfait Négociant* (Paris, 1657), p. 38. See also pp. 40-41. (Translations my own).
[10] See Jacques-Bénigne Bossuet, *De la Connaissance de Dieu et de soi-même* (Paris, 1863), pp. 72-73. (Translations my own).

the more finely developed will be his reasoning faculty. It follows that the rulers of men must be directly inspired by God. Significant expression is given to this line of thought in the *Mémoires* of Louis XIV, where Cartesian innate ideas reappear in the guise of a justification for the theory of divine right:

Wisdom directs that on certain occasions we allow much to chance. In such cases reason herself counsels us to follow some kind of blind motion or instinct above itself which seems to come from Heaven and is known to all men, but is undoubtedly of greater weight and more worthy of consideration in the case of those whom it has itself placed in the first rank. No one can say when we should distrust or obey this motion; neither books, nor rules, nor experience tell us; a certain appropriateness, a certain daring of the mind, always more unfettered in a man who owes no account of his actions to any one, enables us to discover this. [11]

A divinely inspired innate Reason thus emerges as the rationalization of domination, whether the domination be that of an absolute monarchy and the successive rungs of the social hierarchy or of the human over the animal. *Res cogitans* is the realm of unfreedom: part of a preordained Nature, its precepts are universal—unchanging and unchangeable. Revolt is useless, as the post-Fronde generation knew only too well. Such a thorough-going celebration of the realm of unfreedom as is represented by the major works of French classicism leads us to wonder wherein lay, if at all, the realm of freedom. If reason is repressive, that which is repressed will pose a threat; it will be a liberty to be curbed.

Cartesian rationalism is based on the belief that knowledge originates in the intellect. Clear and distinct ideas arise in the mind: "confused" ideas are occasioned by sensory perceptions. The Port-Royal *Logique* goes so far as to deny to the senses any determinant role whatsoever in concept-formation: "In fact, but few ideas originate in the senses, whose sole function is the excitation of the brain" (*Logic,* p. 38). For Pascal the senses are "puissances trompeuses," but as "puissances" they must be combatted. The conflict assumes

[11] Jean Longnon, ed., *A King's Lessons in Statecraft: Louis XIV: Letters to his Heirs,* trans. Herbert Wilson (Port Washington, New York and London, 1970), p. 65.

greater intensity in Bossuet, who views reason as the "captive" of the senses, unceasingly struggling to regain its rightful position of command. The theologian explains the captivity of the mind by the body as punishment for original sin; the individual is predestined to repeat the experience of the race. Accordingly, Bossuet observes that the triumph of the senses over reason in childhood is a phenomenon common to all humans, an innate "misfortune":

But I was born in this misfortune: it was at the moment of my birth, throughout the entire course of my ignorant childhood, that the senses assumed the power which reason, arriving too late and too weak, found already established. All men are born like me in this servitude; and it gives all of us reason to believe what faith teaches us anyhow, that there is something depraved in the common source of our birth." [12]

The Freudian variation on the dictum that ontogeny recapitulates phylogeny, as it is further developed, for example, in Marcuse's *Eros and Civilization,* is entirely applicable here. The childhood of the individual as well as that of the race is considered by Cartesians and Freudians alike to be a period in which the senses dominate; the repression of Eros in subordination to the needs of civilization is a task to be accomplished by the adult, heir to the guilt of the race for having sinned. The Port-Royal *Logique,* echoing Descartes's methodical doubt, counsels in effect total repression of thoughts arising in childhood, because as results of sensory impressions they must be erroneous:

To extirpate the prejudices of our childhood is the only remedy for the impediment to thought offered by confused ideas. We must not believe a judgement solely on the ground that we have made the judgement previously; rather we must believe what we *now* judge to be the case (*Logic,* p. 71).

Childhood belongs to the senses and the body. It is a zone of potential freedom, where the pleasure-principle has not yet come under the control of the reality-principle. Instinctual satisfaction under minimal conditions of repression is a liberation from that historical time which Norman O. Brown has formulated as an ever increasing quest

12 Bossuet, p. 151.

for instinctual satisfaction under ever increasing conditions of instinctual repression. [13] La Bruyère captured the timelessness of childhood in one nostalgic phrase: "For children there is neither past nor future, and they enjoy the present, which we rarely do" (Of Mankind). For La Rochefoucauld, youth is an age when reason exercises no restraint; it is "a perpetual intoxication, a fever of the brain" (271).

Childhood is free from the conflict of dualism. It reproduces, in seventeenth-century terms, that lost state of grace in which man pursued pleasure in all innocence. Dualism is instituted when in the course of human development, individual or generic, the unrepressed desire for instinctual satisfaction would interfere with the satisfaction of society's needs. It is a specifically *human* institution. The thrust of Norman O. Brown's critique of Freud is to destroy the latter's notion of an innate dualism common to all organic life, and in the process to transform dualism into dialectic. As does Descartes, Brown finds that what distinguishes the human animal from the animal is dualism, but which is not the equivalent of a biological given. He would stress rather the discontinuity between the human and animal realms, the distinction of man as a *human* animal. Dualism becomes as it were a cultural artifact, a necessary precondition and product of Western civilization. It is childhood, i.e., a phase of development, and not the body (as in Cartesian rationalism), i.e., an unchangeable given, which provides the link with the biological domain. It is here that Brown would disagree with Freud in postulating a state of undifferentiated unity (as opposed to Freud's universal dualism) as characterizing organic life at the animal level. This same unity is found in childhood, according to Freud's own theory of a first pre-ambivalent stage in infancy. And if instinctual ambivalence is inaugurated in a subsequent phase of development, dialectical reunification of the instincts may yet be envisaged as an eventuality. [14] The shift from dualism to dialectic is coterminous with that from the biologically innate to what we may call the "culturally innate." Such a shift of course opens up the possibility of change, and Brown's critique is motivated by a

---

[13] Norman O. Brown, *Life against Death* (London, 1970), pp. 84-87.
[14] See Brown, pp. 80-82.

desire to avoid Freud's therapeutic pessimism. Lévi-Strauss has suggested that dualism may be the fundamental cultural given, the essence of culture itself:

If... it is true that the transition from nature to culture is determined by man's ability to think of biological relationships as systems of oppositions... perhaps it must be acknowledged that duality, alternation, opposition and symmetry... are not so much matters to be explained, as basic and immediate data of mental and social reality... [15]

Because the area of childhood has proven crucial in a critical reappraisal of the theory of biological innateness in human beings, an examination of the prevalent attitudes toward childhood in the French classical period will help to clarify the scope and function of Cartesian innateness in its various forms.

It is Philippe Ariès's contention that the specificity of childhood was "discovered" in France in the sixteenth and seventeenth centuries. He believes that the high infant mortality rate in the Middle Ages would account for a seeming indifference to children as reflected in the iconography of the time. Perhaps because it was just beginning to be regarded as a singular stage of development, childhood appears as a shadowy realm in the French classical world. The child's identity qua child is not fully affirmed; he is often confused with the adult. All children were dressed just like adults in the Middle Ages, and in the seventeenth century specialization in clothing was limited to boys of the nobility and bourgeoisie. [16] We know from the journal of Héroard that no thought was given by the royal entourage to the sexual education of the infant Louis XIII. Sexuality was apparently treated as openly and frankly in front of the young child as it would be with an adult. [17] Children do not figure in any important manner in French classical literature; when they do appear, however,

[15] Claude Lévi-Straus, *The Elementary Structures of Kinship*, rev. ed., trans. James Harle Bell, John Richard von Sturmer and Rodney Needham, ed. (Boston, 1969), p. 136.

[16] Philippe Ariès, *L'Enfant et la vie familiale sous l'ancien régime* (Paris, 1960), pp. 29-39, 42-55.

[17] Ariès, pp. 102-109. Se also David Hunt, *Parents and Children in History* (New York and London, 1970), pp. 161-163.

Erica Harth

an understandable ambivalence toward them is evident: are they to be considered as children or as adults?

The expression of this ambivalence is striking in La Bruyère's *Caractères*. Children are, on the one hand, nothing but adults in miniature. In a kind of *emboîtement,* the child prefigures the man. He is born a preformed adult; the innate has only to mature and flower:

Children are overbearing, supercilious, passionate, envious, inquisitive, egotistical, idle, fickle, timid, intemperate, liars, and dissemblers; they laugh and weep easily, are excessive in their joys and sorrows, and that about the most trifling objects; they bear no pain, but like to inflict it on others; already they are men (Of Mankind, 50).

But, on the other hand, childhood is still assigned its place in the traditional "ages of man," and is thereby limited to a separate domain. The age of childhood is characterized by a lack of reason, and thus, in conformity with the Cartesian pattern, children are comparable to animals:

There is a time preceding the power of reasoning, when, like animals, we live by instinct alone, and of which memory retains no vestiges. There is a second period, when reason is developed (Of Mankind, 49).

In childhood there is both continuity and discontinuity with the fully human. The child is "unique" by virtue of the absence of reason; his "passions" (i.e. "vices") link him to man:

There seems to be but one character in childhood: at that age morals and manners are nearly all the same, and it is only by paying great attention that we can perceive any difference, which, however, increases in the same proportion as reason does, whilst the passions and vices gather strength as well; these alone make men so unlike each other and so at variance with themselves (Of Mankind, 52).

There are good reasons for this wavering in the attribution of a specific place to childhood. If it is maintained that an innate reason distinguishes man from the beasts, what is to be done about the child, over whom reason appears to hold no sway? If his "uniqueness" resides in his lack of reason, in stressing this aspect we will be forced to stress the resemblance of the human to the animal. If, on the contrary, we assimilate the child to the adult in emphasizing the continuity of "passions," the concept of an innate reason is equally if not more undermined, for the distinction of reason is forgotten altogether. Even when the classic Cartesian schema is not adopted, there is hesitation on the issue of reason in children. In the "Discours à Madame de la Sablière," his celebrated verse meditation on the beast-machine theory, La Fontaine attempts to resolve the question by ascribing a less developed reason to children and animals alike.

For Cartesians and non-Cartesians, childhood is a lost age, a stumbling block, as it would later prove to Freud himself, to the whole argument of biological innateness. The seventeenth century tended to regard this age, in which reason appeared to be absent or quantitatively less, with fear and mistrust. Children are like animals in that they are unrestrained by reason in pursuit of pleasure. They are, in the words of La Bruyère, "maîtres de leur propre félicité" [masters of their own happiness] (Of Mankind, 53). They obey no law higher than their own, and they threaten the adult world with their agressive autonomy. David Hunt observes that adults of the time evidently viewed their children as little animals, constricting them in swaddling clothes to inhibit further development of their animality. [18]

Because it is the prerogative of madmen as well as children to escape the control of reason, it is not surprising that they too were equated with animals in the classical period. Madness was in effect the very negation of that dualism which defined humanity. Therapeutically, insanity was treated as both a *passion* and a *délire*, according to Michel Foucault. It was therefore at once a movement of the corporeal machine and unreason, an error of the mind. [19] The machine infused with soul which is the image of Cartesian man was thus reduced to the animal level:

The animality that rages in madness dispossesses man of what is specifically human in him; not in order to deliver him over to other powers, but simply

---

[18] Hunt, pp. 125-130.
[19] See Michel Foucault, *Madness and Civilization: A History of Insanity in the Age of Reason*, trans. Richard Howard (New York, 1965), pp. 85-116, p. 197.

to establish him at the zero degree of his own nature. For classicism, madness in its ultimate form is man in immediate relation to his animality, without other reference, without any recourse. [20]

Now the animal, Foucault insists, was not relegated to the realm of *nature* in the classical age; it belonged rather to what he terms an "anti-nature, a negativity that threatens order and by its frenzy endangers the positive wisdom of nature." [21] The concept of nature we are dealing with is clearly anthropocentric and is derived from the dualism which confers upon man a privileged place in the Great Chain of Being. An immortal soul links the human to the divine and forms the inherent nature which separates man from the lower levels of life. Innate ideas are natural in the sense that they are ordained by God to determine the nature of the human being as a rational animal. This is the meaning of "natural ideas" which we find in the Port-Royal *Logique*. Its authors amplify the first step of Descartes's method by proposing that the progressive elimination of all ideas arising from sensory impressions will leave us with the desired residue of "idées naturelles," products of pure reason. "Nature" and "Reason" thus establish their classical alliance, and both are the province of man alone.

But if animality as unreason is counter-nature it is also liberty— freedom *from* reason and rational laws. The animality of madness was not looked upon by the seventeenth century as conforming to the laws of a deterministic nature. Instead, madness revealed "a liberty raging in the monstrous forms of animality." [22] Transposed to the human sphere, the freedom of animality poses a threat: madmen and children alike must accordingly be constrained and domesticated like beasts. The seventeenth century saw the first mental institutions in France. Only at this time, apparently, did it occur to people to *enclose* the insane like beasts, as if animality were contagious. When La Bruyère discerns madness in his *caractères* his first impulse is to have

[20] *Ibid.*, p. 74. For madness as animality see pp. 68-84.
[21] *Ibid.*, p. 77.
[22] Foucault, p. 83.

the persons in question locked up. Madmen as nonhumans are supremely asocial and society must be protected from them:

They know you not, they look bewildered, and their brain is turned; their relatives should take care of them and lock them up, lest in time their folly should drive them frantic, and make them harm someone (Of the Court, 61).

The inmates of seventeenth-century insane asylums were treated like beasts to be broken, Foucault tells us. Chained to the walls and beds of their cage-like cells, they were literal monsters to serve as spectacles for those on the other side of the bars. [23] The madman becomes definitively the Other when the irrational in man is totally repudiated and bequeathed to the animals.

The domestication of children proceeded along similar lines. Swaddling clothes effectively limited the child's freedom of movement, as the asylum did that of its inmates. Before he was a year old the dauphin Louis XIII was on a leash in order to learn how to walk. [24] The freedom of the child's animality, like that of the madman, inspired fear. One of the reasons for the widespread use of nurses in the seventeenth century. Hunt suggests, may have been that breastfeeding held many perils: the infant was seen as a predatory animal sucking away what was thought to be the whitened blood of his mother. [25] In a tirade against the agressive bestiality of man, La Bruyère selects as paradigmatic the image of an infant biting his nurse's breast. It is a case in point, for if the child-animal is not held in thralldom, it may rise up as master:

He began betimes to show what he could do, and so severely bit his nurse's breast that the poor woman died of it; I know what I mean, and that is sufficient to conclude: he was born a subject and is no longer one; on the contrary, he is now the master (Of Opinions, 119).

La Bruyère's assertion that children are "born subjects" is indicative of the social role they were assigned in his time. Clearly, all

---

[23] See Foucault, pp. 70-78.
[24] Hunt, p. 128.
[25] *Ibid.*, pp. 117-124.

those participating in animality belong to the sub-regions of humanity. In the one reference he makes to peasants, La Bruyère describes them as "animaux farouches" [wild animals] (Of Mankind, 128). Children, madmen, and the lower classes share a common oppression. That the child belongs to an inferior social group is apparent in La Bruyère's concept of the social organization of childhood. Here again ontogeny recapitulates phylogeny, for the development of this organization mirrors man's political history. The earliest stage is the "popular state," a chaos in which each subject is master. An authentic monarchy can never be established, because the child is governed by pleasure alone:

Children begin among themselves with a democracy, where everyone is master; and what is very natural, it does not suit them for any length of time, and then they adopt a monarchy. One of them distinguishes himself from among the rest... all the others submit to him, and then an absolute government is established, but only in matters of pleasure (Of Mankind, 57).

The danger is that the chaos will become generalized, that pleasure and freedom will reassert their reign, and that children will rise up like peasants. Adult and child stand in a master-slave relationship in which the child continuously attempts to overthrow its master:

The only anxiety children have is to find out the weaknesses of their masters, and of the persons they have to obey; as soon as they have once taken advantage of these, they get the upper hand, and obtain an influence over these people which they never part with (Of Mankind, 54).

A study of the vocabulary of the time reveals that childhood was regarded primarily as a state of dependence. If, during the seventeenth century, "enfance" and "adolescence" became more delimited in their application among the members of the bourgeoisie, the older confusion of the two, reflecting an extension into adolescence of the childhood state of dependence, persisted among the lower classes. Words relating to childhood also designated in the spoken language men of the lower, dependent classes: valets, journeymen, etc. A "petit garçon" could mean a young servant as well. Ariès observes another instance of the assimilation of children with the lower classes

225

in the case of games. Prior to the seventeenth century it appears that adults and children shared the same games. In the seventeenth century, however, adults of the upper classes abandoned these games to children and the *peuple*. [26] We have seen that dress broke down similarly along class lines, the new custom of distinguishing children from adults in clothing being restricted to the bourgeoisie and nobility.

The animal freedom of non-rational beings—be they children, madmen or peasants—was intolerable to those whose belief in an innate dualistic nature required constant reassertion of reason over senses, mind over body. And it is just because the dualism was held to be a biological given, a human *nature* resulting from original sin, that the struggle assumed such intensity. Conquest over the pre-destined is a task suited perhaps to the Cornelian hero, but the weight of the past hangs less heavily on him than on the protagonists of Racine, whose attempts at such conquest always end in failure. Guilt fills the Racinian universe. It is highly significant that the first play of the canon deals with the Oedipal theme, the *original* myth underlying all the succeeding tragedies. The heritage of *sang* understandably becomes a *fatalité* when descendants of the first assassin view themselves as condemned to repeat the Oedipal crime. Étéocle and Polinice in *La Thébaïde* inherit the sins of their father and the duty to expiate his crime:

> Our hatred for each other is fanatic;
> And has not just been fashioned in a year;
> Such hate was born with us; and its dark fury
> With life itself flowed deep into our hearts.
> From tenderest infancy we stood forth foes,
> Indeed, we were so even before our birth:
> Fatal and tragic brood of incestuous blood!
>
> (IV, i, 915-921) [27]

Original sin was after all an Oedipal crime, the overweening pride which led man to believe he could equal God, the primal father.

[26] See Ariès, pp. 13-15, 100-102.
[27] Jean Racine, *Complete Plays (The Theban Brothers)*, trans. Samuel Solomon (New York and Toronto, 1967), I, 44-45.

Conversely, the Oedipal complex of the individual is the ontogenetic equivalent of original sin: "The essence of the Oedipal complex is the project of becoming God—in Spinoza's formula, *causa sui;* in Sartre's, *être-en-soi-pour-soi*." [28] But the Oedipal complex is a developmental process, both phylogenetically (see, for example Freud's *Moses and Monotheism; Totem and Taboo)* and ontogenetically. In French classicism it is a fact of nature; the pride all mankind must pay for is a universal biological given: "Pride exists equally in all men," said La Rochefoucauld (35). "Justice" itself is innate, a divine precept to atone for the sins of our forefathers, as Bossuet instructs: "...a certain something is imprinted on the heart of man to make him acknowledge a justice which visits the sins of the fathers on their children as if it were their lot in life." [29]

Classical reason epitomizes the futile attempt to eradicate guilt through repression. The animal in man, which was the undifferentiated instinctual unity of the pre-Oedipal phase, must be held down or repudiated. The phenomenon Freud termed the "return of the repressed," in its seventeenth-century forms of children, madmen and peasants, had to be dealt with harshly. Freud would have concurred heartily in the widespread opinion that French classicism represents one of the loftier heights of Western civilization, for the more "discontented" is man in the search for instinctual gratification the more impressive will be the products of his sublimation.

Brown, Marcuse and others have wondered if the "civilizing" process analyzed by Freud is irreversible. There would certainly seem to be no way out of the conflict between the pleasure-principle and the reality-principle if it is maintained that man's dualism is biologically innate. Reunification, as Brown has explained, will be possible only when the conflict is recognized as "culturally innate," transmitted from generation to generation in the historical process of civilization. This perspective allows for the margin of change within which reversal becomes feasible. There was, of course, no understanding of cultural innateness in the seventeenth century. On the contrary,

[28] Brown, p. 109.
[29] Bossuet, p. 151.

the biological innateness of Cartesian dualism portended a reunification of a very different sort.

The preceding discussion has been based on the notion that Cartesian dualism laid special emphasis on the mechanistic. Despite the definitive noumenal quality of the *Cogito,* the continuity of the human with the animal is rigorously upheld by Descartes. For the soul to attain its full significance as the essentially human it must be placed within the corporeal machine. And it is well known that Descartes's mechanism, as it was applied in the beast-machine theory, made the philosopher justifiably suspect to his contemporaries, who feared the very conclusions La Mettrie was later to draw. Cartesian dualism is one simple step away from that mechanistic monism which deprives man of his soul altogether.

The fifth part of the *Discours* is a striking illustration of the continuity between mind and matter which contained the seeds of destruction of Descartes's dualism. Descartes informs us that our innate ideas are in effect physical laws, and, following the deductive method he outlined in the second part, he indicates that all laws governing the universe ensue from them:

...I have also observed certain laws established in nature by God in such a manner, and of which he has impressed on our minds such notions, that after we have reflected sufficiently upon these, we cannot doubt that they are accurately observed in all that exists or takes place in the world: and farther, by considering the concatenation of these laws, it appears to me that I have discovered many truths more useful and more important than all I had before learned, or even had expected to learn. [30]

In this fifth part, an apology for Descartes's *Monde,* it is obvious why the treatise had to be suppressed. Descartes had stated therein (p. 37) that all physical laws may be derived from the primary "natural" idea of matter as extension (the Port-Royal *Logic,* p. 66, specifies that *res extensa* is an innate idea).

Innate ideas as elementary scientific principles underlying all physical laws do render God dispensable, and Pascal's accusation

[30] Descartes, pp. 35-36.

that the Cartesian God had merely to give a "chiquenaude" to the world is perfectly justified.

Marcuse points out the implications of the monism inherent in Cartesian dualism. Following Husserl's idea that Descartes's *Ego* was "not really an independent substance but rather the... limit of quantification," he suggests that the quantification of *res extensa* leads inevitably to the quantification of *res cogitans*. The subject-object distinction breaks down when the objective world is dependent upon the quantifying subjective mind. Ultimately, of course, *res cogitans* becomes as quantifiable as *res extensa*. [31] It is noteworthy that those ideas considered innate in Cartesian thinking are strictly mathematical. The classic example is that of the triangle whose perfection is never realized in sensible objects. Bossuet even speaks of an innate mathematics, a "natural geometry" (p. 23). The very idea of God, as Husserl saw, is mathematical in that it is a negation of the quantifiable: God is infinite.

Classical reason, which retains the dualism of Cartesian thought, rationalizes the status quo by justifying the oppression of all those categorized as subhuman. The animal is the Other; man affirms his humanity in denying his senses. Mind and body will be reunited in the new technological rationality ushered in by Descartes. It is not, however, the reunification of Logos and Eros, which would require a readjustment of the reality-principle to meet the human needs for pleasure and satisfaction. Monism is rather a rationalization for more efficient domination. Man becomes a quantifiable unit in the service of the reality-principle. The semi-feudal hierarchy of the absolute monarchy gives way to the democratization of labor: "While science freed nature from inherent ends and stripped matter of all but quantifiable qualities, society freed man from the 'natural' hierarchy of personal dependence and related them to each other in accordance with quantifiable qualities—namely, as units of abstract labour power, calculable in units of time." [32] The fiat of justice is no longer

---

[31] Herbert Marcuse, *One-Dimensional Man* (London, 1970), pp. 120-126.
[32] Marcuse, p. 129.

divine; the men of the eighteenth century established their own justice, which, abolishing class distinctions by ignoring them, let a theoretical equality rationalize inequality in political and economic practice. Secularized reason becomes self-repressive and, as such, still retains the character of biological innateness. All men are assured that they partake equally of "human nature," be they oppressed or alienated. With the new scientific rationality accompanying the French Revolution, the truly liberating concept of cultural innateness receded farther and farther into an unforeseeable future.

Jan Miel

Ideas or Epistemes: Hazard Versus Foucault

At least one critic has remarked—I am sure it has occurred to many—
that Paul Hazard's much admired *Crise de la conscience européenne*
seems oddly old-fashioned and superficial today, and that one reason
for this is Foucault's *Les Mots et les choses*.[1] Certainly Hazard's
book was greeted with almost universal acclaim (in the universe of
French academic life, at least) when it appeared, though one wonders
if readers of, say, Mannheim or Cassirer—they were evidently few
in France in 1935—would not have found it superficial even then.
And certainly Foucault's book immediately gives an impression of
greater depth. But aside from this impression, Foucault's book is a
direct challenge to Hazard's in two ways: it presents a method which
explicitly rejects earlier methods in intellectual history; and it
presents a thesis about the seventeenth and eighteenth centuries which,
if true, must challenge and perhaps supersede that of Hazard. A
reevaluation of Hazard seems inevitable, then, although not without
some critical evaluation of the method and interpretation imposed
by Foucault.

Hazard can scarcely be said to have a method in the sense in
which that word would be understood today. He read enormously
in several European languages, and the results of that reading—that
is, the passages or ideas which interested him, and his impressions
of them—he organized loosely into a general interpretation of a
period. He quotes or resumes his documents faithfully, on the level
described by the French as "vulgarisation." One might almost say
that he is resolutely superficial, in the sense of remaining on the

[1] R. Bellour, "Entretien avec Michel Foucault," *Les Lettres Françaises*,
no. 1125 (31 March 1966); reprinted in Bellour, *Le Livre des autres* (Paris,
[1971]), p. 135.

surface: for, although he gives biographical background on his major figures, for instance, he never draws on biography to provide a "psychological" explanation; and although he alludes frequently to historical, political events, he never attempts to find "historical causes" for the ideas he presents. He remains always on the level of ideas and even the crisis or change in consciousness which is the theme of his work is never seen as something deep which underlies the emergence of new ideas, but rather as being one with the ideas: the change of consciousness which occurs between 1680 and 1715 is, for Hazard, a change in the ideas men had about things.

If we recall the way the book is organized, we might be tempted to think otherwise: there is an opening section on psychological changes, followed by a section on the breakdown of traditional values; then the attempt at reconstruction, and a last section on imagination and sensibility. This suggests that there were profound psychological changes in the later seventeenth century which brought about a breakdown in traditional values, and that in the eighteenth-century attempt to find new values—to reconstruct a new basis for European culture—imagination and sensibility took on added importance. This is a plausible scenario, one that we all tend to accept to some degree, but when we come to look at what Hazard offers us in the way of "psychological changes," we cannot but be disappointed. In fact, the five chapters included under that heading are rather disconcerting: we might accept a change from stability to movement as "psychological," and perhaps even the switch from interest in the ancient to interest in the modern; but in what sense can the shift of the center of European intellectual life from Southern Europe north toward England, Holland, and Germany, be taken to be psychological? And two further chapters on Heterodoxy and on Pierre Bayle scarcely make Hazard's sense of the "psychological" much clearer; nor do we have any sense of depth—that we are seeing the obscure origins, the hidden causes of a crisis.

That Hazard lacks a sociological dimension, which for some writers supplies exactly that sense of depth, is by now a commonplace. Even when he discusses the transition from aristocratic to

Jan Miel

bourgeois ideals (Part III, chap. vii), he says things such as "one no longer admired the aristocratic virtues," and "one turned instead to a bourgeois ideal," as if he were talking about a flock of classless beings who somehow had the choice whether to be aristocratic or bourgeois. But it is not only the lack of sociological analysis which faults his generalizations.

Any student of seventeenth-century France will be struck by his distortion of that period; for in order to make out that there is a crisis after 1680, Hazard must greatly exaggerate the stability, serenity, and unanimity of thought of the period preceding. In the opening chapter, he tells us that the crisis period is characterized by a great interest in travel (as opposed to the stability of the classical period), and by the discovery that other civilizations have other values which call into question the absolutism of Louis XIV's reign. But interest in travel and exotic countries had been strong since the fifteenth century; and the lesson of cultural relativity was common currency at least since Montaigne and was accepted completely by all serious thinkers throughout the seventeenth century. Fortunately, Hazard is sufficiently thorough and comprehensive so that in later chapters this and other oversimplifications are dispelled by his own material. In a similar manner, the aphorism with which Hazard sums up his sense of the crisis—"la majorité des Français pensait comme Bossuet; tout d'un coup, les Français pensent comme Voltaire: c'est une révolution" [the majority of the French thought like Bossuet; suddenly the French are thinking like Voltaire: it is a revolution] [2]—is actually contradicted by the other main thesis of the book, namely, that all the ideas which seemed revolutionary (and led to revolution) in the later eighteenth century had already been expressed before 1680 (I, 10). So then, who were the French who in the seventeenth century thought like Bossuet? Not the Jansenists, nor most of the Jesuits, nor the Cartesians, or Gassendists, or Spinozists, or other assorted *libertins*. Presumably

[2] Preface, I, 7. Further references will appear in the text by volume number and page; they are to the 1961 "livre de poche" edition (Collection "Idées"; Paris, Gallimard).

233

those who thought like Bossuet were those who went to hear him preach: the good loyal Catholics. And fifty years later did good loyal Catholics all think like Voltaire? Hardly.

Such a brief glance at these larger generalizations is of course unfair to Hazard, and is not meant as a real critique so much as an attempt to point up problems concerning which such a work now makes us uneasy. The problem is not simply that Hazard did not write a sociology of knowledge, in the sense of a sociological explanation of a change in ideas—such an explanation would surely have been unacceptable to him, if not incomprehensible. But the lack is felt even at the level of description, and this points to a more general problem: how can one, with any validity, attribute ideas to anyone except the author of the document at hand? Indeed, is there any point in doing so? Whether we wish to attribute them to the "European Consciousness"—or some lesser *Zeitgeist*—or to a socio-economic class, the problem remains the same: there is an extra-polation involved, the justification for which is problematic in the extreme. And yet without such extrapolation and generalization, it is impossible to say anything about the development of intellectual fashions, and the vogue and influence of ideas, which is what Lovejoy said was the primary task of the history of ideas. [3]

Foucault, both in his challenge to Hazard's generalizations, and in his methodology, accosts this problematic. But before seeing how, we may want to ask: If Hazard is not giving us much of the psychology or sociology of the period, nor any very precise knowledge about the development or transmission of ideas, what does he offer? His metaphors are the best guide: the major intellectual figures of the age he calls "les grands acteurs" (I, 250); he sees them as center-stage on the "théâtre du monde" (II, 147); the turn of the century is described as "one of those moments... when the screen becomes blurred" (II, 131). Hazard invites us to be spectators, whether at the theatre or the cinema, of the drama of European intellectual history: the crisis he describes is the turning point in this great

---

[3] In his William James lectures, delivered two years before Hazard's book appeared; see *The Great Chain of Being* (New York, 1965), p. 20.

drama. However we may feel about the value of viewing history in this way, we should at least be aware that the view itself constitutes the history we are presented. One can see the crisis period as a turning point only when one can see how the drama comes out. By seeing the development as dramatic, Hazard manages to remain true to his idealistic approach; but he also reveals what he means by the European consciousness: it can only be a consciousness able to grasp the development of ideas in the seventeenth and eighteenth centuries and see that development dramatically; in other words, the European consciousness is the mind of Hazard himself. If it is not a very profound mind, it at least has a varied and attractive surface; but one can still ask whether the crisis described isn't but a particular convolution of that mind.

Foucault, on the other hand, is deep. The contrast between Foucault and Hazard is very great, on the level of method even more than on that of the interpretation of intellectual history. Even the reception of Foucault's *Les Mots et les choses*[4] in the 1960's contrasts with that of Hazard's work: although it was generally praised for its scope and originality, criticism was immediate and often severe, and, in that Structuralist decade, almost entirely centered on questions of method. In response, Foucault has made several statements on his method and in 1969 issued a whole book in its defence.[5]

His method is what he likes to call an "archeology of knowledge," a term which has several connotations which appeal to him: the notion of depth, of course, of getting below the surface; but also the idea of a science which is not a science and yet is not quite history either, and leans heavily on taxonomy; and again the notion of the past as a succession of layers with little to suggest transition between

[4] Paris, 1966. Important critiques include those of Michel Amiot and Sylvie Le Bon in *Les Temps Modernes*, no. 248 (Jan., 1967), pp. 1271-1298, 1299-1312; of Pierre Burgelin and Yves Bertherat in *Esprit* (May, 1967), pp. 843-861, 862-881; and of Georges Canguilhem in *Critique* (July 1967), pp. 599-618.

[5] *Archéologie du savoir* (Paris, 1969). See also "Réponse à une question" par Michel Foucault, *Esprit* (May, 1968), pp. 850-874, and two "Entretiens" in Bellour, cited in note 1.

them. The object of his study is to discover and define what he calls the "*episteme*," that is, the basic structure of all discursive knowledge of a given period. Although he admits that to carry out this project one should have read "everything," he in fact uses relatively few sources—in contrast to Hazard—and rarely quotes more than a sentence or two from them. This small amount of primary material, presumably selected from very wide reading, is the subject of long developments more or less phenomenological in nature. His debt to Bachelard is explicit, and to the Geneva school of literary criticism is unquestionable, if unavowed. He strongly denies that his method is Structuralist, though in the early 1960s he was associated with that movement, and there are certainly strong affinities; what he wishes most to deny apparently is that his method is simply an application of Structuralist ideas to the realm of history. I might add that Foucault's style is digressive and repetitive, that is, he branches out in unexpected directions and circles back over material already discussed, but always with renewed insight or differences of expression. The result is a richness which renders summation difficult and often unjust; woven into *Les Mots et les choses* are many brilliant and suggestive notions—we must be content here with seeing only the larger pattern.

Starting from the sixteenth century, Foucault characterizes the Renaissance *episteme* as based on similitude: everything resembles something else and in that sense stands for it. Knowledge consists of interpretation and interpretation consists of finding the resemblances; it is essentially additive, may operate by analogy, moves freely between microcosm and macrocosm. There is little distinction between sign and object: objects are read as signs (as they resemble other objects) and signs may relate to other signs or to objects. In this world of printing presses, books, the Book, the world is read as a book.

With the seventeenth century all this is changed. Descartes, mechanization, mathematization, the new empirical sciences, all reflect this; but it is the very nature of knowledge itself which has changed and the new *episteme* is far broader than, and will far outlive the success of Cartesian mechanism. There will be no further significant change in the *episteme* until the end of the eighteenth century. What especially characterizes this classical field of knowledge is the new theory of signs. Knowledge is no longer sought through resemblances but through distinction: when one has truly discerned an object in its distinctness and clarity, one can then accurately represent it by a sign which in turn allows us to assign it its proper place in the order of things. Signification, thus, is not inherent in things but is assigned to them by virtue of our act of knowledge. Restored are older ideas about signs, such as their degree of appropriateness to their objects, the distinction between a metonymic and metaphoric relation to their objects, and between natural and conventional signs. Foucault shows us the new *episteme* at work in areas where mechanization and mathematization were at a minimum: in the construction of a general grammar, in the taxonomy of natural history, and in the analysis of wealth, where money is essentially a sign and therefore can be related to human knowledge and even human desire, but not to the means of production.

Foucault goes on to show that the change which took place in the structure of the field of knowledge at the beginning of the nineteenth century is as abrupt as that at the beginning of the seventeenth. It is at this point that "Man" erupts into history, Man as that which the classical, representational discourse cannot give an account of. For Man has a history: even his language has a history with laws of its own; societies, economies, psyches have a dynamism which becomes the center of every problematic; the "sciences of man" are born. Linguistics becomes historical philology, so-called natural history becomes biology, the analysis of wealth becomes political economy. For Foucault, we are now at the end of this period. It is time to awaken from our "anthropological sleep" which is only an ideology, another form of dogmatism. And although Foucault does not tell us what the new *episteme* will be, we feel somehow it will be closely related to Foucault's own method.

It is obvious in what way this view of the seventeenth and eighteenth centuries challenges that of Hazard: where Hazard sees the major change of modern times—the crisis at the end of the seventeenth century—Foucault sees no significant change at all: the classical *episteme* continues to dominate until the end of the eighteenth century.

On the methodological level, the challenge is even more explicit, and involves a scornful rejection of the history of ideas. Part of Foucault's dismay with such traditional disciplines is simply with their multiplicity. There should not be a history of philosophy *and* a history of ideas *and* a history of science; there should be a history of knowledge. But in addition, the history of ideas has proved to be totally incapable of showing us how ideas develop or have their influence. In the *Archéologie du savoir* (pp. 182-183), Foucault actually spells out four ways in which his method differs from the history of ideas, namely, 1) whereas the history of ideas seeks to find the ideas, themes, etc., which are expressed in the documents under study, his method analyzes the structure of the discourse itself; 2) the history of ideas attempts to trace the emergence of ideas as well as their development and disappearance, while Foucault's method takes a given discourse in its specificity without regard for what precedes or follows; 3) the history of ideas seeks psychological or sociological explanations—he does not; and 4) the history of ideas tries to reconstruct past thought by replacing it in the context of its age, while Foucault rejects such a process as false and futile and wishes only to give a systematic description of that thought in its own terms. Oddly enough, if we line up Hazard against these charges, he would stand convicted of only two of them: of seeking a continuity (2), and of reconstructing the context of the past (4). Of (1) and (3), namely the attempt to find ideas, or psychological and social causes behind the documents, Hazard is largely free, saved by his very superficiality, his impressionistic style of approach.

And if we turn on Foucault with the same problematic we raised in regard to Hazard, Foucault's greater rigor may turn out to be only apparent. If we ask how Foucault can impose a single *episteme* on two centuries of diverse writers, he is of course ready with a reply. He does not pretend to present us with the *Weltanschauung* of a period, still less with a statistic of opinions held. [6] He is not concerned with who said or wrote what because the Subject is a notion belonging to the very anthropologism he rejects. He studies only the utterance, the structure of the discourse itself. He is an archivist, not at all concerned with the realities (human personalities, psychologies, sociologies, etc.) one can imagine to lie behind the documents studied, but only with the classification and analysis of the documents themselves. The rigor of this as a methodological principle is undeniably attractive. But it does not really avoid the problem. As at least one reviewer, Pierre Burgelin, has pointed out, [7] when one tries to define one *episteme* for an age, one still runs into the problem of writers (Burgelin cites Nicolas d'Autrecourt and Pico della Mirandola for the Renaissance, Harvey, Lavoisier, and Montesquieu in the classical period) who simply can't be made to fit Foucault's schema. They may be a minority, but Foucault's claim is not based on statistics: it is a claim that the structure he describes is so fundamental that it is impossible in the age of one *episteme* to think by means of another. Yet clearly there is something like foreshadowing and lag and even a certain independence of privileged *epistemes* (for example, that of mathematics, and even, by Foucault's own admission, of poetic language) which Foucault's theory offers no way to account for.

Now Foucault's method involves an explicit rejection of the category of change; [8] not that he denies that changes occurred, of course, but rather the whole notion of change is "put in parentheses" (in the manner of the phenomenologists) in order to facilitate an investigation of *what* has changed. What this makes possible is the isolation of the Renaissance and Classical *epistemes* with the result of greater clarity and profundity in our understanding of each. Once we have seen what Foucault shows us in this way, it is difficult not to be convinced. So, for instance, I have been struck with how the exchange of letters between Pascal and the Père Noël on the question of the vacuum bears out Foucault's analysis. It is a veritable

6 See, for example, *Les Mots et les choses,* p. 46.
7 *Esprit* (May, 1967), pp. 854-856.
8 See, for example, *Les Mots et les choses,* pp. 64-65.

dialogue between a Renaissance mind and a Classical one: the Père Noël daws analogies with the circulation of the blood, with the four elements and the humors, and ends with a definition of light which is a masterpiece of redundancy and confusion. Pascal shows him (if he were capable of understanding) not only that his comparisons are arbitrary and his definitions tautological, but that his whole approach to the problem cannot lead to any certain truth: if, when the mercury drops away from the closed end of a tube, we can discover that particles of matter remain in that space, then let us name them, but if none can be found let us not hesitate to call that space empty, i.e. a vacuum, and not imagine that Nature has such passionate feelings about vacuums that she must have rushed to fill it. In other words, Pascal is pleading for an unequivocal use of terms (or signs) to represent distinct and isolable objects, as against the kind of analogical thinking which attributes passions to Nature and sees in the theory of the humors a model for the natural sciences. Foucault's brilliant analyses of the Renaissance and Classical *epistemes* certainly shed light on this exchange; but the fact is both men were writing in 1647-48, and Foucault offers no way to account for the epistemical lag of laggards like the Père Noël.

To take an example within the fields Foucault discusses, we can say that it is only because Foucault (and incidentally Chomsky) has shown the enormous importance and scope of the Port-Royal Grammar that historians of grammar have been able to see the essential and important way in which certain Renaissance grammarians, notably Scaliger and Sanctius, figured in the formulations of the Port-Royal thinkers. [9] Once again the light shed by Foucault's analysis is real and valuable; yet again it is at the expense of chronology, and in this case, since the Port-Royal Grammar is so important to Foucault, the chronology, if we let it intervene, seems even more troubling.

[9] See J.-Cl. Chevalier, *Histoire de la syntaxe: Naissance de la notion de complément dans la grammaire française (1530-1750)* (Geneva, 1968); also his "La *Grammaire générale* de Port-Royal et la critique moderne," *Langages,* no. 7 (Sept. 1967), pp. 16-33. Cf. also Roland Donzé, *La Grammaire générale et raisonnée de Port-Royal: Contribution à l'histoire des idées grammaticales en France,* 2nd ed. rev. (Berne, 1971).

The Port-Royal Grammar didn't appear until 1660, while Scaliger and Sanctius were writing in 1540 and 1587 respectively; furthermore, by the middle of the eighteenth century, the most basic of the Port-Royal distinctions was completely misunderstood by the grammarians writing for the *Encyclopédie*. [10] If we want to make the Port-Royal Grammar the basis for an analysis of the Classical *episteme*, and then reintroduce chronology, doesn't it seem rather that we ought to date the Classical Age from the later sixteenth century to the early eighteenth, and try to define a new *episteme* for the Enlightenment, thus making room for Hazard's *crise de conscience* after all? In other words, if Foucault's analyses are unquestionably more profound than those of Hazard, his attempts to extrapolate from his material to generalizations about historical periods pose the same problems and offer no more satisfactory solutions.

But Foucault and Hazard both share another fault of even greater significance: if Hazard seemed to offer us no very satisfactory explanation of why there was a crisis or change in ideas, Foucault, as we said, explicitly rejects the category of change: the very notion of change, of becoming, is part of the anthropologism of which we must rid ourselves. So we must be content to investigate a series of discontinuous layers without concern for the transition between them. When two distinguished intellectual historians, applying such divergent techniques, find it impossible to offer any adequate explanation for change in intellectual history, it may be worth our while to speculate on the reason why, in the hope that such reflection might shed some light on their divergent methods, but also because without some sort of explanation, we would not seem to be dealing, in any usual sense, with history at all.

To "account for" or "explain" change implies, almost inevitably, that we are talking about some sort of causality. If causality has long been a vexing problem for historians generally—we certainly cannot go into their problems here—it may be that it is peculiarly so for intellectual historians. It is certainly true, for instance, that it is never

[10] Chevalier, p. 32.

correct to say that one idea is the cause of another, at least on the conscious level; a logical relation is not a causal one. Likewise one idea cannot "influence" another, it can only influence a person who may in turn think other thoughts or influence other people. Nor do ideas grow (like turnips) even though historians of ideas talk about the "influence" and "growth" of ideas as if these things did occur. Such notions not only fudge on the whole issue of causality, but also suggest that ideas have some sort of autonomous existence, which they clearly do not.

On the other hand, to see ideas only as the product of historical forces—a sort of froth on the tide of history—is equally false. The idea of "historical forces" is itself highly suspect: economic systems or social structures are not forces in any proper sense and can become the source of movement or change only through the reactions or interpretations of men. The true source of change in history, then, is the way in which men interpret their situation. To understand historical change, one must not only be aware of the situations, but also of the ideas men have about their situation, and the method by which they arrive at these ideas. One can then attempt to isolate what in the interpretation and the method may lead to change. Put this way, it would seem obvious that the principle motive for change will have to be the inadequacy of a given interpretation or method. What I am suggesting—it is only a suggestion: I do not intend to solve these difficult problems simply because I have raised them—is that Foucault and Hazard, for all their differences, share one assumption which is probably false, and that is that it is the *new* ideas, *epistemes,* thoughts, systems of thought, which are important and constitute a new era in intellectual history. I suggest that new ideas, *epistemes,* etc., are always lying about waiting to be pounced upon, and they often have to lie about a good long while before anyone does anything about them. Scholars have proven very skillful at tracking the emergence of new ideas, often ferreting them out (or at least "anticipations" of them) a century or more before anyone was supposed to have thought of them. Many of the ideas of the Port-Royal Grammar have been traced not only to Renaissance sources,

Jan Miel

but even to Scholastic or Augustinian ones. And many of the ideas which created the Enlightenment are, as Hazard shows, of Renaissance origin and had considerable currency among seventeenth-century *libertins*. But if we want to know what brought about the creation of the Classical *episteme*, or of the complex of ideas we know as the Enlightenment, we must look not for the first appearance of new ideas or *epistemes* but for what made men feel the need of them, what was missing in the old ones. It is simply true that the emergence of a new idea or method is never as decisive as the refutation of an old one. The really critical moment in the Cartesian revolution, then, is not the decision to apply geometrical method to other areas, still less is it the revival of the ontological proof of God's existence; the *first* book of the *Discourse on Method* is the crucial one, in which Descartes tells us how he went from one book to another, from one subject to another, one teacher to another, even one country to another, and amid all the resemblances and differences found no principle of order, no basis for certain truth. It is that moment of discovery that all knowledge is hollow at the center which needs far more attention than it has yet received. Kant, at the end of the eighteenth century, will give us another such moment, and these are the moments of the great changes in the *episteme* in Western Europe. What we may want to ask however—or rather what we may want Hazard to ask Foucault —is whether the end of the seventeenth century is not a similar moment. In Locke's critique of knowledge, or perhaps even better in Pierre Bayle, when he speaks of Reason as a "coureuse" [libertine], and a "voie d'égarement" [pathway to error], and says she is proper only to destroy, not to build, only to give man doubts and a knowledge of his own intellectual impotence, [11] do we not see the same despair over the current means to knowledge, the sense again of a lack of foundations? It is true that neither Locke nor Bayle sets about creating a new method of knowledge, a new *episteme*, but profound changes occur in the old one even so. If, as Foucault maintains, the status of the objects of knowledge remains unchallenged until the end

[11] In the articles "Pyrrhon" and "Manichéens" in the *Dictionnaire historique et critique* (Rotterdam, 1697).

of the eighteenth century, along with the capacity for signs adequately to represent them, the nature of signs and the ways in which they relate to each other change drastically. The recognition of the arbitrary or conventional nature of signs becomes more acute as the knowledge of more varied languages increases; and if the historical development of languages is not well understood, there is, as in many other areas, a significant nostalgia for origins: not only will Condillac write an *Essay on the Origin of Languages,* almost all the *philosophes* have something to say about language being a creation of nature, not of Reason. Signs do not *naturally* signify the rational elements of the universe, they must be made to do so: it is no accident therefore that Bayle, in his despair over Reason, is also the great desperate organizer of the Republic of Letters, the community of intellects necessary for the establishment of the conventions by which signs operate. Reason is no longer that which is naturally and equally distributed to all men, as Descartes would have it, but that which is created and maintained by an intellectual Establishment: that is why the word '*philosophe*' comes to mean less a man with a particular vocation than a member of a club.

The other problem concerns the way in which the signs are ordered. Reason, as it was understood in the Cartesian model, namely as a deductive process based on the model of geometry, was obviously far too restrictive. Pascal notes, in the *Préface sur le traité du vide,* that it is at best appropriate only to geometry, arithmetic, music, physics, medicine and architecture, and totally inappropriate to history, geography, law, and religion. If Reason were going to tell us anything about these latter areas, she had, as Bayle saw, to prostitute herself. In any case, the *philosophes* clearly no longer felt bound by either dialectical or deductive reason: to make clear distinctions, and to assign clear terms to one's ideas was enough; the way in which the ideas were then associated was unimportant, as long as new ideas went on being generated. Lockean psychology was not so much an original philosophy of mind as it was a description of the way his own mind and other minds of the later seventeenth century operated. Neither of these two changes—the questioning of the origin and status of signs; and the abandonment of a deductive method of reasoning as the main mode for ordering them—had an immediate effect on the relation between sign and object, and so for Foucault the *episteme* remained constant throughout the seventeenth and eighteenth centuries; Hazard, sensitive above all to ideas, cannot help but see as critical the period which actually gave birth to "ideas" in the sense in which most historians of ideas actually use that term. Both emphases are important; neither taken alone gives us an accurate sense of the history of knowledge in the period.

Finally as for the role of History in these matters, well, Foucault assures us that History, and indeed Man, are inventions of the nineteenth century and soon will be, or perhaps already are *passés*—about to be reabsorbed, apparently, into the great Discourse. But Foucault's very rejection of historicism is actually a radical critique of our means of historical knowledge, and so future historians may look on Foucault as one of those figures who, like Descartes or Bayle or Kant, turn up at key moments (like the return of the repressed) to show us that at the center of the Discourse is contradiction and nothingness; that our language is always both rational and historical, both presence and absence; that, if it constitutes man in his uniqueness, it also constantly calls him into question; and that our history is not only what historians will make of it, but what it will make of them.

Contributors

Stillman Drake is Professor of the History of Science in the University of Toronto and Acting Director of the Centre for Renaissance Studies. Translator into English of most of Galileo's major works, he is author of *Galileo Studies* and of many essays on the scientist.

Karsten Harries of the Yale Philosophy Department, has written many articles and a volume on *The Meaning of Modern Art*. He is currently preparing work on Renaissance and baroque aesthetic theory.

T. A. Heinrichs teaches in the Department of Political Economy in the University of Toronto and is presently writing a dissertation on language and politics in Hobbes.

Olivier René Bloch, Director of the Philosophy Section at the University of Paris XII (Paris - Val de Marne), has recently published a highly-regarded study, *La Philosophie de Gassendi: Nominalisme, Matérialisme et Métaphysique.* Already author of articles on the subject, he is presently working on Aristotle's fragments and on epicureanism in antiquity.

D. E. Curtis, currently preparing a doctoral dissertation on Bayle for the University of Paris III, is author of a monograph on Gabriel Naudé's theory of history and progress. He teaches in the University of Hull.

Timothy J. Reiss, author of several articles and a book, *Toward Dramatic Illusion,* is presently teaching in the Comparative Literature programme of the University of Montreal, and preparing work on the literary structure of mind in the Renaissance and working towards a history of meaning in the same period.

Sylvie Romanowski teaches in the Department of French and Italian at Northwestern University, and has a volume on *L'illusion chez Descartes: la structure du discours cartésien* in press with Klincksieck.

Buford Norman, of the Department of Foreign Languages at Iowa State University, wrote his doctoral dissertation on Pascal for Yale.

Virginia Howe is a graduate student in the Yale French Department.

J. D. Hubert is well-known as author of many articles on French Literature and of three notable books on Baudelaire, Racine and Molière. He teaches in the Department of French and Italian at the Irvine campus of the University of California.

Herbert De Ley teaches in the French Department of the University of Illinois. He is author of a volume on Proust and Saint-Simon, and has in manuscript a further work on Saint-Simon while completing another on epistemology and literature in the seventeenth century.

David Lee Rubin, author of a monograph on Malherbe's odes and editor of John Napier, is preparing a work on structural problems in the early seventeenth-century French lyric. He teaches at the University of Virginia.

Beverly Ridgely, well-known for his many essays on the role of the new science in French literature, teaches in the Department of French Studies at Brown University.

Jacqueline Van Baelen, author of *Rotrou: le héros tragique et la révolte* and co-editor of the forthcoming *Théâtre complet* of Tristan l'Hermite, is presently working on a book on Racine and an edition of three *Oedipus* plays as she teaches Romance Languages at SUNY (Binghamton).

Jacques Neefs, of the University of Paris VIII (Paris-Vincennes), is author of a recent work on *Madame Bovary* and co-author of another on modern French literature.

Maurice Laugaa, of the University of Paris VII (Paris-Censier), is author of many articles and a volume on the criticism of Madame de Lafayette. He is currently working with the notions of Digression and Description in their effect on the continuity and discontinuity of narrative chains.

Erica Harth, author of an Ansley Award winning book on Cyrano de Bergerac and of several articles since, teaches Romance Languages and Comparative Literature at Brandeis University.

Jan Miel teaches in the College of Letters at Wesleyan University. Besides articles on Chomsky, Lacan, and others, he is author of a volume on *Pascal and Theology,* and is presently working on a structuralist theory of tragedy.

Issues still available through the office of YALE FRENCH STUDIES, Room 323, William L. Harkness Hall, Yale University, New Haven, Conn. 06520 (at $1.50 per issue)

Handling and postage charge:
United States and Canada: $.25. Each additional volume: $.12
Foreign Countries: $.35. Each additional volume: $.12

19/20 Contemporary Art (a double issue now offered at a single price, many illustrations); 23 Humor; 25 Albert Camus; 26 The Myth of Napoléon; 32 Paris in Literature; 33 Shakespeare in France; 35 Sade; 38 The Classical Line; 40 Literature and Society: 18th Century; 41 Game, Play, Literature; 42 Zola; 43 The Child's Part; 44 Valéry; 45 Language as Action; 46 From Stage to Street; 47 Image and Symbol in the Renaissance; 48 French Freud: Structural Studies in Psychoanalysis.

39 LITERATURE AND REVOLUTION: $2.50 (a special issue)

36/37 Structuralism is now out of print. It has been published by Doubleday as an Anchor Book and may be ordered from their office at 277 Park Avenue, New York, N. Y. 10017.

Issues which are out of print—now available through
Kraus Reprint Co., Route 100, Millwood, New York 10546

1 Critical Biography of Existentialism; 2 Modern Poets; 3 Criticism and Creation; 4 Literature and Ideas; 5 The Modern Theatre; 6 France and World Literature; 7 André Gide; 8 What's Novel in the Novel; 9 Symbolism; 10 French-American Literary Relationships; 11 Eros, Variations on an Old Theme; 12 God and the Writer; 13 Romanticism Revisited; 14 Motley: Today's French Theatre; 15 Social and Political France; 16 Foray through Existentialism; 17 The Art of the Cinema; 18 Passion and the Intellect, or, Malraux; 21 Poetry Since the Liberation; 22 French Education; 24 Midnight Novelists and Others; 27 Women Writers; 28 Rousseau; 29 The New Dramatists; 30 Sartre; 31 Surrealism; 34 Proust.

FUTURE ISSUES

50 Literature and Intoxication—May 1974
51 Medieval Romance—Nov. 1974

PRINTED IN SPAIN